DEFIANT BRACEROS

DEFIANT
BRACEROS

How Migrant Workers
Fought for Racial, Sexual,
and Political Freedom

MIREYA LOZA

The University of North Carolina Press
Chapel Hill

Designed and set in Miller and Caecilia by Rebecca Evans
The University of North Carolina Press has been a member of the Green Press
Initiative since 2003.

Cover illustration: Leonard Nadel, "A Bracero Lies in Bed and Smokes in a Living
Quarter at a Californian Camp." Item #2470, Leonard Nadel Bracero Photographs,
Archives Center, National Museum of American History, Smithsonian Institution.

Library of Congress Cataloging-in-Publication Data
Names: Loza, Mireya, author.
Title: Defiant braceros : how migrant workers fought for racial, sexual, and political
    freedom / Mireya Loza.
Other titles: David J. Weber series in the new borderlands history.
Description: Chapel Hill : The University of North Carolina Press, [2016] |
Series: The David J. Weber series in the new borderlands history | Includes
    bibliographical references and index.
Identifiers: LCCN 2016009978 | ISBN 9781469629759 (cloth : alk. paper) |
    ISBN 9781469629766 (pbk : alk. paper) | ISBN 9781469629773 (ebook)
Subjects: LCSH: Foreign workers, Mexican—United States—History. | Mexicans—
    Race identity—United States. | Foreign workers, Mexican—Political activity—
    United States—History. | Foreign workers, Mexican—United States—Social
    conditions—History. | Foreign workers, Mexican—United States—Economic
    conditions—History. | Seasonal Farm Laborers Program.
Classification: LCC HD8081.M6 L67 2016 | DDC 331.5/440973—dc23 LC record
    available at http://lccn.loc.gov/2016009978

Sections of chapter 3 previously appeared as "Alianza de Braceros Nacionales de
Mexico en los Estados Unidos, 1943–1964," in ¿Que Fronteras? Mexican Braceros and
a Re-examination of the Legacy of Migration, ed. Paul Lopez (Dubuque: Kendall
Hunt Publishing, 2010), and will appear in an upcoming issue of the journal Diagolo.

For Marcelina, Pedro, Rosalba, and Juan Loza

CONTENTS

ILLUSTRATIONS

ACKNOWLEDGMENTS

This book was written with the support of many communities. As an under-graduate, I was fortunate enough to take a class with someone who would change the course of my life. Matt Garcia introduced me to bracero history in an academic setting, and I owe him a debt of gratitude for all of the time and energy he spent preparing me to write this book. Vicki Ruiz's gener-ous guidance broadened my scholarship. Kristin Hoganson and Adrian Burgos provided thoughtful edits, feedback, and, most of all, unwavering mentorship. Natalia Molina, Jason Ruiz, José Alamillo, and Anitra Grisales engaged in my ideas and helped map out new terrains. Stephen Pitti and George Sanchez graciously transformed this project. Near and dear to my heart is my University of Texas community: Gilberto Rosas, Korinta Mal-donado, Isabella Seong Leong Quintana, Pablo González, Nancy Rios, Fer-nanda Soto, Jamahn Lee, Jennifer Nájera, and Peggy Brunache. At Brown University, I was also fortunate to receive amazing guidance from Evelyn Hu-Dehart, Ralph Rodriguez, Steven Lubar, Elliot Gorn, and Susan Smu-lyan. Felicia Salinas, Marcia Chatelain, Matt Delmont, Jessica Johnson, Monica Martinez, Monica Pelayo, and Eric Larson made my time on the East Coast memorable. Sarah Wald was a great virtual writing partner, checking in and keeping me focused. My colleagues at the University of Illinois at Urbana-Champaign created an environment of open support: Ricky Rodriguez, Fiona Ngo, Lisa Cacho, David Coyoca, Isabel Molina, Soo Ah Kwon, Jonathan Inda, Julie Dowling, Alejandro Lugo, Edna Viruell-Fuentes, and Sandra Ruiz. Andrew Eisen and Veronica Mendez worked hard to digitize documents, track down footnotes, and secure copyrights. University of Illinois graduate students Raquel Escobar, Carolina Ortega, and Juan Mora and undergraduate Emmanuel Salazar kept me on my toes. Many others helped me with advice and support: Bill Johnson-González, Simeon Man, Julie Weise, Geraldo Cadava, Kathleen Belew, Michael Innis-Jiménez, Lori A. Flores, and Perla Guerrero. This project was funded by the University of Illinois, the Ford Foundation, the National Endowment for the Humanities, the Formby Research Fellowship at Texas Tech University, Historical Society of Southern California, Smithsonian Institution, the Mexico-North Research Network, and Brown University.

None of this would be possible without the Bracero History Project and the collective effort it took to get it up and running, from folks at George Mason University's Roy Rosenzweig Center for History and New Media and the University of Texas at El Paso's Institute of Oral History to Brown University's Center for the Study of Race and Ethnicity. Amazing people came together to document extraordinary experiences, and I was fortunate enough to work alongside Kristine Navarro, Steve Velasquez, Peter Liebhold, Anais Acosta, Sharon Leon, and Alma Carrillo. Their commitment to public history continues to inspire me. I am also indebted to every person who collaborated with the project and recognized that these oral histories are important. I also want to thank every community member, undergraduate student, and graduate student who was committed to this endeavor and pressed the record button, asked great questions, and captured these oral histories. Most of all, the Bracero History Project thrived because of individuals who shared their stories and went on record to make sure this history was remembered.

Wonderful friends helped sustain my life outside the academy: Marisol Lopez, Chinyere Osuji, Veronica Cortez, Grisel Murillo, and Martiza Santibañez. Rosa Maria Corrada always brought a positive perspective to everything. Keisha Banks picked up her backpack and joined me when I needed help crisscrossing Mexico carrying out research. Over tons of takeout and television, Mimi Nguyen lent an ear in moments of frustration or laughter. My partner in crime, Alma Carrillo, contributed to this book through her fantastic oral histories and her incredible sense of friendship.

I am extremely fortunate to have an awesome family, who, like my friends, supported my writing when they needed to but also reminded me that I was much more than my job. First and foremost, I want to recognize all of the efforts of the Loza, Soto, Villalba, Perez, Loera, and Miranda families. I want to express gratitude to my family in El Sitio de Maravillas, Guanajuato, especially my Tías Concha, Victoria, Guadalupe, Marta, Cleotilde, and Socorro. I have always known that "cousin" was never the right word to describe my relationship with Daniel Loza, Benjamin Perez, Oscar Loza, and Johnny Loza. Daniel Loza spent hours and days of his life reading drafts and pushing me to make my ideas clearer. His presence in my life shapes the way I see the world. Whether it was for a quick trip to the store or to offer me a much-needed drink, Benjamin made time for me when I needed it.

Oscar always set a high bar, while Johnny forged a path to the University of Illinois. Juan Soto, Eric Peña, Ivonne Loza, and Leon Schnayer contributed greatly to my supportive family life. Eric Loza, Brian Soto, Christian Loera, Magaly Villalba, and Melissa Villalba provided fun times when I was looking for a break. Gerarda Loera, Abdon Loera, Carmen Villalba, and Policarpio Villalba sustained my academic work through kind acts along the way. Even when I was a difficult person, my sister, Patricia Peña, worked hard to get along with me, put things in perspective, and helped me move forward. I cannot imagine finishing this project without my partner, Mike Amezcua. He packed up our things for archival trips, stayed in when I needed to write, and changed his plans when I needed more. My heart is full of love and gratitude for everything he's done!

For the grandchildren of a bracero, Isa, Ale, and Sammy Loza, I hope you carry this book as a reminder of the long road that got us here. And for the grandchildren of a self-proclaimed "mojado," Grace and Gabriel Peña, I hope you always honor that. My Tía Rosalba and my Tío Juan are the rocks that anchored my Chicago family. They opened their home to everyone and created a world for me that was never predicated on nuclear family but on extended family and ties of chosen kinship. As a child, I spent every day with my Tía Rosalba, and she taught me through example the value of public service. I carry her lessons into the field of Public History. My father, Pedro Loza, always told me that I had a choice—I could work with my hands or with a pen in my hands. He preferred I do the latter. My mother, Marcelina Loza, supported my decision to study whatever I wanted, even when people whispered in her ear that I should study engineering or law. She worked seven days a week to put me through high school and undergrad. Their love and guidance has always filled my world with possibility.

DEFIANT BRACEROS

INTRODUCTION
Making Braceros

On a warm Saturday morning in June 2008, I attended a large meeting of ex-braceros—men who had served as Mexican guest workers in the United States—in a public plaza in Jiquilpan, Michoacán. Jiquilpan is best known as the birthplace of former Mexican president Lázaro Cárdenas, but behind the picturesque cobblestone streets and colonial archways live hundreds of aging, ex–guest workers who cluster together on street corners and in the plaza. That day, both indigenous and mestizos took turns sharing stories about their time laboring in the United States on contracts they had secured through the Bracero Program. They recounted long travels to contracting stations, the jarring medical examinations, and the chemical DDT that was sprayed on their naked bodies at the border. They pointed out the physical toll the work took on their bodies, like soldiers sharing war scars. One man pointed to a ring finger now missing, another pointed to an old lesion, and so many others clung to the crooks of their backs in pain. They remembered long hours as stoop laborers, life in labor camps, and their fight for long-lost wages that the government had systematically deducted from their paychecks. Counting out loud and figuring conversions in their heads, they attempted to calculate how much they were owed. I witnessed this scene play out over and over again throughout parks and plazas in Monterrey, Nuevo Leon, and Paraíso, Tabasco, in Mexico; at La Placita Olvera in Los Angeles; and outside of warehouses on the South Side of Chicago.

The United States had called upon these men to alleviate a labor shortage in the agriculture and railroad industries during World War II. The agricultural need continued long after the war, as growers became more and more dependent on low-cost Mexican labor. Because the great majority of braceros worked in the fields, stories about crops, seasons, cultivation, and harvesting live on. Men invoked the minute details of this work, as if the minutiae stood as proof of their labor. They traveled from every state in Mexico by train, bus, boat, and on foot to reach contracting stations in hopes of working in areas across the United States. Many families took out loans,

1

pawned family heirlooms, and sold their livestock to pay for travel, food, and the bribes required to get their loved ones to their destination. The majority of these men know the California landscape intimately, as the names roll off their tongues and are spoken in accented mispronunciations: Bly (Blythe), Hiber (Heber), Estockton (Stockton), Osnard (Oxnard). And then there are those they say with ease: Santa Paula, San Bernardino, and Coachella. One man confessed his disdain for cotton work in Texas, while a few called out towns in Arizona, Arkansas, Michigan, and Oregon. Some of the oldest men, those in their nineties, were able to share stories about the first years of the program. And the youngest men—in their mid-sixties—talked about their experiences during the final years of the program.

These men represent the over 4.5 million contracts issued to Mexican guest workers from 1942 to 1964, during the various agreements between Mexico and the United States that came to be known as the Bracero Program. They were called *braceros*, a term that referred to their *brazos*, or arms. Though "bracero" had long been synonymous with "Mexican laborer," during those years it became the specific designation for Mexicans who had contracts to work in the United States. Despite the distinctions that officials drew, the line between bracero and undocumented worker quickly blurred as men left contracts to work as undocumented laborers, or as undocumented workers found their way into the program.[1] But for many of the aging men who participated in the program and have fought to collect their full salaries, it is important to distinguish themselves as a class, a group of people who had all belonged to the "legal" contingent of workers.

That morning, before the group discussion, I met with Luis Barocio Ceja. His niece was an activist with the Bracero Justice Movement, which is dedicated to recuperating the back wages that braceros are still owed.[2] She introduced me to her uncle in hopes that he would consider telling his story for the Bracero History Project, which I was working on at the time. For several years before our meeting, I had been collaborating with the National Museum of American History in its large undertaking to document the bracero experience, and that summer I had been sent to collect oral histories from across Mexico. Ceja kindly accepted my invitation to share his experiences in the Bracero Program. As I began reading him the release forms he needed to sign, he interrupted me to explain that he was literate, and that, although he was from a modest agricultural community in Michoacán, his parents had insisted he attend the Universidad Nacional Autónoma de México in Mexico City. This was an extraordinary accomplishment for his parents, who had been born into the hacienda system and worked as peons until they received their own communal land holdings through redistribution policies in the early 1930s. He, like many others in Mexico impacted by the Bracero Program, understood agricultural systems of exploitation long before setting foot on U.S. soil.

As he leaned over to sign the release forms, I pressed the record button and began the interview. Ceja's memories were vivid as he recounted stories that carried me from contract to contract, from the beginning of the program through its final years. Ceja painted a picture of neighborly aid and conduct that contributed to the workers' sense of patriotism during those first years of the Bracero Program. However, as time went on and exploitation increased, that patriotism disappeared. Ceja had begun his journey as a single nineteen year old who could no longer afford to attend the university. *"Me aventuré,"* he told me, meaning he decided to take a risk and seek out an adventure.[3] On March 31, 1943, along with many other men, he started making his way to the border by train. Part of the contracting process included enduring invasive medical exams, but what he found equally troubling were the incessant inspections of the agriculture and science textbooks that he had decided to bring with him. The program targeted agricultural workers from rural communities, and Ceja at least fit that part of the bill; but his high level of literacy was disturbing to the people screening him. Perhaps the books signaled a dangerous difference among bracero communities that officials in the program, as well as growers, wanted to sweep under the rug. Maybe officials interpreted his literacy as a sign that he could cause trouble because he could read the terms of his contract and hold growers accountable.

Despite this, he gained entry into the United States through the program. Ceja recalled arriving in Corona, California, to a welcoming party organized by a special greeting committee, along with a band that played "Que Viva Mexico." Over the next twenty years, he would obtain several contracts until the program ended, noting that he received the best treatment during the early years, when employers and supervisors tried to make these braceros feel comfortable. He also recalled the social incorporation of braceros, as local girls invited them to their homes and to dances.[4] Individuals in receiving communities like Corona saw braceros as a vital component for winning the war. Braceros embraced these patriotic discourses, which elevated the purpose of their migration.

Historian Manuel García y Griego describes this period, from 1942 to 1946, as "wartime cooperation," which was followed by "turbulence and transition" from 1947 to 1954. This second period is marked by a dramatic increase in bracero contracting, a rise in undocumented labor in the United

States, and governmental disputes between the two nations. The final years of the program, 1955 to 1964, represented the "apogee and demise," during which exploitation of braceros rose to a degree that caught national attention.[5] While many braceros stayed in the United States after the termination of the program, others went back to Mexico, expecting to benefit from the modernized nation they were meant to help build from across the border.

These shifts came into focus for me as Ceja recounted his story. When I asked about his experience working in the Imperial Valley of California in 1953, he said, "The Americans are racist. . . . They want us when we can serve them, when we can work hard."[6] He was treated well during the war years, not because the braceros were liked or truly wanted, but because, as he explained, they labored. He believed that after the war, the growers shed their guise of acceptance and welcoming to reveal their true feelings: they only valued him as a beast of burden. Despite his openness about Corona in 1943, I was surprised when I found him reluctant to give more details about camp life in the Imperial Valley in 1953. I wondered why this was. What else had changed and how did those changes affect the dynamic social world of the labor camps? As I went on to speak with more braceros over the course of six years, their stories revealed details that framed camp life and bracero subjectivity in new ways.

In collecting the oral histories for this book and for the Bracero History Project, I encountered others who, like me, were attempting to answer a deceptively simple question: Who were the braceros? The Bracero Justice Movement, the social movement that Ceja's niece was working with, needed to answer this question to help these men recover stolen pay and right a historic wrong. The National Museum of American History was looking to provide the public with a history of "legal" Mexican immigration, and thus an avenue by which to integrate Latino migration stories into the national historical narrative. And policy makers looked to the figure of the bracero in hopes of finding a temporary solution to the challenge of legislating true immigration reform. All of these efforts drew on a politics of commemoration that required that the subjects included be appropriate and respectable as a means to gain visibility for this particular group of workers. Once again, the narrative about these men was controlled, contained, and deployed in the service of a greater good.

The Bracero Justice Movement drew on narratives of hardworking fathers and family men in order to build a historical narrative that acknowledges the contributions of these men and simultaneously shames both the U.S. and the Mexican governments into doing more for these men in their twilight years. The movement embraced politics of commemoration in order to recognize these workers but challenged its limits by utilizing unlikely images of remembrance that highlighted alienation, marginalization, and emasculation. In doing so, they helped usher in a *política de la dignidad*, a politics of dignity that challenged the Mexican nation-state to meet its obligation to its worker citizens abroad. This politics of dignity, I argue, invoked questions about the place of human rights for the transnational worker. The National Museum of American History, on the other hand, needed to create a figure that was worthy of commemoration in the halls of the nation's museums and to convince the general public that these men and their families deserved a place in American history. By doing so, this program challenged perceptions that the history of the Mexican migrant was synonymous with "illegality." Policy makers, for their part, needed to create a positive image of guest workers in order to gain support for their idea to create a new temporary migrant workforce.

Obscured by all of these political projects, however, were the narratives of men who had deviated from the official representation of the bracero and defied the ways the Bracero Program attempted to control every aspect of their lives. The stories of people like Ceja, who traveled as a young, unmarried man looking for adventure and better opportunities—indigenous workers who faced both racism and upward mobility, women who also participated in the program through informal and elicit economies, and guest workers who fought the labor and political establishments for better working conditions—have been pushed to the sidelines in order to commemorate braceros as good family men and great laborers.

Defiant Braceros recounts collective, individual, and institutional memories of the Bracero Program to highlight the narratives that Mexico, the National Museum of American History, policy makers, and the Bracero Justice Movement have ignored or relegated to the margins. The stories of those in the bracero community who fall outside romanticized notions of *mestizaje*,[7] masculinity, and family and who defy perceived norms in terms of race, sex, and political involvement rupture the official history. *Defiant Braceros* focuses on braceros who do not always fit the normative narrative and incorporates their stories about the social worlds they inhabited, which included wives, children, parents, and brothers, but also growers, foremen, sex workers, mistresses, and alternative family structures. Some of the subjects in this book deviate from Mexican and American visions of ideal workers. They embraced nonconformist identities and purposely engaged in acts that defied state aspirations and norms. Their oral histories thus provide an entry point for unpacking the politics behind the transnational creation of the "respectable" bracero subject, both during the time of the Bracero Program and in its contemporary historicization. These narratives dislodge official accounts to reveal how the Mexican and U.S. nation-states prepared a class of workers for cyclical migration, thereby paving the way for the unjust and unequal system we have today. These histories help inform our current debates and the decisions that are made about immigration reform, labor, and the real people impacted by these politics.

Beyond the Normative Narrative

While I was traveling on collection trips for the National Museum of American History, policy makers were debating models for immigration reform that resonated strongly with the Bracero Program. At the turn of the twenty-first century, President George W. Bush imagined a guest-worker program as part of his vision of reform. He set the tone for his introduction to a potential program by talking about his experience with Mexican families in Texas who valued faith in God, love of family, hard work, resilience, and military service. Through these descriptions, Mexican migrants were deemed worthy of working in the United States and of benefiting from immigration reform through what he called a "temporary worker program." Bush argued, "If an American employer is offering a job that American citizens are not willing to take, we ought to welcome into our country a person who will fill that job."[8] In essence, instead of reforming exploitative labor practices or addressing the deplorable wages or work conditions that make these jobs undesirable to begin with, Bush suggested that Mexican laborers could fill those jobs. This attitude resonated with Ceja's comment, "They want us when we can serve them," suggesting that immigrant laborers were welcomed if they served the system. Indeed, Mexican workers could satisfy capitalist desires for a flexible, deportable workforce with little change to the current labor conditions.[9] This was not a new idea, of course, though by the time Bush suggested it in 2004, it is likely that many had forgotten its earlier model, the Bracero Program. To be sure, guest workers had not disappeared from the U.S. economy after the termination of the Bracero Program, as foreign laborers found their way into the H-2A and H-2B programs.[10]

At the time the Bracero Program first started, supporters painted a similar picture of respectable braceros as hard workers and family men. This narrative framed the program as providing an opportunity for families in need and posited family as an essential component to an individual's decision to labor abroad. It also helped create the belief that familial bonds would ensure that these workers would go back to their homeland. These discourses were articulated by proponents of the program and were disseminated through news articles that introduced what readers would come to discern as "typical" braceros. These archetypes held certain common characteristics — the men were often described as fathers and husbands, hard workers, well meaning, and invested in family uplift.

In 1957, Fred Eldridge introduced his reading audience in the *Saturday Evening Post* to one of these men. His article, "Helping Hands from Mexico," even circulated beyond the United States when the Mexican newspaper *Excelsior* printed a translated version. Eldridge opened the article by suggesting, "When you drink your morning glass of orange juice, put sugar in your coffee, enjoy your tossed salad for lunch or buy a new cotton dress, it probably never occurs to you that Señor Rafael Tamayo, thirty-three, the father of five, and a legal resident of Ocotlán Jalisco, republic of Mexico might be entitled to a short bow for services rendered."[11] He presented the reader with an understanding of Tamayo through the items he produced, but also mentioned his age and number of children to highlight his identity as a father and family man. Eldridge described Tamayo as "a handsome man with a well-groomed mustache and dimples."[12] Despite his departure, or perhaps because of it, Tamayo continued to be the primary breadwinner of the family. Tamayo is quoted as saying that his wife would not work in his absence because, in his words, "it would shame me. It is not the custom."[13] Despite the reality that many women in Mexico had to work outside of their homes, Tamayo's wife fulfilled nuclear domestic visions as a stay-at-home wife. Eldridge acknowledged that some Mexicans did oppose the program, but explained, "One bracero camp of 1,700 men in Fullerton, California, sent $316,000 home during three months of 1956."[14]

Sending remittances took on a larger role than merely providing for the necessities that money could buy. The remittance reinforced structures of patriarchy and took on both material and symbolic roles within bracero families. Its meanings could be read as long-distance fathering, as securing fidelity, and as proof of these men's strong moral characters. These narratives became configured around fatherhood and family in such a way that family became the only logical explanation for accepting highly exploitative work abroad. According to Eldridge, Tamayo articulated this by explaining that his only reason for seeking out a contract was to raise "his family's standard of living above that of barest subsistence."[15] This scene of fathers departing

Mexico to improve their families' standard of living played out over and over again in articles that introduced braceros to local communities.[16] Fulfilling their families' economic needs trumped their absences from their families' everyday life. This was also true for other men who came to the United States in the same period but not through the Bracero Program.[17]

Some critics of the program demonized these men in terms that also relied on narratives of family, as they cast the braceros as unfaithful husbands and irresponsible fathers. They pointed toward the economies of vice that flourished around the program, the "broken" families left behind, and the American women seduced by these men. In his 1958 thesis, Daniel Martínez argued that community members of Cucamonga, California, felt "infuriated" as braceros left local girls in an "unhappy circumstance." He also blamed braceros for social ills related to an increase in bars, liquor stores, and prostitution in the community.[18] The Catholic church agreed with Martínez that the program placed braceros in moral peril because they were exposed to a world of "vice" and "are denied a family life," which led to the "breaking up of innumerable families in Mexico."[19]

Mexican modernization efforts held the patriarchal nuclear family as a central vehicle for transforming the lives of poor mestizos and indigenous communities alike. Like Eldridge's journalistic account in the *Saturday Evening Post*, the Mexican government also "anchored its public promotion of the Bracero Program" through idealized notions of "*la familia mexicana*, the Mexican family."[20] As the program grew in popularity, reifying the importance of this structure was also essential for ensuring remittances. By 1950, remittances for those working in the United States had become the country's third-largest source of hard currency.[21] The program made it normal for one family member—often the husband/father—to cross national borders in an attempt to make a living and support those who stayed behind. It also reinvigorated the Mexican economy with the hard, cold cash that braceros sent home. For this revenue source to continue flowing, the picture of the nuclear family needed to be revised to account for a transnational structure where manhood, and specifically fatherhood, could be defined by labor and remittances from afar. Family, usually wives and children, became imbedded in the logic of taking on this arduous labor. The level of exploitation that these men endured could only be justified in the name of family, and thus men who joined the program for an "adventure" or who were motivated by self-exploration embodied a contradiction in this logic and as such were of little use to Mexico.

As family became a powerful symbol within the program, it also became a racialized logic that impacted indigenous subjects. Discourses of Mexican indigeneity intersected with the premise that the program would "modernize" Mexican populations viewed as "primitive" and "backward." While other scholars point toward the implications of this project of modernity on mestizo men and their transnational families, I turn my attention to those who stood at the center of this racial project of modernity, the *"indio."*[22] The *indígena* family needed to be modernized in particular ways that emphasized reorganization into nuclear family units, disciplined labor, and practices of pleasure that distanced them from long-standing stereotypes of the "drunken Indian" and "lazy Indian."[23]

Prior to the program, the Mexican state engaged in various efforts to "civilize" indigenous communities. But when the Bracero Program appeared, it provided a unique opportunity to incorporate them into the national project of modernization abroad. In the decade prior to the program, the Mexican state had invested in programs to modernize indigenous and rural peasantry that focused on education, irrigation, rural outreach, village health programs, and the organization of communal agricultural lands known as *ejidos.*[24] Attention was also turned to systems of management that would "remake" Indians.[25] The Bracero Program was part of this, as it provided a system of labor management and an avenue to modernize populations without implementing costly state programs in Mexico. In the eyes of state officials it was essential to change indigenous communities and aid in their transformation toward mestizaje, in order to alleviate problems that were long tied to racialized discourses of poverty. Historian Devra Weber emphasizes that an examination of the movement of indigenous populations "upsets the still-popular image of rural peasants remaining in static and 'un'-historical isolation until brought into the modern age."[26]

The stories of indigenous groups in the Bracero Program also shed light on racialized structures of management that developed in the camps and intra-ethnic tensions within bracero communities. Growers drew on this presumed knowledge of race to place indigenous guest workers in areas deemed appropriate for their bodies. They developed different management structures to deal with language barriers, which were compounded by the use of Mexican indigenous languages that were not commonly understood in the United States. Men like Heriberto Flores Sotelo, who arrived in the United States in 1956, created their own sense of racial identity vis-à-vis indigenous communities. He carefully explained that he did not speak a *"dialecto,"* an indigenous dialect, but *"castellano,"* Castilian Spanish.[27] Drawing such subtle and not-so-subtle lines of distinction, many mestizo guest workers came to see themselves as more "civilized" than their indigenous counterparts, who needed a more stern management system.

Most of the scholarship concerning intra-ethnic tensions in the program has focused on Mexican Americans and Mexican immigrants.[28] I argue, however, that viewing Mexican immigrants as a cohesive whole conceals both the experiences of indigenous communities and the Mexican nation-building efforts that pushed for mestizaje as the only means to incorporate indigenous populations into modern society. Anthropologists have long noted the importance of the bracero generation in shaping the migration of contemporary Mexican indigenous communities, but historians have largely ignored the ethnic and racial diversity among Mexican migrants. As early as 1916, Mexican intellectual Manuel Gamio advocated for the incorporation of indigenous communities into the national project, which would render Mexicans a "homogeneous" race as mestizos and unify the culture and language.[29] Mexico would not become indigenous, but indigenous populations would meld into the nation as mestizos.

The absence of indigeneity in historical studies of migration is a product of both the Mexican national project of mestizaje and the difficulty of examining a category that can fluctuate within the life span of one individual.[30] Mexican understandings of race and ethnicity allow subjects to shift identity from indigenous to mestizo, making it challenging to ascertain the exact number of indigenous people entering the program. Systems of racism and discrimination made it more common for an individual to go from being indigenous to mestizo, rather than the other way around. The inclusion of indigenous Mexicans in the program created expectations that Indians could, while in the United States, learn to be modern Mexicans and then potentially be reincorporated into the Mexican economy, and hence the nation. The Mexican state and U.S. growers viewed indigeneity as a form of racial deviancy that could be corrected through modernization and mestizaje. Some fellow mestizo braceros held similar views, as they believed themselves to be distinct not only on racial grounds but also in terms of class and education.

Intra-ethnic racial tensions also informed labor-organizing strategies among braceros. The Alianza de Braceros Nacionales de México en los Estados Unidos (Alianza), one of the leading bracero organizations that focused on unionization, saw uneducated and "primitive" braceros as impeding its efforts. Frustrated with the failures of Alianza, one of its leaders, Benito Hernández, expressed the difficulties he encountered when working with men who scratched out symbols on boxes instead of writing numbers, stating that he had never encountered such "primitiveness," a euphemism for Indians.[31] He believed that it was this primitiveness that made them much more likely to break the law and work in the United States as undocumented workers, even though the particular indigenous laborers he was working alongside were also on legal temporary work contracts. He also argued that they were difficult to organize because they did not understand the benefits of unionizing. Their racial deviancy thus led to perceptions that also called their political potential into question.

While the relationship between Alianza's leadership and membership sheds light on intra-ethnic racial tensions, it also reveals that guest workers who participated in the organization also defied public images that confined guest-worker aspirations to family uplift. These men articulated much more complex political goals that demonstrated an understanding of the Mexican systems of agricultural exploitation that made it necessary for these workers to leave Mexico in the first place. They wanted more than a mere temporary labor contract; they sought a transnational labor union. This ambitious goal demonstrated that they understood the U.S. dependence on low-wage Mexican labor and Mexico's inability to protect them.

Not only was the Mexican government unable to shield these workers from exploitation, but it exacerbated their mistreatment by directly stealing wages from them. Bracero transnational activism arose as a form of defiance against exploitation in the fields and at home, beginning with Alianza in the 1940s, and that activism has extended to the Bracero Justice Movement's present-day efforts to recuperate wages and demand reparations. Through the example of bracero wage theft, activists in the movement connect past exploitation with contemporary marginalization, deploying discourses of family, morality, and citizenship to expose the corruption of the Mexican nation-state. Braceros use memory in order to create narratives that can be utilized strategically to serve a political goal and contribute to a seemingly cohesive collective identity. Kinship and family are called upon again, but their meanings are now subverted in order to seek justice for this aging population of workers and their descendants. This book draws attention to the Bracero Justice Movement, in an effort to further the cause of social justice for bracero communities while also including the voices that have been silenced in the construction of the politically and strategically useful bracero subject produced by the Bracero Justice Movement.

Opening the Archives

This research is largely based on my six-year experience working with the National Museum of American History's Bracero History Project as an intern, research assistant, pre-doctoral fellow (2007–8), and oral historian.[32] Through this project, I carried out interviews and trained faculty and students to amass over 800 oral histories for the online Bracero History Archive. I personally documented over ninety oral histories, digitized hundreds of documents, and collected dozens of artifacts for the National Museum of American History in six states in the United States and nine states in Mexico. These oral histories are also the cornerstone of the digital archive, www.braceroarchive.org, and the Smithsonian Institution's traveling exhibit, "Bittersweet Harvest: The Bracero Program, 1942–64," which opened at the National Museum of American History in September 2009 and traveled through 2015.

One of my goals for this project was to collect oral histories and digitize materials not commonly found in existing archives. I focused on indigenous communities, the family members of these guest workers, and members of receiving communities in the United States. These individuals' oral histories embody the complexities and contradictions of the program. Methodologically, I allowed the oral histories to guide my archival research at the National Archives in College Park, Maryland, and San Bruno, California; the Archivo General de la Nación, Mexico City; the Archivo Histórico del Estado de Guanajuato; Stanford University's Special Collections; and the Southwest Collections at Texas Tech University.

Many public historians working on the project, myself included, often felt a manic sense of urgency in documenting these oral histories, as many in the bracero community were nearing the twilight of their years. As these individuals passed, the project's oral historians experienced a sense of loss for the archive. Scholar of memory and history Pierre Nora sheds light on this sense of urgency by explaining, "The fear that everything is on the verge of disappearing, coupled with anxiety about the precise significance of the present and uncertainty about the future, invests even the humblest testimony, the modest vestige, with the dignity of being potentially memorable."[33] We all documented as much as possible, often explaining the importance in personal terms, as many oral historians on the team felt a deep sense of belonging in this community and the urgent need to preserve what could be potentially forgotten. Nora explains this exhausting effort by stating, "What we call memory is in fact a gigantic and breathtaking effort to store the material vestiges of what we cannot possibly remember, thereby amassing an unfathomable collection of things that we might someday need to recall."[34]

The end result was a digital archive containing oral histories and thousands of digitized documents that expressed a myriad of contrasting stories. At times, these two types of documentation overlapped, corroborating information; at other times, they stood in stark contradiction. For example, an ex-bracero might pull an identification card out of his wallet that contradicted his narrative by disputing a so-called fact, such as year of entry, address, or even name. A year of entry or address could easily be collapsed with some other piece of information. A name could appear differently in official documents if a bracero used a family member's identity to obtain a contract, or if a typist misspelled a guest worker's name. As I shared my experience carrying out oral histories for the project, I was constantly asked, "How do you know what they say is true; that their memories are accurate?" The contents of the archive reflect this dilemma. And the only answer that could address this contradiction was that oral history documented one particular performance/rendition of memory, but that there is, in fact, a larger repertoire of expression.

Diana Taylor points out the inevitable rift between the archive of supposedly enduring materials (texts, documents, buildings, bones) and the so-called ephemeral repertoire of embodied practices/knowledge (spoken language, dance, sports, ritual).[35] But in the case of oral history, the practice of producing a record (an audio/video recording or transcript) turns the ephemeral repertoire of embodied practice/knowledge into an enduring, unchanging material of record. The interpretation of that material can change, but the material itself is frozen. Unlike the variable repertoire of performance, oral history is expected to provide a singular text or object, and in failing to do so, historical suspicions arise about the validity of that particular oral history.

Although oral history relies on the ability to access and express memory, the act itself resembles the ephemeral nature of performance. As Erika Doss explains, one allure of memory is that it refuses to stand still, as it is elusive, unstable, open-ended, and unresolved: "It is further embraced as an active agent that is performative, personal, and presentist."[36] The lived aspect of memory exceeds the archive's ability to capture it.[37] Because memory refuses to be frozen in time, recording oral history is a multivalent act that cannot be duplicated with exactness. We remember by retrieving past events that interest us from our present position.[38] Furthermore, our interest in past memories is anchored in present-day concerns and thus shifts with the tides of each day. Many factors shape this performance of memory, from the relationship of the oral historian to the interviewee to the location of the interview and the time it took place. Beyond the relationship of the oral historian and the interlocutor, the race, gender, class, and sexual orientation of the interviewer leave legible marks on the recorded product of oral history. Maurice Halbwachs suggests that the most accurate of memories are communicated between a narrator and listener who share the same social, physical, and historical frame of reference.[39] I do not suggest that accuracy is the primary goal of oral history, but that this formulation of narrator/listener is rarely achieved; instead, we must think about an oral history interview as one performance produced by a particular scenario and acknowledge that a different scenario might produce a different oral history. This appears to pose a problem, because, unlike the slight distinction of a particular performance, the goal of oral history has always been to produce a singular record.

But why was it so important to provide a fixed narrative of bracero memory? As Allan Megill explains, "When identity becomes uncertain, memory rises in value. . . . Memory is oriented *toward* the subject and is concerned with a real or imagined past only because that past is perceived as crucial for the subject, even constitutive of it."[40] In the present day, the identity of ex-braceros has become crucial for making claims in the Bracero Justice Movement, of belonging for a generation caught in a moment that called for immigration reform, and for policy makers attempting to address immigration and labor issues. Megill suggests, "An identity that solidly exists has little need for an explicit, thematized appeal to memory."[41] Bracero identity relied heavily on memory, in part because the term "bracero" has had a longer history and has been used as an overarching term to mean any Mexican worker. Politicians, public historians, Bracero Justice Movement activists, and Mexican guest workers drew strong lines to distinguish those who came through the official program from those who entered the United States as unauthorized laborers. The experiences and memories of these guest workers were constantly deployed to harden these lines of separation and create an official narrative about the program based on images of respectable labor. Ultimately, their collective identity as authorized, state-sanctioned migratory laborers "saving our crops" in a time of war created a figure worthy of being honored at the National Museum of American History. Narratives that provided a complicated vision that included deviations from this image could not be acknowledged for fear of showing these men in a negative light that would make them unworthy of commemoration.

Deviant and Defiant Braceros

I focus on deviance and defiance in order to reveal the power and interest of both Mexico and the United States in normalizing a particular type of masculinity tied to family, ethnicity, labor, and modernity. Despite both states' attempts, however, workers deviated from their interpellation and blurred the boundaries between "legal" and "illegal," indigenous and mestizo. They challenged heteronormative constructions of the nuclear family and gender expectations, organized for better labor conditions, and even now continue to fight for full compensation and recognition of the hard work they performed for both the United States and Mexico. They not only deviated from certain norms but they also purposely engaged in acts that defied the limits and the expectations that Mexico and the United States placed on them. In each chapter of this book, I move through examples that highlight particular types of deviance—from racial, to gender and sexual, to political—in an effort to examine how bracero identity is configured and how braceros are deploying those configurations to organize themselves in the contemporary moment.

Some subjects deviated from state norms, and through their defiance openly challenged and rejected the logic behind them. As scholar Lisa Cacho explains, examining deviance need not always pathologize or rationalize an individual's choices.[42] Instead, it can lead to the inclusion of previously silenced groups and, as Cathy Cohen writes, "generate new models of power, agency, and resistance."[43] We can see these new models in some of the braceros' defiant rejections of the schemas of state control and exploitation. By including dissenting voices that did exercise, and in some cases still are exercising, their agency and by demanding fair treatment from Mexico and the United States, this book attempts to chart out modes of defiance that make alternative models of bracero agency and resistance visible.

As I mentioned above, one major reason that Mexico entered into a labor agreement with the United States was its perception that this arrangement could help usher rural peasants into the next stage of modernity. The Mexican Revolution's promise of inclusion failed to come to fruition for many mestizo and indigenous populations alike. The Bracero Program provided an avenue of incorporation for these communities and relieved the state of this perceived burden. Although scholarship on the Bracero Program recognizes the discourses of race and modernity that permeated it, I unpack its effects on the indigenous populations that the Mexican government sought to transform.[44] Chapter 1, "*Yo Era Indígena*: Race, Modernity, and the Transformational Politics of Transnational Labor," examines the experiences of Mixtec, Zapotec, Purépecha, and Mayan communities in the Bracero Program. Although many Americans came to view braceros as one homogeneous group, the regional, racial, and ethnic differences among braceros shaped their social relations. Recognizing the shifting meanings of race that indigenous migrants experienced in the United States, I explore the formation of mid-twentieth-century racial constructs in Mexico and the subsequent role of indigeneity in the context of U.S. and Mexican nation-building projects.

The experiences of indigenous braceros differed on multiple levels. Some of them struggled with both Spanish and English, relying on hometown social networks in order to work and meet their daily needs. Language impacted systems of labor management in the fields, as growers and over-seers prized multilingual indigenous guest workers for their interpreting and recruitment skills. In many cases, though, indigenous communities were also more vulnerable, as some mestizo braceros reified Mexican racial hierarchies by engaging in racist practices of subjugation. Largely based on oral histories, this chapter opens up the discussion on workers' experiences to include the perspective of indigenous men and their families. With the program, the Mexican state could bypass more costly social programs that would address the modernization and integration of indigenous populations.

As both mestizos and indigenous groups left their families for prolonged periods of time, many men built new community networks in predominantly homosocial spaces in the United States. Chapter 2, "In the Camp's Shadows," examines constructions of masculinity, the maintenance of transnational families, and complex forms of sexual desire. Based on data from oral histories of indigenous and mestizo braceros located in Mexico and the United States, I argue that transnational experiences expanded gendered social relationships and practices of sexuality that redefined notions of the family and masculinity. Though women often appear only in the margins, if at all, in histories of the Bracero Program, they actually played an important role.[45] In addition to shifting into head-of-household roles in Mexico in the absence of their guest-worker husbands, some lobbied to allow women to participate in the program, and others followed their male counterparts, either to work in the informal service industries that developed along the border or to look for opportunities in the United States.

Braceros who did not have strong ties to wives or families back home were often viewed as a moral threat: by host communities as a threat to local women, by Catholic clergy as adventurers, and by growers as men who overindulged in their off-hours. Indeed, economies of vice and sex developed along the border, in local bars, at the camps, and sometimes in cars parked in the fields. Of course, many of these men enjoyed gambling, drinking, and prostitution back in their hometowns, but I argue that this type of leisure took on different and new meanings in the context of the Bracero Program and in the predominantly male spaces of the camps. Pleasure fell outside the goals of the program, so guest workers created their own spaces where they could reclaim their bodies for enjoyment instead of labor. Within these marginal spaces, they could also engage in sexual practices and create intimacy that functioned outside the binaries of heterosexuality and homosexuality, or feminine and masculine constructs.[46]

Camp life gave men an opportunity not only to express shifting desires but also to create a politics that challenged their sense of citizenship, belonging, and both Mexico and the U.S. aims for the program. Chapter 3, "Unionizing the Impossible: Alianza de Braceros Nacionales de México en los Estados Unidos," describes the trajectory of a transnational labor organization, the National Alliance of Mexican Braceros in the United States. This organization, Alianza, founded by braceros, initially challenged policy restrictions that prohibited braceros from organizing through unions. However, the eventual demise of Alianza ended up solidifying the divide between Mexican and American labor-organizing efforts in the United States. In this chapter, I trace Alianza's trajectory and explore the organization's relationship with Ernesto Galarza, a prominent labor activist. Galarza began by working to incorporate guest workers into his American unionizing efforts. However, after he grew frustrated with the Mexican government's repressive treatment of Alianza, he changed his tactics from unionizing braceros to working to terminate the Bracero Program itself. Alianza drew on larger narratives of Mexican agricultural labor exploitation that predate the program, but it was unable to connect these with systems of marginalization that created documented and undocumented, mestizos and indígenas, and literate and illiterate subjects. Although their political visions defied the norm, these visions could not include those whose undocumented status, indigeneity, or illiteracy placed them outside their unionizing efforts.

The narratives of exploitation before, during, and after the Bracero Program shape the community's present-day political strategies. Chapter 4, "*La Política de la Dignidad*: Creating the Bracero Justice Movement," chronicles the contemporary organizing efforts of the Bracero Justice Movement, which seeks to recuperate the back wages that were withheld from braceros in the form of a 10 percent deduction from each paycheck. This money was to be placed in a savings account to which braceros would have access upon their return to Mexico. However, the Mexican government never implemented a system by which braceros could access these funds effectively, and thus the vast majority of braceros never received their full salary. In 1998, Bracero Pro-A, a binational organization, began investigating the wage theft, and since then, it has led transnational efforts to regain these wages by suing Wells Fargo Bank, which managed the deductions before turning the funds over to the Mexican government. This struggle represents one of the largest transnational legal cases for the recovery of back wages in the Americas.

In this fight, the Bracero Justice Movement utilizes narratives of family and labor to set the stage for images of exploitation and emasculation, thus exposing what it sees as the Mexican government's complicit role in cheating these workers out of their full wages. Their *política de la dignidad* pulls from Mexican discourses of family to cast braceros as "sons" of a nation that has abandoned its obligation to protect them. In this way, they subvert the traditional visions of bracero labor and provide a shaking accusation of state corruption, ultimately revealing the limits of citizenship for migrant workers.[47] But the collective memory that emerges from the Bracero Justice Movement still limits stories of deviance based on pleasure and adventure, as these memories stand in the way of the goal of incriminating the U.S. and the Mexican nation-states in their failures to protect braceros. However, it privileges narratives that highlight racial deviance in order to reveal longer histories of exploitation that critique the "*mal gobierno*" or failed state that refuses to protect its citizens. The Bracero Justice Movement's political vision has shaped the production of collective bracero memory in ways that have had a lasting imprint on the oral histories documented for the Bracero History Project.

The National Museum of American History drew from this particular collective memory of braceros but placed more focus on the contracting process and labor. The epilogue focuses on the dilemmas of documenting memory for the Bracero History Archive and the reception of the National Museum of American History's exhibit, "Bittersweet Harvest: The Bracero Program, 1942–1964." The present-day political and social context in which these oral histories were collected left indelible marks on how the program is remembered. The retelling of bracero history also reveals contemporary concerns with the role that Mexican agricultural workers play in American society and sheds light on the national dilemma of immigration reform, which has been unable to address the concerns of indigenous, queer, and other deviant migrants. Indeed, reform efforts suggest that rights should be allocated unequally, based on conceptions of normativity that are currently contested within the United States as well as across borders. Thus, immigration policy serves to police not only immigrants, but also the boundaries of belonging for everyone.

Together these chapters trace the experience of the Bracero Program from the perspective of workers, and they reveal the overlooked complexities of bracero subjectivities. By critically examining memory, race, sexuality, and state power, this book reframes the material experiences of braceros and the discursive power the guest-worker program has wielded. I show the political implications of this subjectivity and the present-day efforts to create braceros as a class of laborers who stand in contradistinction to undocumented workers. By focusing on bracero memory, I demonstrate that these memories are not perfectly bound time capsules of the past, but instead are unwieldy expressions about the past that are indelibly tied to the circumstances of the present.

Through these memories, braceros themselves reveal contradictions within U.S. immigration policy that renders Mexican labor as necessary and Mexican settlement as unnecessary and unwarranted. Braceros' memories also wage strong critiques of the Mexican nation-state, demonstrating the Mexican state's twisted vision of civil rights as this now-elderly community demands reparations. Former braceros call attention to the dehumanizing nature of the program and the Mexican state's profiteering and complicity in creating a stateless class of workers primed for exploitation. They trace their marginalization to a period before their departure to the United States. This book takes the multiple dimensions of that marginalization as a starting point. What follows are indigenous workers who journeyed to the north not simply as contract laborers, but as people who complicated the racial schema of the program itself.

INTERLUDE *Me modernicé*

On Friday, May 12, 2006, I found myself carrying out an oral history at
Casa del Mexicano in Los Angeles, where I met Nemecio Meza. He and
his wife agreed to be interviewed for the project, and we made our way
toward the basement of the building. She headed into one room for
her interview, and he followed me. There, in a quiet room with a basic
table, two chairs, and a broken glass window, the interview began in the
ordinary manner in which extraordinary stories are collected. I asked
questions from an oral history guide and Nemecio graciously answered
with detail. But then, about forty-five minutes into the interview, he mentioned something that was not included in our oral history guides, even
though for him it was the greatest challenge he faced during the program:
language. He, an indigenous Nahuatl speaker from Puebla, Mexico, had
not been speaking Spanish for very long before he received his bracero
contract. I was dumbfounded at the obvious shortcoming of our guides
and quickly realized that they failed to encompass Nemecio's experience.

At that point, I revised my call when the Bracero History Project
was introduced to the public, specifically asking indigenous families to
participate by sharing their stories. A few stepped forward in small towns
in southern California, but I knew I had to learn more, so I decided to
travel to Mexico. In the summer of 2008, I asked a friend to join me on
a collection trip organized by activists that would take me across Mexico.
Equipped with a backpack containing a digital recorder, computer, and
scanner, we began in the northern city of Monterrey, following Bracero
Justice Movement organizers from town to town until we reached southern Mexico. In Cansahcab, Yucatán, I met Julio Valentín May-May, who
offered assistance after I explained to him what I was researching. He told

me, "*Yo era indígena* [I was indigenous]." The word "*era*," meaning "was," rang over and over in my mind, even after our interview ended. Coming from a different experience, I could not fully grasp how he used "was" as a racial and ethnic identification of the past. What was it about his experience that moved him away from being indigenous? Was indigeneity a fluid racial and ethnic characteristic that could be changed? I listened for answers to these questions as other indigenous braceros spoke of their experiences in the program and stated, "*Me modernicé*," I became modern, or "*Me civilicé*," I became civilized. As I interviewed more braceros indígenas, others understood Mexican modernity and mestizaje as a whitening project tied to claims of a "Spanish" identity and defiantly rejected this change by stating, "Why would I say that I am Spanish if I am indígena?"[1]

ONE   *YO ERA INDÍGENA*

Race, Modernity, and the Transformational
Politics of Transnational Labor

Their sombreros and serapes undoubtedly hung in those
dreary bunkhouses, for they were bareheaded, and their
rough black hair look[ed] as if [it was] never combed.
These *mestizos* and Indians varied in skin color.
—TED LE BERTHON

Indians from Tlaxcala, small wiry men who spoke only
the tribal tongue, showed up in Yuba City.
—ERNESTO GALARZA

Published seven years after the initiation of the Bracero Program in 1949,
Aventuras de un Bracero: Relatos de Seis Meses en Estados Unidos, remains
one of the few bracero memoirs depicting the conditions Mexican workers experienced in the United States.[1] Bracero-turned-author Jesús Topete
has his protagonist recount his six-month experience in the United States
as a guest worker. His narrative not only reveals details about the bracero
experience but also highlights popularly held notions of race in Mexico. In
one anecdote, he writes about the excitement that the protagonist and his
fellow workers felt when they heard that women would be coming in to
work alongside braceros harvesting potatoes in California. The men were
looking forward to working alongside tall, beautiful *"gringas,"* because they
spent so much time laboring only in the company of men. The protagonist
was then extremely disappointed when *"chichimecas* speaking English"
arrived. Here he used a term that technically refers to the Nahua people
of Mexico, but it is also used as a derogatory way to indicate indigeneity.
Thus, he both insulted the women and emphasized racist concepts of idealized Mexican beauty in which indigenous women are unattractive. He even
claimed that some of the men in the camp were better looking than these
groups of women.

indigenous
women

Topete says he developed a tense relationship with these Mexican American women because they made fun of the braceros, viewed them as unmodern, and often asked them if cars and telephones existed in Mexico. When one of the women asked him why he did not speak to them, he told her that he did not like to be mocked. Furthermore, the women spoke English boastfully in front of the braceros as if they were gringas and Spanish in front of the gringos, claiming they were Mexican. But the Spanish she spoke, according to him, was not even that good because it was clear that she used terms from the most remote mountains in Mexico. He went on to say, "*La cara de totonacas se les ve a tres kilómetros* [You could see their *totonaca* (indigenous people of Totonacapan) faces from three kilometers away]."[2] Here he references another indigenous population as a way to insult these women, while he also maps indigeneity onto Mexico's rural and remote areas.

The protagonist saw himself as belonging to a group that stood above rural indigeneity; as he explained, he was a cosmopolitan man from Guadalajara who had experienced modern Mexican cities with skyscrapers, movie houses, theaters, and parks. The memoir thus reveals the racialized perception that indigenous communities conflicted with or only existed outside of cosmopolitan modernity, in both Mexico and the United States. In Topete's schema, one could not be both "Indian" and modern. Although these women also strived for a cosmopolitan identity, the protagonist felt he could decipher their true identity as "Indian." His indictment also illustrates racialized relationships of power, where his modern cosmopolitan identity trumps what he perceived as these women's "true" racial identity. The protagonist intended the words "*totonaca*" and "*chichimeca*" to be insulting and belittling. Although these women inhabited new lands in which these notions of racialized appearance were understood differently, they continued to be racially inferior in his eyes, and many braceros shared this sentiment. Mexican racial systems were at once flexible and rigid. Indians could become mestizos, but a hierarchy still existed, with whiteness at its pinnacle. That is to say, although mestizaje functioned as a spectrum of mixture, whiteness had more value, and Topete felt more entitled to it.

Topete's description of this scene reveals popular perceptions about the place of indigenous communities in Mexican racial hierarchies, while it also demonstrates how race is an important construct that defined social boundaries in the transnational communities of Mexico and the United States during the Bracero Program. Although many braceros were in the process of inhabiting new geographic areas, they rooted their racial frameworks in Mexican social hierarchies and discourses of Mexican moder-

mestizo = indin erasure

nity. In the United States, migrant workers challenged and reconfigured Mexican meanings of beauty, belonging, and labor, thus reframing racial categories. Braceros negotiated American and Mexican racial constructs, as well as their implications, when being managed by American growers. While Topete's novel demonstrates how braceros grounded racial meanings in perceptions of Mexican indigeneity, his writing simultaneously renders indigenous braceros invisible. By 1940, the Mexican census estimated that "Indians" composed about 20 to 25 percent of the population.[3] However, the population of Mexican indígenas was perhaps much higher, given that census takers, politicians, and anthropologists held the power to determine whether an individual was "Indian." Furthermore, the state was invested in decreasing the population identified as Indian in order to reinforce the national racial identity of mestizo.[4] The state pressure to transform indigenous communities into mestizos makes it very difficult to determine the numbers of indigenous braceros that participated in the program.

Scholars have explored the racism embedded in the discourses of Mexican president Manuel Ávila Camacho and other government officials as they envisioned guest workers to be the racially undesirable members of the Mexican nation and most in need of modernization. Historian Ana Rosas argues that the Mexican government viewed braceros as an "intellectually, culturally, and socially inferior race."[5] They constructed the indigenous subject as socially and racially deviant and an impediment to Mexican modernity. This racism was based on the Mexican history of colonization, the oppression of indigenous communities, and nation-building strategies that focused on the mestizo as the ideal citizen. If the mestizo rural peasantry was marginalized because of its indigenous heritage, where did that leave populations that identified only as indigenous and did not claim whiteness or mestizaje? Historian Robert Buffington keenly observes, "In Modern Mexico . . . Indians would be productive citizens or be damned!"[6] That is to say, there was no place for a modern indigenous future. The Bracero Program thus became a way for indigenous communities to become "productive" citizens by learning to labor in the United States. Their bodies would be disciplined abroad and ready for integration upon their return to Mexico.

This chapter focuses on the experiences of indigenous braceros and their crucial role in shaping narratives of Mexican modernization through the Bracero Program. Mexican elites viewed indigenous people as deviant subjects who needed to be remade into Mexican mestizos for incorporation into the nation.[7] Their stories reveal how some indigenous bracero communities strived for this inclusion in the project of Mexican modernity by marking their transformation from indigenous peasant to Mexican laborer, while others rejected this premise. In learning the framework of modernity, bracero communities increasingly used the discourses of civilization, class, and race to explain the changes happening in their families, towns, and rural villages. Indigenous women evoked these discourses and argued that their husbands became more "civilized and modern" because of the program.[8] Indigenous braceros often highlighted the impact of language and attire as manifestations of the modernizing power of migration. In indigenous communities, such as the Zapotecs of Teotitlán del Valle, braceros recalled buying their "first pair of shoes and coming home with tailored pants."[9] In this context, they viewed the Mexican rural past as uncivilized, and dress standards signaled a world of difference.[10] Changes in attire became emblematic of the transformative power of bracero modernity. Men experienced the modernizing powers of the program through the Mexican and U.S. states' management of their bodies, through their new purchasing power and consumption, and finally through language and literacy, all of which shaped racial and ethnic identity and changed how these men understood and represented themselves.

The racial and ethnic identities of distinct bracero populations also shaped how individuals understood their place in the racialized landscape of the United States and their relationships with other braceros. Examining the experiences of indigenous braceros can help us question assumptions that these guest workers were racially and ethnically homogeneous. Furthermore, placing indigenous workers at the center highlights how American labor management created and perpetuated a distinct racialized system when hiring Mexican migrants. Some indigenous communities yearned to secure bracero contracts, but American officials informally barred them from the program simply because of their inability to speak Spanish proficiently. As a result, indigenous migrants were more likely to enter the United States as undocumented workers. In Mexico, official documents and processing stations utilized the dominant language of Spanish, making it more difficult for non–Spanish speakers. Conversely, other employers targeted populations to work in specific crops deemed suitable for indigenous bodies, such as picking dates. Discriminatory practices often placed these groups in dangerous jobs. This forced many indigenous braceros to rely on assistance more from hometown social networks than from other immigrant communities. For example, while many mestizo braceros from northern states like Jalisco had prior experience working in the United States and could rely on their social networks for support, many of the indigenous braceros from the central and southern states of Mexico did not share this advantage.[11] Some men from these geographic areas were the first of their communities to enter U.S. territory.[12]

The communities I focus on include the Purépecha residing in Michoacán; Mayans residing in the Yucatán; and Mixtecs, Nahuas, and Zapotecs from central Mexican states who relocated to Southern California. These communities created strong ties with the Bracero Justice Movement and were willing to be interviewed for the Bracero History Project. I trace indigenous populations through archival documents that label individuals as "Indian" and through oral histories with indigenous populations and nonindigenous populations. Many within the bracero community claimed indigenous identities because of language, while others did so through narratives emphasizing family history and culture. The lines of racial and ethnic identity were not always clear-cut; accordingly, interviewees spoke about their complicated dances across these lines and along spectrums of mestizaje. While few historians have focused on these intersections of Mexican indigeneity and migration, several anthropologists, such as Seth Holmes, Lynn Stephens, Liliana Rivera-Sánchez, and Adriana Cruz-Manjarrez, have produced pioneering works that document the contemporary migration of these communities.[13] In addition, organizers in the Bracero Justice Movement have identified indigenous communities affected by the Bracero Program in almost every geographic region of Mexico, from the northern border to southern states like the Yucatán. While my research does not encompass all the indigenous communities that participated in the Bracero Program, it does include some of those who settled permanently in the United States.

Like mestizos, indígenas wrote to the Mexican presidents pleading for work contracts. These letters reveal not only the conditions that caused them to seek out contracts, but also the additional burdens they faced. In March 1944, a group of Purépecha wrote to President Manuel Ávila Camacho requesting entry into the program because of the disaster caused by the eruption of the Paracutín volcano in Michoacán. They asked the president for the immediate "immigration of the Purépecha race," because the eruption had ruined their crops.[14] Once in Mexico City, the group of indígenas spent more then sixty days trying to enter the program. Their situation grew "precarious" because they had been lied to and deceived by false promises of contracts.[15] The next month, they wrote to the president yet again, explaining that they could not return because many had sold everything they owned to get this far and that their poverty in Mexico City had driven the men to sleep in public parks. Returning home would mean that they had "failed."[16]

Over 200 indígenas signed the letter. Some wrote their names confidently in cursive, while others had shakier signatures or wrote in block print, and still others simply left their thumbprint in lieu of a signature.

Situations like these had become such a problem that a group of women in Mexico City wrote to the president to complain that their streets and sidewalks had become "dorms" and "public urinals." They saw these men as a "danger to families" and children.[17] Three years later, Josefina González Flores, a fifteen-year-old young woman from the predominantly Purépecha area of Pátzcuaro, Michoacán, wrote to the president. "For the sake of God, can you give my father, Zacarias González Flores, a card so he can go work?" In the past, her father had held a six-month contract that had enabled him to buy a small lot, and with much sacrifice they had managed to cover their small home with a roof. Josefina added that if they had to sell it, "Where will we go?"[18] While indigenous men from Michoacán traveled a long way in the hopes of enrollment, those from southern states with large indigenous communities traveled much further, adding to their costs. Félix Aguilar gave up after he found it nearly impossible to enter the program in Mexico City in March 1944. He wrote to the president simply requesting fare to return to his home state of Yucatán.[19] Aspiring braceros continued to write the president in hopes of securing contracts, citing the need to work. By the late 1950s, Abel Matamoros, a Mixtec, pleaded for contracts for his group that had traveled from Oaxaca to Empalme Sonora.[20]

The class position of these workers shaped their decisions to settle in the United States or to return to Mexico. Families who owned their own homes and arable land in Mexico, as well as those who had other viable means to make a living, were more likely to return home. While some men had more economic and social reasons to return to Mexico, others found ways to ease their transition into life in the United States. Spanish-speaking indigenous braceros found avenues of social incorporation within the program, and some built friendships with mestizo braceros and people in Mexican American communities. Some men believed that their experiences laboring in the United States altered their sense of self, as Julio Valentín May-May's statement, "*Yo era indígena*," indicates. Other men, like Pedro Domínguez, openly embraced their indigenous identity on American soil despite the marginalization and the stigma, defying the Mexican state project that characterized their indigeneity as deviant and in urgent need of change.[21] Ultimately, the statements of both of these men reveal racialized logics of modernity.

Solving the "Indian Problem"

Modernizing Mexican indigenous communities through an emerging mode of labor management was a central concern of the dictatorship of Mexican president Porfirio Díaz (1883–1911). Scholar Jason Ruiz explains that the Mexican elite invested in the notion that "Mexico had much to gain if Americans saw the potential in Indian labor, and it appeared that the regime actively strove to spread the message that Indians could become better and more modern workers." At the turn of the century, a bureaucrat in Mexico's Ministry of Development, Otto Peust, claimed that Indians were "inert and only cultivate what is indispensable for their own consumption. Higher salaries do not make them more active; to the contrary, they make Indians work less, because they acquire what they need a little faster."[22] Here Peust creates a logic that justifies indigenous labor exploitation. Despite their resistance, "Indians" urgently needed to be transformed into modern workers so that they could become valuable citizens. Moreover, this discourse posited that "Indians" required rigid systems of management so that they could be "remade into something better."[23] The Bracero Program drew on these Mexican discourses of race and labor to create a sense that U.S. systems of labor management offered an opportunity for Mexican indígenas from the most rural areas of Mexico to recast and remake themselves into modern Mexican subjects and thus better citizens.

After the Mexican Revolution, policy makers, anthropologists, and intellectuals identified the Mexican Indian as the "problem" that Mexico faced in its efforts to create a cohesive national project that would unify and modernize the state. The perception of the "Indian problem" was based on three assumptions: first, contemporary indigenous populations were "the tired, tattered remnants of once-great races"; second, Indians represented an "obstacle to national progress"; and third, "only racial and cultural *mestizaje* could unify the nation."[24] In the 1920s, intellectuals, such as José Vasconcelos, argued that Spanish and indigenous miscegenation in Mexico created the racially ideal national subject: the mestizo. However, these discourses of mestizaje obfuscated the realities of marginalization and racism that Mexican indigenous communities faced.[25] Vasconcelos's ideas of miscegenation amounted to whitening projects whereby indigenous populations would move away from their indigeneity in order to become incorporated into the nation. Through racial mixing, "the inferior traits of non-whites would be replaced by those of the whites."[26] In an effort to build a national identity, mestizaje was coupled with *indigenismo*. Historian George Sánchez explains that, as a construct, indigenismo was "a product of non-Indians, which sought to exalt the native Indian of Mexico while destroying his culture and land base," and its goals were "to construct a sense of unifying nationalism among a diverse and unwieldy population."[27]

By the 1920s, Manuel Gamio, a prominent Mexican intellectual and the father of Mexican anthropology, pushed for the temporary migration of rural peasantry to the United States as a means of modernizing Mexican populations and to "*forjar patria* [forge a sense of nationhood]."[28] Many of Gamio's ideas were shaped by his doctoral work in American anthropology with Franz Boas, who specialized in the study of Native American communities.[29] Gamio's U.S. training and vision for Mexico demonstrates what historian Natalia Molina describes as racial scripts, or the "ways in which the lives of racialized groups are linked across time and space, and thereby affect one another, even when they do not cross paths."[30] His work was premised on a cultural relativist approach in which "cultural manifestations of different peoples" could not "be placed in a single and unique hierarchy of values, as unilineal evolution had required."[31] Gamio borrowed from the ideas of anthropologists working with Native American populations and adapted these ideas to challenge Mexican ideas about the racial inferiority of indigenous Mexicans. He wanted to fold indigenous populations into the Mexican national project, explaining, "Our end should be to make the national race homogeneous, unify the language, and make the different cultures that exist in our country converge into one."[32] Leading intellectuals thus "redefined the term Indian, making culture rather than race a determining factor."[33] As a result, they reduced the number of Mexicans who were considered Indians, making mestizaje easier to achieve, as there was no longer a need for racial mixing, because culture, "not biology, distinguished the Indian from the non-Indian."[34]

While Vasconcelos and Gamio ideologically incorporated indigenous populations into state-building projects through mestizaje and indigenismo, Mexican president Lázaro Cárdenas (1934–40) created an economic vision of incorporation through agricultural reform. Cárdenas redistributed lands through *ejidos*, a communal land system in which many indigenous populations could hold lands that could not be bought or sold as private property.[35] This was one element of the *cardenista* program, which could be used to assimilate indigenous communities into the national polity.[36] His plans of progress rested on the idea of Mexicanizing the Indians, not indigenizing the Mexicans.[37] These ejidos were not seen as the end point or the fruits of the Mexican Revolution but instead as a tenuous opening from which to incorporate these populations into a modern industrial future.[38] If they could learn to labor on their own communal lands under the strict state regulations of the ejido system, they could perhaps cultivate "modern" work habits that would allow them entry into industrial systems. This ejido system "would serve as an indispensable tool for managing change and introducing peasants to new habits of work, consumption, and clock time."[39]

Mexican politician José Gómez Esparza illustrated these concerns by explaining that the Indian problem was fundamentally economic and that they could be "first taught to work" in order to make them "productive subjects" with the subsequent desire to "eat, dress, and live better."[40] While President Manuel Ávila Camacho worked to undermine the agrarian reform put in place by Cárdenas, he also looked for new ways to incorporate the rural peasantry and indigenous communities into the national economy that were not predicated on land redistribution.[41] The Bracero Program represented one method for "modernizing" the Mexican Indian, even as artists, poets, and archaeologists deployed discourses of indigenismo to carry out the cultural work of casting indigenous populations as foundational to Mexico's past but in need of change to find a place in Mexico's future.[42]

In a current propelled by indigenismo, by 1945 mestizo intellectuals and artists were attempting to recover Mexican indigenous histories in a celebratory and romanticized fashion; however, this did not change the fact that these communities faced racism and inequality as part of their everyday lives.[43] Earlier efforts to emphasize "culture" rather than race in the formation of indigenous identities resonated, as signifiers of racial identity became more tied to class, patterns of consumption, language, and labor than to strict assessments of phenotypical racial features. In this period, indigenous populations could take on a mestizo cultural identity if they consumed items that represented the modern Mexican subject and learned to labor in ways that disciplined their bodies. This is not to say that phenotype was irrelevant, but that racial identity could shift on the spectrum of mestizaje.

To be sure, this was not the first time Mexican government officials placed hopes of modernization on migration. In fact, during the first iteration of a Mexican guest-worker program, begun during World War I, officials emphasized the skills that workers could gain.[44] In the 1920s and the 1930s, the Mexican government used land-reform policies to "lure U.S.-resident Mexicans and the U.S.-acquired skills back home."[45] During this period, the Mexican consulates encouraged the return of immigrants to their homeland with headlines like "*México llama a sus hijos* [Mexico calls to her children]."[46]

They represented powerful pleas rooted in ideas of family and belonging that aimed at moving Mexicans across the border once more.

By 1942, the Bracero Program held the potential to introduce the Mexican peasantry and indigenous populations to modernization in the American fields, without needing to redistribute wealth through Mexican land reform. Mexican officials cloaked the program in the racialized terms of Mexican modernity and as serving as a social and technological project for rural peasants of Mexico. Learning to be managed by Americans would also make this population more malleable for reincorporation into the Mexican economy. In this state-to-state project, braceros were essentially socialized into modernity in an effort to push Mexico forward technologically in the areas of agriculture and industry.[47]

Being a modern Mexican meant one would wear commercial shoes and pants instead of village-made sandals and clothes. Similarly, one would speak the national language of Spanish instead of an indigenous language. According to scholar Stephen R. Niblo, leading Mexican intellectuals, such as Manuel Gamio, argued for models in which indigenous transformation could take place through consumption. They believed that these groups needed to "live better" and that their needs should be satisfied with "goods and services," thus "overcoming the old customs that oppose every change."[48] For indigenous Mexicans, the border-crossing journey and the experience of working in the United States could bring about these changes and thus take these communities one step closer to the racial project of mestizaje.

Gamio's investment in studying both indigenous populations in Mexico and the migration of Mexicans to the United States shows how racial scripts could cross national boundaries. Ideas of race were not tightly attached to one nation but bled across borders. Mexican and U.S. racial scripts about indigeneity intertwined in this historical moment when Native Americans were also being relocated from reservations to urban centers. Federal policy shifted so that Native Americans would be encouraged "to live like other Americans without federal restrictions."[49] Proponents believed that "moving to urban areas to work and live would improve their standard of living."[50] As it was for Mexican indigenous communities, the promise of integration into the nation was premised on migration, work opportunities, and consumption. These indigenous communities across borders had similar problems framed within discourses of poverty, and the proposed solution was migration to sites of labor that could teach these populations capitalist agendas of labor rooted in measures of work and time. Unlike the Mexican nation-state, however, the United States did not provide a national racial identity that

ILLUSTRATION 1

Hoy 747 (June 16, 1951).

Native Americans could strive for. In Mexico, mestizaje was presented as the solution to integrating indígenas, and there were a myriad of avenues to transform indígenas to mestizo. The Bracero Program represented one such avenue in which the Mexican state invested little but reaped great rewards.

Indigenous Mexicans in the Popular Imaginary

Not everyone believed in the modernizing potential of the Bracero Program or its ability to recast the racial identity of indigenous communities. Some middle-class Mexican critics problematized the consequences of the program; they infantilized indigenous Mexicans and represented these individuals as children in need of state protection. Shortly after the implementation of Public Law 78 in 1951, which extended the Bracero Program, the Mexican magazine *Hoy* depicted the plight of the bracero through a caricature on its cover (ill. 1).[51] Standing on either side of a small indigenous boy are two larger male figures. The boy wears a *serape*, with the word *campesino* (peasant) written across it. On the left side is the American grower with a gun in his holster, and the words *humillaciones* and *discriminaciones* (humiliation and discrimination) written along the bottom of his Western shirt. On the right side stands a Mexican mestizo with the words *malos tratos* and *humillaciones* (poor treatment and humiliation) inscribed across his large belly. Both figures peer down with wide, menacing grins as if they are waiting to eat the child. The barefoot child is dressed in *pantalones de manta* (white linen pants) and a *serape,* symbols of his indigeneity. While his wide-open arms signal that he is waiting to be picked up by one of these patriarchal figures, the look on his face does not communicate excitement. Instead, it is as if he recognizes his poor and limited options, as Mexico is depicted as just as menacing as the United States. In fact, the Mexican character is fatter and fuller than the American figure, whose mouth is closer to devouring the child. The image articulates the indigenous bracero's dilemma anchored in racial discourses.

Mexican visions of indigeneity resonated with racial scripts in the American Southwest, in which Mexicans were already considered more "Indian" than Spanish, and this status held strong implications in the area of agricultural labor.[52] Their perceived indigenous ancestry made them exploitable labor because they were viewed as an inferior race with little potential for self-governance. American representations of the labor of Mexican indigenous populations "implied that the Mexican Indian was racially suited to primitive forms of labor—and that the subordination of Mexicans in general was justifiable on racial grounds."[53] Historian Natalia Molina explains that in the United States, "Mexicans were considered nonwhite because of their indigenous heritage, but access to resources, land, and money moved them up the social hierarchy."[54] This was also true in Mexico, as "Indians" could climb the social ladder similarly via resources, land, and money, which laboring as a bracero could provide.

Braceros were commonly depicted as indigenous in the popular culture of Mexico. Another image, titled "*Salto Mortal*," or deadly leap or somersault, was provided by cartoonist Arias Bernal and printed in *Siempre,* a Mexican political magazine (ill. 2).[55] In the image, a bracero under the circus big top leaps toward Uncle Sam, positioned on a trapeze. With his legs tightly hooked around the trapeze, Uncle Sam appears made up to look like a clown performer. His arms are firmly extended in an effort to catch the worker, and money flows out of his pockets. The bracero is wearing white cotton pants, a shirt, and a sombrero, and he is the only figure without shoes. It is unclear whether the indigenous bracero is looking toward Uncle Sam or toward the money fluttering around him. It is also unclear whether the

ILLUSTRATION 2 *Salto Mortal*, by Arias Bernal, *Siempre! Presencia de Mexico* 4, no. 31 (January 23, 1954).

worker will be successful as he attempts to grasp Uncle Sam's hands. The Mexican mestizo looking on from the background is dressed, like the figure in the previous cartoon, in a *charro* outfit. The figure of the *charro*, a traditional Mexican horseman with much more social status than a ranch or field hand, gained popularity in the Mexican golden age of cinema and was elevated to a national symbol that embodied mestizo ideals of masculinity. His outfit, shoes, fair complexion, and full mustache connote not only that he is of a higher class than the indigenous worker, but he is also racially distinct. On the mestizo's shirt appears the message, *"Falta de Seguridad en el Camino* [lack of security or safety on the road]," meaning that he does not care that the road to becoming a bracero is not safe, suggesting that the indigenous worker is expendable. The mestizo looks toward the spectacle from the safety of his trapeze, recognizing that the only person in danger is the worker. He and Uncle Sam are secure, while the bracero is in mid-flight with no trapeze or safety net in sight.

To the vast majority of Americans, the men who came through the Bracero Program were indistinguishable from one another, thus solidifying a national and racialized identity that was imposed on them. In addition to marveling at their physical appearance, Americans gawked at these men's clothes, sandals, and hats because these objects represented racial difference and aided in the depiction of these figures as "primitive" and "unmodern."[56] Photographers like Leonard Nadel captured the brownest bodies on the way to work camps and in the fields. Writers such as Lawrence and Sylvia Martin became captivated by these laborers' brown flesh and clothing, describing the braceros as including "every Indian type in the republic and every mixture of Indian with Spanish"; their regional identities could be deciphered through their attire.[57]

As men entered the United States in sandals and returned to Mexico with shoes and boots, they embodied modernization.[58] The sandals were not only a functional piece of attire but, like sombreros, also connoted regional identity, as many areas of Mexico created distinct styles. While on a guest-worker contract, Gabriel Martínez Angel compared the sombreros and sandals of his compatriots from different regions and explained that these articles suggested not only where workers were from in Mexico but also their class background, as laborers with more money would have more complicated woven leather straps on their sandals.[59] In the processes of becoming modern, some braceros did away with symbols of indigeneity and regional identity in order to adopt a broader Mexican national identity that incorporated American consumer goods. In order to assess these changes, American academics looked to Mexican intellectuals to make sense of the racial world of Mexicans. Vocal critic and scholar of the Bracero Program Henry P. Anderson noted in his studies the impact of the Bracero Program on indigenous communities. He utilized racially charged categories presented in the demographic studies of Gilberto Loyo and Lucio Mendieta y Nuñez to illuminate the place of indigenous populations in Mexico on their journey toward a teleological transition into the "modern world."[60] Language and footwear became one of the key indicators of moving away from an "Indian world" and into modernity. Anderson described those who belonged in the core segment of the "Indian world" as barefoot and as "native"-language speakers. He viewed the attire of Mexican braceros as a key sign of indigeneity and noted the malleability of this racial and ethnic category, as Mexican laborers transitioned from bare feet, to *huaraches*, and finally to shoes.[61] For these intellectuals, language closely follows these transitions. Class distinctions are implicit in the scholarship on which Anderson drew for his understanding of the movement of braceros from the "Indian world" to the "modern world."[62]

Since attire signaled modernity, many indigenous braceros were eager to consume the proper symbols of entry into the Mexican nation. Indigenous braceros argued that the program fundamentally changed the dress styles of some indigenous communities, because braceros who left for the United States with *pantalones de manta* (typically simple white cloth pants) returned wearing the newest American apparel. These *pantalones de manta* were similar to those popularly worn by many mestizo communities but were considered part of their enduring indigenous heritage. American anthropologist Oscar Lewis described these pants as "ancient white *calzones* [underwear]" that villagers pair with "huaraches."[63] For Lewis, this supposedly primitive underwear signaled not only poverty but also indigeneity. Poverty had become so interwoven with indigeneity that embracing mestizo modernity also became a route to escape poverty. The Bracero Program gave Mexicans the economic opportunity to do away with these symbols of poverty and adopt the consumer symbols of modernity, progress, and uplift, such as boots and Levi's. Although the change from "sandals to shoes" affected all poor braceros, the meanings ascribed to this change became particularly complex for indigenous communities as narratives of modernization collided with shifting meanings of race.

While the Bracero Program could transform the male indigenous rural peasant into a productive mestizo citizen, it did not hold the same potential for indigenous women. Social workers turned their eyes toward indigenous women who could not participate in the program and who needed the attention of the state in order to "adapt" to their newly modern husbands, fathers, brothers, and children.[64] *Christian Science Monitor* author Lucile Rood explained in a 1944 article, "Many of the Indian women and children from the hinterland made their first journey to the big city capital of their country when they accompanied their men to the point of debarkation last spring." Fascinated by "primitive" ways of life and fixated on tattered yet colorful attire, Rood cast this group as the greatest beneficiaries of the Bracero Program. These women dealt with intense repercussions from the departure of their loved ones: "[The] primitive unity of the Indian family dependence has made the grief of separation doubly hard for some of these women, but they have accepted it stoically."[65] The families of indigenous braceros in this article faced deplorable living conditions in Mexico City, which, coupled with their lack of knowledge of how to cash checks, write letters to their bracero family members, and adapt to a modern environment, created situations that in Rood's mind could only be addressed by a social worker. Mexican social workers focused on women living in camps along

How much do you know
about your nation's agriculture

Agricultural Life

United States Agriculture	California Agriculture	Agricultural Life
Its troubles, virtues, growth.	Its oddities, importance, economy.	Its contents— facts from this issue.

United States Agriculture — Its troubles, virtues, growth.

1. What is National Farm-City Week and why is it celebrated?

2. What do most authorities agree will eventually solve our surplus farm products problem?

3. What is a basic crop in the eyes of the Federal Government?

4. In addition to federal income taxes, how much do U.S. farmers pay each year in state and local taxes?

5. Are farmers exporting more or less of their products each year?

California Agriculture — Its oddities, importance, economy.

1. How much does California agriculture contribute each year directly and indirectly to the state's economy?

2. How many different commercial crops does California produce?

3. California produces more than 90% of the nation's supply of 11 crops. Can you name at least six?

4. How do California farm wage rates compare with the national average?

5. How much do California farmers spend each year for supplies, equipment, living expenses, etc.?

Agricultural Life — Its contents— facts from this issue.

1. What penalty does a farmer suffer when he employs Mexican Nationals when qualified U.S. workers are available?

2. How do wage rates paid Mexican National workers compare with those paid to domestic workers for similar work?

3. How much does a Mexican National worker pay for his room and board?

4. How many Mexican Nationals may a farmer employ?

5. What is the daily highlight in the life of Policarpio Ruiz?

U. S. Agriculture

1. National Farm-City Week has been proclaimed by the President each fall, beginning in 1955. President Eisenhower's proclamation in 1956 called for public recognition of the contributions of the farmer to the nation's economy and concluded, "The public should understand the needs, problems, and opportunities of all the people of the United States whose main concern is agriculture." 2. Our growing population, estimated to reach 220 million people in 1957, and to increase consumption of farm products by 50% in the next 20 years. 3. A "basic" crop is one designated by law as so important to the economy of the country that its price is supported by the government. At present, they are: wheat, cotton, rice, corn, peanuts and tobacco. 4. Farm property taxes have been climbing steadily for the past several years. Latest rise was 7% with a record $927 million collected in 1955. 5. Though exports of farm products are down from the highs of war years, recent government effort, more liberal import policies, and greater foreign economic activity have jumped farm exports to $4 billion this year, highest in 5 years.

California Agriculture

1. California's farmers contribute directly more than $2½ billion a year to the state's economy. The total swells to $10 billion by the time these farm products are processed, handled, and shipped. 2. California produces 269 commercial farm crops — more than any other state. 3. California produces more than 90% of the nation's lemons, almonds, artichokes, walnuts, olives, dates, prunes, tomatoes, lettuce, figs, and brussels sprouts. 4. California farm wages are over 50% higher than the national average. 5. California farmers spend about $2.4 billion every year.

Agricultural Life

1. An employer may lose the Mexican Nationals in his employ and his right to contract them if it is found he is not giving preference to qualified U.S. agricultural workers. 2. Mexican Nationals must be paid at a rate no lower than the employer pays his domestic workers for similar work, and domestic workers must be offered a rate no lower than that paid to Mexican workers. 3. He pays nothing for his room and the use of all camp facilities. His meals are to be at cost, but in no case more than $1.75 for 3 meals a day. 4. As many as he wishes as long as all practicable sources of our own workers have been exhausted. Mexican Nationals are imported only because a sufficient number of U.S. workers is not available. 5. Policarpio Ruiz, young bracero who is the leading character in the picture story on pages 10 and 11, says dinner time is the best part of his day.

ILLUSTRATION 3 "Boots and Sandals," featured in *Agricultural Life.*

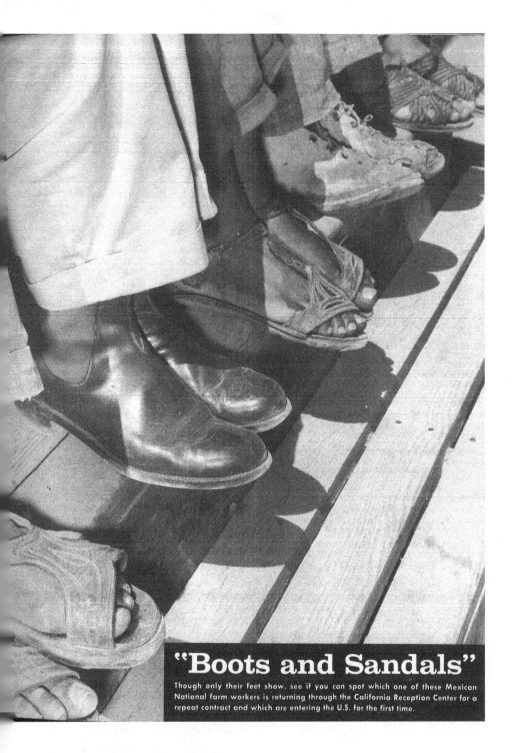

"Boots and Sandals"

Though only their feet show, see if you can spot which one of these Mexican National farm workers is returning through the California Reception Center for a repeat contract and which are entering the U.S. for the first time.

roadsides and in the "slums of the great city," to offer "free instruction in child hygiene, home and personal sanitation, knitting, sewing and cooking." These social workers also tailored programs for the families of braceros that taught the "rudiments of reading and writing so they might communicate with their husbands and sons."[66] Snapshots of indigenous women sitting and standing with striped *rebozos* (shawls) wrapped around their shoulders or placed over their heads accompanied the article. Rood described them as the "typical" group of wives affected by this migration.

Ultimately, what these and other popular perceptions of the time made clear was that "Indians" needed to be prepared for the modernization that the Bracero Program would bring. Rood argued that the income from bracero remittances could be used to buy "better clothing" and "better housing" that more closely resembled model homes that would reorganize their "primitive" way of life. It was essential for these indigenous women to learn new ways of living so that they could be "given" a "broader point of view" that would improve their condition. They would have to shed their "Indian" ways in order to accept modern comforts, moving them from the "hinterland" to incorporate them into broader Mexican society. Because indigenous women would not learn to be modern by traveling and laboring in the United States, Mexican social workers would prepare these women to adapt to the changes brought home by their bracero husbands and fathers. They could not gain entry into modernity through their own experiences in Mexico; instead, that would require mediation by their male bracero family members.

These post–Mexican Revolution depictions of indigenous Mexican communities emerged as central to Mexican national identity. And although intellectuals of the day superficially celebrated indigenous history and culture, they continued to perpetuate the popular notion that indigenous people were historic relics, not subjects of a modern Mexico. During the Bracero Program, receiving communities relied on both Mexican popular culture and American scholars of Mexican "Indians" in order to address the social needs of indigenous braceros and develop systems of racialized labor management.

Racial Imaginaries, Indigenous Imaginaries

Depictions of Mexican indigenous populations circulated throughout areas where braceros were heavily employed, such as Southern California. In the early period of the program, growers in San Bernardino County attempted to address the compounded social isolation indigenous braceros felt by urging them to attend public events specifically organized for them. In the first years of the program, growers and receiving communities attempted to address concerns of braceros by creating social spaces that were at times anchored by racially essentialized perceptions of who the men were. On July 26, 1944, the Claremont Colleges created an event for braceros featuring Mexican American performers called the Padua Players, from the Padua Hills theater troupe.[67] The Padua Hills Theater was managed under the Padua Institute by Bess and Herman Garner, who thought that the theater could expose the general public to Mexican culture and teach Mexican Americans the dance, music, and history of Mexico and California.[68] A group of indigenous braceros with six-month contracts attended the event, held in the Balch Auditorium of Scripps College.[69]

During this period, many of the Padua Players' productions featured young Mexican American women, as many young men were off at war. Furthermore, the scripts featured "Mexican women soldiers during the Mexican Revolution (*soldaderas*) and Mexican matriarchs (*Tehuanas*) in southern Mexico."[70] Productions, such as *Como Siempre*, featured young women dressed in colorful *huipils*, embroidered blouses, and headdresses in an attempt to depict indigenous populations of Oaxaca. Historian Matthew Garcia argues that although the play provided young women the opportunity to portray strong female roles, it also catered to the prejudiced sensibilities of American audiences by portraying "Mexican men as effeminate, lazy alcoholics" and indigenous women as "wedlock tyrants."[71] These ideas further reified the notions in the world of growers and labor management that these men required not only close guidance, but also labor structures that could make them productive workers and patriarchs. Although indigenous braceros were encouraged to attend this play, the image that they encountered of Mexican indigeneity seemingly supported American visions that positioned these workers and men in need of American cultural guidance.

Like this early group of braceros, Pedro Domínguez, a Purépecha from Janitzio, Michoacán, confronted an unexpected depiction of his own community while attending a film with his *patrón* (boss or landowner). At one point, the patrón invited Domínguez to take the day off and accompany him to the local theater to watch the Mexican movie *Maclovia*, which was set in Janitzio. Perhaps the patrón felt drawn to cinematic depictions of Mexicans so he could further his knowledge of his workers. Released in 1948 in Mexico, this movie became a popular frame of reference for Domínguez's patrón and his fellow braceros for understanding Purépecha communities. The film depicts a legendary love story between a Purépecha couple in

Janitzio: Maclovia, played by Maria Félix, and José Maria, played by Pedro Armendáriz. The movie explores relations between the indigenous people and outsiders as they fight over the military occupation of Janitzio and the abuse of power by a self-identified "white, with blue eyes," sergeant who is in love with Maclovia.

During the golden age of Mexican cinema, indigenous images flourished as directors placed brown bodies among scenic vistas. Mestizos were cast as the indigenous protagonists, while indigenous communities were relegated to the backdrop. These images commonly circulated across the border.[72] Sharing a movie experience with his patrón was an extraordinary experience for Domínguez, as guest workers rarely shared spaces of leisure with management. The patrón expressed surprise when he found out that the beautiful site of the movie was, in fact, where Domínguez was from. "That *patrón* did not believe I was from there." The patrón replied, "You're not from there, only rich people should live there because it is so beautiful in the movie." To which Domínguez responded, "I am from there. . . . I felt really proud."[73] For the patrón, beauty was reserved for the rich, and it seemed like a contradiction that indigenous people could live in such a picturesque landscape.

Pedro Domínguez recognized that his patrón and others did not know he was Purépecha because language was one of the key markers of racial and ethnic identity. "No one knew I was indigenous," he explained, until they heard him speak Tarascan.[74] He pointed out that many men from indigenous communities felt embarrassed and hid their indigenous identity by not speaking languages that would irrevocably racialize them as indígena. Popular depictions of Purépechas caused many in his camp to express fascination with them. He and his friend from Janitzio spoke in Tarascan, and other braceros listened with curiosity to what they were saying. Domínguez said, "They [monolingual Spanish speakers] were very interested in learning Tarasco,"[75] because being bilingual in Spanish and an indigenous language could make them indispensable employees in the context of managing indigenous communities. Speaking an indigenous language also came at a risk because it would racialize a Mexican bracero as indigenous and hence make him vulnerable to shaming, additional exploitation, and marginalization. But Domínguez did not hide his indigeneity, emphasizing, "Why should I be embarrassed? Why would I say that I am Spanish if I am indigenous?"[76] His statement provided a challenge to the hegemonic discourses that positioned transitioning away from indigeneity as a vital function of the program. Implied in these racial scripts is the assumed desire of indigenous populations to embrace racial and ethnic change as the only entry into the national project of mestizaje. Domínguez acknowledged that the core of this project privileges whiteness coded as "Spanish," and he rejected that notion and challenged the assumption that indigeneity should cause embarrassment. Through his rejection of mestizaje, he defiantly stood against the racial project of Mexican modernity and embraced indigeneity. He posed a critique of the narrative of racial transformation that both Mexico and the United States promoted within the program.

Although many could not tell the specific ethnicity of Mexican guest workers, some contractors, farmers, foremen, managers, and community members noted these differences in order to more effectively develop systems of labor management. As Elizabeth Esch and David Roediger explain, "Racial managerial knowledge was often tantalizingly close to being systematized but remained more effective if informally wielded by lower managers who hurried and pushed workers, and often hired and fired them."[77] In the case of contractors and farmer-owners, some specifically targeted or avoided indigenous braceros based on their racialized perceptions that specific groups were better suited for certain types of agricultural labor. Although indigenous labor was incorporated into the railroad component of the program, there is more evidence in both oral histories and the archives of their use in agriculture.

Reading and managing brown bodies informed behaviors at several points in the contracting process: first at the contracting station; then in medical examinations; and finally in being selected or assigned to a particular growers' association or grower. Elvon De Vaney, a former contractor for the cotton industry in Texas, described his preferences for laborers using biologically racist terminology. "There was only one type of individual or group of individuals we kinda shied away from and this was the little bitty short Indian fellas from way down on the southern end of Mexico." His knowledge of Mexican geography intersected with his understanding of racial difference, as he went on to explain:

> They was so short . . . they couldn't get the tube up . . . it's about a
> forty-foot pipe. . . . So we had to shy away from them little guys especially in the [irrigation]. . . . They were kinda dwarf, midget type. . . .
> The closer to the border, usually the better educated in our ways of
> farming they'd be. . . . We tried to get boys . . . if they were from the
> states of Durango or Zacatecas, San Luis Potosi . . . what we'd call the
> mountain states . . . those boys were generally bigger and stronger.

They were meat eaters, ranch country-type folk. . . . They were bigger and stronger and more stable. A lot of time, Chihuahua and border state boys were kinda rascals, just a little bit a lot of times, so if we had a choice we'd get your mountain type fellars.[78]

For De Vaney, indigenous braceros were not as sought after as the taller mestizos from the mountainous areas of Mexico because the "dwarfs" or "midget" types were seen as unviable for working in cotton production. De Vaney went on to explain that when choosing braceros he also avoided men from the border, as the ideal bracero came from the country and not cities. He perceived mestizos from the border as more assertive and indigenous populations as more docile. Perhaps because of the proximity to the United States, braceros from borders areas were more likely to have experience working in the United States and therefore more knowledge of how to maneuver through and resist exploitative practices in the fields. Defiant braceros could use the program to enter the United States and skip out on their contracts if better opportunities presented themselves. It was the job of contractors like De Vaney to find a workforce that could stick out the contracts and would not complain when growers violated the terms of the contract.

Braceros understood what the various visual markers meant and manipulated them to perform particular identities to their advantage. De Vaney stated, "Our selectors learned this first, you see an ol' kid coming and if he had on pointed shoes, kinda high top boots and zoot suit britches . . . you'd kind of just thumb him over the side . . . and get the ol' boy with the hat behind him. That had on him a big ol' straw hat and the rubber tire shoes cause you'd know more or less that he was a farmer. . . . This other might be a ukulele player over on Juárez." Migrant workers became aware of this, and, as De Vaney explained, "it wasn't too long before till they wised up, to what was taking place, they'd pack their zoot suit britches and their sharp pointed shoes in a suit case and get the ol' tire casing sandels and that's the way they'd come through the selection line. . . . And then as soon as you'd select them they'd put on their sharp pointed boots."[79] Cosmopolitan men, border dwellers, and urban zoot suiters learned to perform indigeneity, poverty, or general naïveté about the program in order to garner favor. These new performances of race and class upended the visual knowledge of growers. Laborers utilized managements' symbols of identification in order to recast themselves as "ideal" braceros. They understood how to navigate American racial ideologies and used that knowledge to their own advantage.

Some Mexican workers along the border also had English-language skills that could make them more difficult to exploit. Bracero Rosendo Alarcón Carrera explained that on one contract near the final years of the program, he worked in Pecos, Texas, with a grower who, in his eyes, broke the rules of the contract by having the braceros work for other growers. The group of workers found out because, as Alarcón Carrera described, one bracero in his group "knew a lot of English and spoke to us." This English-speaking bracero, from Juárez, Mexico, understood what other braceros could not because of the language barrier and organized the braceros into reporting the grower to the growers' association.[80] Situations such as these led growers and contractors to view men whom they caught "passing" as country folk as more troublesome and less effective field workers.

Growers, like foremen and contractors, believed that their ideal laborer was a man from an agricultural community with little to no education and few literacy skills. These values were embedded throughout the contracting process as officials in Mexican processing stations inspected the hands of braceros in search of calluses that were indicative of agricultural work.[81] This set of characteristics sought by employers placed indigenous laborers in a double bind: going from the most desirable because of their exploitability to the least employable because of their perceived low level of intelligence and presumably weaker physique. The simultaneous attractiveness and unattractiveness of utilizing indigenous labor demonstrated how labor management's narratives of race impacted workers. Esch and Roediger argue that this is a larger trope in American histories of labor management, as being "able to preside over such contradictions require[d] that managers pretend to possess a knowledge of race and of human behavior that they could never have had."[82] As I will describe later, indigenous men with some Spanish-language skills could, like the zoot suiter playing the role of campesino, manipulate these understandings to their advantage.

Other industries that participated in the Bracero Program, such as date-palm cultivators, specifically targeted indigenous men because of the perception that they were physically and psychologically suitable for this kind of work. The medical community validated these ideas by deploying "scientific" and "statistical" language deemed objective. In one such report that appeared in *Today's Health*, a publication of the American Medical Association, Thomas Gorman explained, "An interesting recent development in the examination of workers is the testing of their physical aptitude for different crops. The accident rate in working on date palms has been cut noticeably by using young men who work well at heights."[83] The medical community backed the date-palm growers' racialized ideas of labor by deploying discourses that tied the men's physical bodies to aptitudes for working with particular crops.

Mestizo and indigenous braceros understood the racialized discourses of labor management and the scientific racism at the core of these logics. When I first met Nahua bracero Nemecio Meza in Los Angeles in 2006, he broadened my perceptions of the bracero experience by confiding in me that speaking little Spanish was his biggest challenge in the program, as he was raised in the state of Puebla-speaking Nahuatl. I was also interested in the way he sensed growers' perceptions of indigenous communities. He explained that the date-palm industry targeted Zapotecs and Mixtecs from Oaxaca, because "they were not a tall people, they were short. They could withstand [high] temperatures because their land was very hot."[84] Nemecio drew a parallel between Oaxaca's climate and Southern California's hot and arid date-growing area. This assessment also rested on racist scientific discourse of human adaptation, and although Nemecio claimed an indigenous identity, he saw himself as very distinct from Zapotecs and Mixtecs. This belief also pointed to a hierarchy and tensions within Mexican indigenous populations that deemed certain indigenous people ideal for particular work.

As many employers targeted rural peasants who supposedly had little education, it became counterintuitive to provide formal education programs in the United States. In some geographic areas, English and literacy courses fell out of favor quickly. Ernesto Galarza recorded the perceptions of E. C. Rosenberger, a manager for the Upland Heights Orange Association, stating, "His idea was that the more the Mexican worker was educated, the harder he became to handle. As far as he was concerned, he preferred to have them left alone."[85] Education could have serious implications for the management of guest workers. According to Galarza, growers "felt that [the workers] were already getting far more out of life than they had ever before enjoyed; they were learning habits of spending totally out of proportion to their needs or condition in life; and the more they earned, the more they wanted. Educating them was just another way of looking for trouble."[86] Literacy meant that these men could also read their contracts and come to a better understanding of their rights as guest workers in the United States. Many managers and foremen chose men they felt they could easily handle and oversee. Some went so far as to take advantage of these men based on illiteracy in both the English and the Spanish languages.

The Language of Modernity

Non–Spanish-speaking braceros often experienced exploitation that was compounded by their inability to express themselves in the dominant languages of Spanish and English. Employers and fellow braceros could take advantage of these workers, knowing that it was more difficult for them to protest. Employers created discourses that pathologized indigenous workers in order to reinforce power relations and limit their recourse. Zapotec men, like Antonio Feliciano Ramirez and his friend Juan F. Torres, experienced this firsthand when they found themselves working in Plainsboro, New Jersey, for the Pennsylvania Railroad Company in 1945.[87] It is likely that this was not Torres's first guest-worker contract in the United States, as he had some rudimentary English skills but spoke little to no Spanish.

In the summer of 1945, Feliciano Ramirez injured himself at his work site. Although other workers witnessed the accident, he did not report it immediately. The nature of the incident is not exactly known, but he suffered severe back pain and lesions to his left eye. When he decided to inform his supervisor, J. P. Zealy, about his injury, he asked his friend Torres to act as his interpreter. Zealy did not believe that the accident had indeed occurred at the workplace, and he also downplayed the severity of the injuries. In the formal report, Zealy wrote, "My observation reveals that he [Ramirez] is either slightly demented or greatly faking." Moreover, Zealy found it difficult to believe Ramirez because he could not establish the precise date of his injury. Zealy could have answered this question by asking Ramirez's co-workers, but he did not show any interest in interviewing witnesses to the accident.

Ultimately, Ramirez signed off on an injury report that did not recognize his rights to proper settlement for his injuries. His case was reviewed, and a formal hearing took place. Ramirez also visited a doctor who verified his injuries, but he was still unable to establish that he had been, in fact, wounded on the job. Management asked Ramirez to return to work, but when his injuries prevented him from carrying out his job, the company terminated his contract, thus forcing him to return to Mexico. Before his departure, Ramirez signed documents that authorized his friend Torres to represent his interests and collect compensation for his injury. During a review of the hearing, many questions about translation arose, as Torres acquired legal counsel that argued that Ramirez's language abilities could not accurately express his answers to the questions he was being asked during the hearing. His representative pointed out:

The last question in the record of the July 28 hearing is: "Has this investigation been conducted in a fair and impartial manner according to the rules and regulations?" The answer recorded is: "Yes, this investigation has been conducted in a fair and impartial manner. I have—the statement in its entirety and it is true and correct to the best of my knowledge." The irrelevance of this question and answer given is obvious. Ramirez is an illiterate. The rules and regulations covering the proceedings in which he was involved were totally beyond his knowledge and understanding. He could not possibly have read the statement in its entirety. Neither could it have been read to him, since the interpreter did not know how to read either in English or Spanish.[88]

The hearing revealed that the company did not provide Ramirez with a proper translator, as Torres was not literate in either English or Spanish, and the extent of his ability to speak Spanish was also not clear. The legal representation to the case argued that there were many additional errors in translation and that Ramirez had signed documents that were not made clear to him.

Additionally, Ramirez's legal counsel took offense that Zealy pathologized Ramirez as either demented or a liar. They wrote:

> A moment's thought will suggest that Mr. Zealy did not have to venture into psycho-logics and neurology to find probable reason for Ramirez' inability to remember dates and places. If the American, English speaking supervisor were to find himself in the midst of Zapoteca Indians; if he were to be interviewed by a Zapoteca Indian with the aid of a Mexican who could not read or write Spanish or English; and if the supervisor did not know a word of Zapoteca and only a few words in Spanish, it is likely that he would not be able to remember dates, places, and names to the satisfaction of his questioner.[89]

It is unclear whether Ramirez did in fact receive compensation in Mexico for his injury, but what is clear is that Zealy believed that he could manipulate the circumstance because of Ramirez's inability to express himself in the dominant languages of Spanish and English. Despite his vulnerability, Ramirez created avenues to attempt to address grievances. He authorized Torres to work on his behalf in hopes that his bilingual friend would be able to resolve the conflict. Though allowing his friend to represent his interests ultimately did not work in his favor, Ramirez's story is an example of how indigenous braceros relied on fellow community members for support. Similar linguistic networks of support arose in agricultural fields across the United States as monolingual indigenous men attempted to secure contracts and navigate their daily lives. These linguistic circles became an important resource for indigenous people to make their way through the program and deal with discrimination.

As early as 1944, racialized systems for managing indigenous braceros emerged and were heavily shaped by linguistic circles. In one of Ernesto Galarza's studies of Mexican guest workers in San Bernardino County, he noticed the growing presence of indigenous populations, specifically Purépechas: "In one camp there is a group of nine Indians from one village in Mexico. They speak only their own Tarascan dialect." Galarza further explained that, in addition to the field foreman, who only spoke English, the employers also hired a Mexican who understood Tarascan to work as a translator between the foreman and the workers. "Through him, orders and instructions are relayed to the Indian group."[90] Monolingual Tarascan speakers strategically stuck together during contracting to ensure that a functional linguistic circle could be developed once at the work site. Some growers took it upon themselves to reinforce these circles by purposely hiring groups from shared linguistic communities. This also streamlined communication with management. Another grower went so far as to employ an assistant camp manager who was described as "a local well-educated Mexican Indian." Perhaps the grower felt compelled to emphasize that this person was "well educated" in order to validate the valuable role the local would come to play in the camp. Even mestizo braceros noted that indigenous laborers were preferred for certain types of agricultural work and deployed racist logics that highlighted the indigenous body in order to understand growers' preferences.[91]

In these labor-management systems, bilingual indigenous braceros became prized employees and took on what we might call middle-management roles. Nemecio Meza described how, ten years after Galarza's study, these systems of labor management of indigenous groups persisted. He explained to me that "for every ten people, they looked for a Oaxacan who spoke Zapotec and Spanish to serve as a translator for his people. And then the boss would ask the translator of the group of ten Oaxacans . . . he would tell them what they needed to do or how to work. Everything their boss wanted he would tell the translator. That's how they did it at that time."[92] Unlike Spanish-speaking braceros, indigenous workers directed complaints and concerns toward indigenous middle management, and those individuals could choose whether to translate these concerns and raise them or to ignore them. Furthermore, they also held the power to shift translations as they saw fit. Language centralized power into the hands of a few and thus streamlined the use of indigenous braceros in American systems of labor. This also makes it highly likely that these prized laborers would be given preference for special contracts, ensuring their return to particular sites and giving some the opportunity for family reunification.[93]

Contractors and management in the date industry believed that indigenous braceros were ideal for the type of labor needed in date harvesting and also relied on the social networks of indigenous braceros to recruit more temporary laborers. Isaias Sánchez was an indigenous bracero who spoke Spanish and actively sought out date-palm work. Although he had experience tending to several different crops, he acquired skills working in date-palm fields specifically because he valued how easy it was for him to obtain contracts working in that industry. Some braceros considered it undesirable work because falling from a tall palm tree could mean death or permanent disability. Sánchez, on the other hand, found it made it easier for him to obtain contracts. While many other men waited for days, weeks, or months at processing centers in Mexico, he recognized that he could capitalize on a specialized expertise in order to avoid long waits. On one of his trips, Sánchez arrived at the contracting center to find that there was a slight shortage of braceros to work the date palms. A center worker approached him and asked if he could bring him thirty laborers. Sánchez went back to his hometown and recruited friends. Eventually, after Sánchez gathered enough experience as a date worker, he was given an identification card that helped him obtain bracero contracts more quickly (ill. 4). During one call for date workers, only five men had an identification card, making him the envy of other workers who awaited contracts. Because Isaias spoke Spanish as a first language and was connected to indigenous communities, he became a prized employee. Although language could easily have marked him as mestizo, he identified with indígenas and understood the power of language and identity.

As other indígenas learned to speak, read, and write Spanish, they could also take a step closer toward projects of mestizaje, whereby the nation could imagine and celebrate indigenous culture and history from the vantage point of the mestizo. Educational volunteers, fellow workers, foremen, and growers could all provide moments of linguistic learning in the accepted dominant languages. In Mexico, language was a powerful symbol of race,

ILLUSTRATION 4 Isaias Sánchez's identification as an experienced date worker. Bracero History Archive.

and monolingual speakers of indigenous languages were cast in more rigid racial terms, as anthropologists, census takers, and government officials were more likely to label a monolingual as indigenous. Spanish-speaking indígena braceros could more fluidly alter their own racial identity and assert a mestizo identity in Mexico. This racial claim could be augmented by Spanish literacy. While growers in the United States could see physical difference and could decipher contours of indigeneity, Mexico provided a setting where racial identity could work in a fluid spectrum, which, of course, had its limits. Indigenous populations could work toward a mestizo identity, but they could never solely assert the Spanish or European identity that composed a prized part of mestizo identity.

Indigenous communities understood the power of language in Mexico through a racializing lens long before they went to work in the United States. Some families who sought greater economic opportunities and incorporation, or simply wanted to bypass the labor discrimination tied to indigeneity, encouraged their children to learn Spanish. Mayan bracero Alonso Ayala explained, "My father didn't like us to speak Mayan, and my mom spoke Mayan."[94] Harking back to a colonial period of indigenous labor exploitation, he explained that he had gotten tired of working in a hacienda system. *Patrónes* in this system often viewed indigenous populations as an exploitable source of labor. Ayala explained, "It was like slavery."[95] He finally decided to leave in search of a guest-worker contract, because, "well, because things were difficult here. We worked hard and we earned very little."[96] According to Ayala, in order to increase economic opportunities, indigenous parents encouraged their children to speak Spanish. This proved to be a valuable skill, because during the program Ayala experienced less isolation than workers who could not speak Spanish or English.

Even multilingualism did not lead to complete integration with fellow braceros because many workers brought with them mestizo Mexican attitudes toward indigenous populations that affected whether some workers would express an indigenous identity. Like Julio Valentín May-May, Ayala recalled that other braceros made fun of Mayans and caused some Mayans so much discomfort that they would not speak their language. He remembered that "many . . . were embarrassed to speak Mayan."[97] Braceros who held a command of Spanish, like Ayala, could potentially distance themselves from indigenous racialization by refraining from speaking indigenous languages.

Some braceros took advantage of educational opportunities to learn Spanish, not only because it held the potential to circumvent discrimination but also because it provided an avenue for social incorporation into camp life and into a broader social world upon their return to Mexico. In the early years of the Bracero Program, growers and receiving communities often offered English classes and literacy courses, but some educators quickly determined that they would have to include basic education in Spanish as well. Patricia Sahera, a resident of an agricultural community in Salem, Oregon, joined a group of young women who taught such courses. Many of these women studied Spanish during high school, and their command of the language ranged from basic to advanced. During her time as an instructor, Sahera came in contact with indigenous braceros who challenged her notions of the racial and ethnic homogeneity of Mexican migrant workers. Twice per week, during the evenings, she taught an English-language course using a Sears catalog for illustrations. Sahera recalled, "I can remember using the Sears' catalog a lot to get pictures of things because some . . . of the Mexicans, well they were from Mexico but they were Indians who did not speak Spanish and they would relate to the picture well and you could give them the Spanish and the English or the ones that spoke Spanish, we tried to stress the English and we all laughed, some of those ladies were quite good with their Spanish."[98] Perhaps it was amusing that these young women held a better command of Spanish than these native-born Mexicans. Sahera also explained that many of the Spanish speakers assisted the non–Spanish speakers. Many of these young volunteers taught indigenous men basic Spanish so that they could then teach them a bit of English. Through the program, non–Spanish-speaking Mexicans gained language skills that would prove useful upon their return to Mexico. Sahera's incorporation of the Sears catalog also further exposed laborers to modes of popular consumption. As braceros turned the pages, they saw a cornucopia of American goods and imagined themselves in the newest Levi's jeans and dapper shoes.

Braceros, such as Nemecio Meza, explained that it was through their guest-worker contracts that they gained much greater exposure to the Spanish language than they had had in Mexico. He was raised speaking

Nahuatl and learned Spanish at the age of fifteen. As a traveling musician, Meza's father became very fluent in Spanish, even though Meza's mother and grandmother never learned Spanish. In 1959, Meza found himself traveling with his father to Empalme, Sonora, to try to obtain a bracero contract. This was familiar terrain for Meza's father because he had gotten several contracts previously. They waited for a contract together in Empalme, but officials in the contracting center sent them to two different employers. Meza ended up working in a very large farm in Cucamonga, California, and later obtained two additional contracts in King City, California, and Lorenzo, Texas. Meza encountered many contracting and work difficulties but lamented that his greatest struggles were with language. He had been practicing Spanish for only five years by the time he arrived in the United States as a bracero. Meza explained that his experiences as a bracero in the American Southwest strengthened his command of Spanish, which later facilitated his migration from Puebla to the Mexican border after his bracero contracts ended, and eventually during his move to Los Angeles. While the acquisition of Spanish-language skills could lead to their reincorporation into the Mexican economy upon their return home, the ability to speak Spanish also became a key factor that affected a bracero's decision to stay, as he could find support and social integration into already existing Mexican communities in the United States.

Although indigenous bracero Isaias Sánchez did speak Spanish, his family attempted to dissuade him from pursuing a contract because of his illiteracy. "You don't know how to read, you don't know how to write," his father angrily noted.[99] So how could he venture out of the country? But Sánchez was convinced that he, like many other laborers with limited literacy, could figure it out. By the time Sánchez was eighteen years old, his father was already in the United States on what Sánchez called an "adventure." When his father came back, Sánchez told him he had obtained the paperwork he needed to seek out a bracero contract. After a previously unsuccessful attempt to secure a contract, Sánchez made his way to the border in April 1955. Since his efforts to obtain a contract in Irapuato failed, Sánchez believed he could find success at the contracting stations on the border. He did not know how to read and write well, but in 1959 a maternal great-uncle, Bruno, taught him how to write his name. Prior to learning, Sánchez used his fingerprint in place of his signature. Bruno approached him and said, "Look, Shorty, you have a chance to at least learn to sign your name. I am going to show you."[100] Sánchez accepted and said, "That man taught me. He went to the store and brought me back a chalkboard, the Coca-Cola kind. And on it he started writing letters and all of that."[101] Bruno told Sánchez, "Let's renew our contract and you will not use your fingerprint,"[102] meaning he would use his signature in lieu of his fingerprint. He learned enough to write his wife a letter. This was a great triumph for Sánchez, as he was able to work and learn in the United States in ways that he could not in Mexico. Through the Bracero Program, he continued to go back and forth from his hometown to the United States until 1964. Eventually, after the termination of the program, he settled in California.

Navigating Ethnic and Racial Hierarchies

While bilingual indigenous braceros like Sánchez could rise to the ranks of middle management, those who only spoke indigenous languages could feel intense alienation. In the chaotic contracting centers, separation from their linguistic circle could open indigenous men up to additional isolation, exploitation, and violence. For many mestizos, these experiences could be associated with Anglos and Mexican Americans, but indigenous workers often experienced these at the hands of their mestizo counterparts. Unlike mestizos and bilingual indigenous people, monolingual speakers of indigenous languages were also less likely to find the support they needed to break contracts and move to urban centers on their own. Their dependency on the few bilingual workers who played the role of interpreters also meant they could easily be taken advantage of by these same men.

As one of only two Tarascan speakers at his work site during his first contract, Pedro Domínguez felt intense isolation. He was a guest worker in the United States for three consecutive years, for approximately six months per year. Braceros from other indigenous communities in Oaxaca attempted to communicate in their native language with Domínguez and his friend, but they were unable to understand each other. He said, "There were the Oaxacans as well and they spoke to us, but we could not understand them because they speak in another way and we could not understand them, and the same goes for them. I think they could not understand us either."[103] They made efforts to build broader social networks. Domínguez described how he sought out relationships with other Tarascan speakers: "We looked for each other, because we were unhappy."[104] In an attempt to feel less isolated and help each other, they built networks of community and support based on their language group.

Managers in the fields noted the tensions between mestizos and indigenous braceros, and in some cases attempted to mediate it. Felix Flores, a Purépecha from Janitzio, Michoacán, explained the racial and ethnic tensions in the program. In order to deal with the discrimination that could potentially arise, one of the men who brought Felix Flores to a field in Texas gave a speech about equality as he dropped off the new braceros. Flores recounted, "In the barrack he would tell them . . . 'Look, guys, *paisanos* [fellow countrymen], here are the other *paisanos*. You're going to treat each other like people. You're going to treat each other like brothers. You're going to treat each other like nephews. You're not going to fight. And they speak another language, and you another language, and others speak other languages.'"[105] This particular camp employed braceros from various mestizo and indigenous communities, and the contractor knew that the indigenous braceros were susceptible to intra-ethnic tensions and racially discriminatory practices. The contractor attempted to circumvent these issues early on by addressing mestizo braceros directly. Some Tarascan braceros avoided speaking in front of other braceros because they did not want to call attention to themselves and be stigmatized. Many Mexicans recognized the relationship the Purépecha community had forged with ex-president of Mexico Lázaro Cárdenas and viewed the Purépecha as leftists and communists. Flores recalled that non-Tarascan speakers would at times tell them "that we were Bolsheviks," because they were speaking Tarascan.[106]

Flores recalled mestizo discrimination and social marginalization of indigenous braceros. He recounted how men working at his camp called a group of workers with large sombreros *venados*, or deer, because they used blankets with deer on them, while the indigenous braceros were referred to as *enanitos*, or dwarfs. These taller men intimidated the indigenous braceros. When the *venados* teased them, the men from Janitzio said, "Relax don't pay attention, if we pay attention they will throw us over there."[107] Flores thought they could be easily tossed aside and physically assaulted by the *venados*. He explained, "They are tall and we are short."[108] They felt their stature prohibited them from defending themselves physically, but they found the support and advice they needed to face the situation within their close-knit circle. They created networks of solidarity to deal with unfair treatment and the menacing presence of the *venados*.

Isaias Sánchez also illuminated these tensions, but he experienced them across the country in Southern California's date industry. He remembered that when he was fifteen, men from his largely Zapotec hometown of San Pedro Apostol, Oaxaca, returned from the program: "The first ones that came [back] in 1945, the first men that came here, they had gone over there and they said that the United States is, 'cool, there is a lot of work, and you make a lot of money.'"[109] After several failed attempts to obtain a contract in 1955, he finally succeeded in becoming a bracero, making him one of the 126,453 men who left the state of Oaxaca as a bracero in the years 1951–64.[110] Sánchez used to get angry with fellow braceros who would make fun of the indigenous braceros who spoke to each other in their native languages. "They humiliated them, they said things to them," he explained.[111] In response, Sánchez recalled, "I said to them, 'Don't say anything to them. What they are speaking, they speak it because they understand each other that way. And why do you get involved, you have no right to offend them.' 'And who are you' 'I am part of them!' We got into it."[112] He explained, "Well they would insult them, they would say bad words to them, and that's not fair, that's not fair."[113] Sánchez pointed out to his friend, "They don't even understand you if you insult them, because they only know how to speak very little Spanish."[114] He took the treatment of other indigenous braceros personally and felt compelled to stand up to the injustices committed against them.

Julio Valentín May-May, a Mayan from the Yucatán, also experienced racism and discrimination directly. In May 1962, he left his hometown of Cansahcab to embark on the long and arduous journey of obtaining a contract. When he was finally issued one, May-May entered the United States through Calexico, California. Officials of the Bracero Program sent him to work in Blythe, California, which is located in the Sonoran desert near the Arizona state border. The grueling work and hot climate killed eight people, by May-May's count. It was common for the temperature to climb into the high 90s and over 100 degrees Fahrenheit in May and June. Many men from his town decided to return to Mexico rather than work in these harsh conditions. The high mortality rate May-May witnessed demonstrated that indigenous populations were targeted as expendable laborers who could work in dangerous conditions.

During his time in the United States, it was clear to May-May that some people did not like him because he was Mayan. In the fields, one worker stole May-May's boxes of produce in order to take credit, and payment, for May-May's work. "He hates me," May-May concluded and explained that just because braceros spoke Mayan, "[the mestizo bracero] disliked them."[115] This bracero was prejudiced against indigenous Mexicans and thought he had the right to exploit their labor by stealing their boxes of produce and receiving payment for them. Some mestizos worked toward implementing racial hierarchies in order to claim positions that placed them above indígenas.

In the face of this blatant racism, May-May could have chosen to stop speaking his language, but instead he explained that when he found another

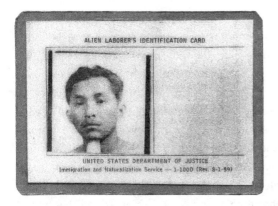

ILLUSTRATION 5 Julio Valentín
May-May's bracero identification,
front side, June 19, 1962. Bracero
History Archive.

Mayan speaker he would speak Mayan, "so that others could not listen."[116]
He found many advantages to speaking Mayan and creating linguistic social
circles. Many of the large-scale farms in Blythe used barracks lined with
bunk beds to house braceros. The housing was sparsely furnished and personal space was very limited; privacy was almost nonexistent. There was very
little space for personal items, and many men struggled with the inability to
find privacy. Under these dehumanizing conditions, Mayans found ways of
creating private social spaces in public through the Mayan language. Non-
Mayan speakers could not eavesdrop or join the conversation, and Mayans
shared information and advice in this private sphere. They connected with
each other through conversations in indigenous languages and fought to
create confidential and intimate spaces in public settings.

One of several Nahua braceros working in the grape industry in Fresno,
California, in the late 1950s, Florencio Martínez Hernández utilized indigenous language circles to organize a strike around pay. "We spoke in *mexicano*
and they couldn't understand us, [and] in that way we could organize even
though it was prohibited, and fight for a just salary. We created the strike
in *mexicano*," Martínez Hernández said.[117] He used the word *mexicano* to
refer to Nahuatl because it is popularly known in Mexico as the language
of the Aztecs. For the duration of the strike, Nahuatl speakers decided to
speak solely in that language. After a month on strike and several threats of
deportation, the grower finally agreed to meet the demands of 160 braceros,
the majority indígena. Martínez Hernández proclaimed, "We didn't understand English and they didn't understand *mexicano*, so we were even."[118]
For Martínez Hernández, Nahuatl became a critical tool for challenging
exploitation and unfair practices. Braceros used the private linguistic circle
created by speaking Nahuatl to fight for their labor rights and in the processes dispel the myth that indígenas were a docile workforce.

While some men remember how indigenous languages helped them form support networks, other bracero indígenas were wary of placing too much trust in each other. Felix Flores pointed out the threat of braceros being assaulted on their return trips, which, as he explained, were just as dangerous, if not more, than the departure because of the cash they were often carrying. Flores was deeply disturbed by the reality that many of the assaults were perpetrated by men from the same hometown, as they often knew how much their friends had saved. But the real root of the problem of theft was that illiterate and indigenous-language–speaking families had few avenues for communication. Domínguez points out that since his contracts only lasted forty-five days, he did not write his family. He also explained that even if he had written them, they did not know how to read. Their lack of Spanish literacy led Domínguez to believe that his effort to communicate with his family through letters was in vain. Although other illiterate mestizo braceros experienced the same hurdles in communication, Domínguez's problem was compounded by his family's lack of Spanish-language proficiency. This uncertainty with the process of communicating the instructions his wife needed to cash money orders led him, along with other braceros, to carry large sums of their earnings back to Janitzio.

Isaias Sánchez noted that indigenous families could overcome these hurdles through the help of their children or friends who were well educated and spoke Spanish. Starting from the moment of their departure, this support network helped them gather the paperwork necessary to obtain a guest-worker contract. They then continued through the contracting process with indigenous bracero support networks, which functioned through language groups. When Sánchez worked in Arkansas, he was approached by a group of indigenous men from Oaxaca, and someone in the group pleaded with him, "Paisano don't leave us, if you are going to leave, we will leave with you. You can tell us when we will change money, when we will leave to Oaxaca. You can help us."[119] Sánchez responded, "Of course."[120] There were about eighteen in the group that Sánchez led back to Oaxaca. Once in the state, they knew how to get back to their hometowns. During his many contracts, Sánchez filled various roles within indigenous communities, including guide, translator, and barber—all of which were facilitated by his learning to read and write in Spanish after he became a bracero.

Indigenous braceros stood at the center of narratives about the modernizing potency of the program, and their experiences illuminate the contours of this racial project. These oral histories challenge mestizo-centered histories of the Bracero Program and narratives that solely focus on Anglo-Mexican racial tensions or intra-ethnic tensions between Mexican migrants and Mexican Americans. Both these schemas look past the racial and ethnic heterogeneity of Mexican communities. The experiences of indigenous communities disrupt long-standing ethno-normative constructs developed around the Bracero Program, chief among them the assumption that the United States was hiring (and that Mexico was providing) "fixed" national subjects. Indigenous bracero experiences draw our attention to new dimensions of this modernity project by pointing to their own self-representations, the program's bureaucratic dealings with them, and the limits and possibilities of their relationships to mestizo braceros. Moreover, issues of consumption, language, and migration brought on by the program changed the lives of indigenous bracero families and thus brought them closer to the racialized nation-building projects intricately tied to mestizaje. Although indigenous communities have much in common with mestizos in terms of the economic situations that drove families to participate in the program, the uncertainties of the contracting process, labor exploitation in the United States, and the difficulties of family separation, oral histories shed light on the ways indigenous bracero families dealt with these specific issues differently than their mestizo counterparts. They created systems of support centered on linguistics in order to participate in the program and to cope with marginalization, violence, and ethnic and racial tensions.

The experiences of Mexican indigenous communities affected by the program bring Mexican racial and ethnic relations into relief and offer up a distinct perspective of the guest-worker program. The racial discrimination, threats of violence, experiences of marginalization, and solidarity that indigenous communities felt draw out the conflicting place of indigenous communities within Mexico and in historical transnational circuits. Indigenous communities were incorporated into the Mexican national project through their labor as braceros, as some strengthened their command of Spanish, learned to write, and changed their attire. From pants to shoes to language, these shifts signaled an entry into modern Mexico. These shifting terrains also signaled that not only was it possible to enter the project of Mexican modernity by working abroad, but it also bolstered the assumption that these communities needed to be modernized. In addition, it perpetuated the false logic that mestizaje was the only avenue toward a Mexican modernity that created no space for the future of Mexican indigenous populations. Ultimately, indigenous populations deviated from the ideals of a Mexican modern future. While some remade themselves as mestizos abroad, others defied the racial national project by reasserting their identity as indígenas.

Mestizaje is such a powerful racial ideology that it naturalizes a person's transition from indígena to mestizo, obscuring the national, political, and economic forces behind this transition. This complicated shift demonstrates the charged racialized underbelly of discourses of modernization. The ideology of mestizaje split communities, repeatedly placing studies of indigenous populations in the hands of anthropologists and archaeologists, leaving indígenas with a rich body of ethnography and ancient history but a slim history as modern subjects. It also naturalizes the role of mestizos as central subjects in modern Mexican history. This, in turn, renders the historical imprint of Mexican indigenous communities' migrations across the United States virtually invisible. Nationalist mestizo ideologies have not only obscured the social production of race but they have also propagated heteronormative romanticizations of the Mexican family. As a result, bracero practices that deviate from these norms have been hidden in the camp shadows. But, as I learned in speaking with braceros, the Bracero Program gave some men the opportunity to remake themselves and occupy a space in the predominantly homosocial world of braceros.

INTERLUDE *¡Yo le digo!*

On July 1, 2008, I was on a bus headed to Oaxaca with Antonio Aragón's phone number scribbled in a notebook. A Bracero Justice Movement organizer and ex-bracero, Aragón had agreed to arrange several meetings with the local chapter of the organization. On July 3, I made my way to San Pedro Ixtlahuaca, Oaxaca, where a group of ex-braceros sat on a patio waiting for me to explain the goals of the Bracero History Project and to decide if they wanted to participate. Unlike other collection sites, the group insisted on sitting quietly and listening while their fellow members were being interviewed. I had wanted to ask more questions about sexual practices, but I did not want the men to feel uncomfortable talking about it in such a public setting. One of the biggest challenges in collecting oral histories for the project was establishing trust and encouraging openness in a very short period of time.

We took a break, and Gustavo Eloy Reyes Rodríguez invited me into his kitchen for lunch. As we chatted, I asked in an intentionally naive tone, *"Existían los gays en ese tiempo*? [Did gays exist at that time?]" I knew that the term was not a historically accurate one to explain homosexual practices in Spanish-speaking migrant communities at the time, but it served as a starting point for the discussion. *"Claro!* [Sure!]," he responded.[1] Here I asked him to tell me more for the record. After the break we went to the front patio and waited for the group to return. When everyone made their way back, Rodríguez stood up, called for the attention of the other ex-braceros, and said *"Esta señorita quiere saber de los gays, díganle!* [This young lady wants to know about the gays, tell her!]" The patio fell silent. The word "señorita" echoed in my mind at that quiet moment, and I felt acutely aware of my gendered body in a room full of men who just that morning had eagerly waited for a chance to speak and were now speechless. It was as if speaking about queerness might be a suggestion of one's own deviance. Rodríguez placed his thumb inside the loop of his belt, as if he was purposely taking a more masculine and authoritative stance, and boldly declared, "¡*Yo le digo*! [I will tell you]."

TWO **IN THE CAMP'S SHADOWS**

Intimate Economies in the Bracero Program

Pos, yo jamás había estado . . . así revuelto entre tantos
hombres. (Well, I had never been mixed up among so
many men.)
—JUAN VIRGEN DÍAZ, ex-bracero

La seducción de este país es el control. (The seduction
of this country is control.)
—JOAN, *Pito Pérez se va de Bracero*

In 1957, Ted Le Berthon, a journalist for the *Commonwealth*, explored the
conditions of Mexican guest workers and shed light on illicit camp economies: "It is impossible—also illegal—not to give these male captives a day
off, usually Sunday. Then prostitutes, professional gamblers, and vendors of
liquor, narcotics and worthless jewelry, all hovering close by, relieve *braceros*
of a sizable portion of their pay. True, most foremen could not more admit
such parasites within camp confines than they would admit a labor organizer. But the parasites are endemic wherever large bodies of men are far
from home, especially on payday."[1] Le Berthon vividly described the conditions in which vice and illicit economies flourished in bracero labor camps,
and, unlike other journalists and academics, he did not base his argument
in terms of bracero morality. For him, these illicit economies thrived on
the margins in isolated camps, away from the purview of most Americans.
He tied this underworld to the conditions of "captivity" within the labor
camp, referring to the braceros' lack of mobility, isolation, and loneliness.
He recognized that the Bracero Program provided thicker, more malleable
margins, where arduous labor collided with opportunities for pleasure and
a reconfiguration of gender norms.

Le Berthon's perspective contrasted with beliefs that these men brought
their questionable "morals" with them to the United States, disrupting
heteronormative visions of nuclear family life in both Mexico and the
United States. Daniel Martínez, a Mexican American graduate student in the

Claremont Graduate School, expressed this perspective in his study on the impact of the Bracero Program on Mexican American communities. Within it, he recorded popularly held perceptions that braceros came to the United States as philanderers and men looking for adventure and vice.[2] Through general fieldwork and interviews carried out from 1957 to 1958, Martínez's study captured Mexican American concerns about the Bracero Program. He found that some Mexican American critics thought that the program needed to end because the men created moral problems in the United States and tainted images of Mexico abroad. Many Mexican Americans worried that Mexican nationals courted Mexican American women for casual sexual relationships that lasted only as long as their contracts.[3] The apprehensions of these communities point to glaring questions about bracero sexuality and sexual practices: Could braceros suspend sexual urges for the duration of their contracts? If not, how would they find sexual partners? Would sexuality present problems for public safety and health concerns? How would this affect bracero families? Did economies of vice follow braceros? Historian Erasmo Gamboa argues that these "sweeping generalizations about the men's values obscured the public's ability to recognize that vice was already present and not introduced by the bracero."[4] Although the vices practiced by braceros were not new, they flourished in the camps because the options for leisure and pleasure were limited in those spaces, which themselves provided sites outside of the purview of the general public.

Le Berthon's view of the underground economies that sprang up would not have been published during the program's early period, when visions of "Good Neighbor" cooperation permeated press coverage. These depictions projected American ideologies of nuclear family life and Protestant values onto the Mexican guest workers through narratives that characterized braceros as fathers, brothers, and husbands who worked hard and spent their earnings piously to ensure their families' economic advancement.[5] While the Catholic clergy opposed the program, American ideologies of advancement meshed well with Mexican ideals of modernization and uplift that normalized ideas of patriarchal family structures, which were implicit within the program and its modernizing agenda.[6] Conceptions of "advancement" or uplift narratives were presented in connection to the "primitive" and "Indian" family that needed to be modernized. Stories of life in the bracero camps reveal how some men reclaimed their capacity for pleasure in the face of a system that attempted to cast their bodies solely in terms of the ability to labor. Historian John D'Emilio has argued that by the 1920s, through the free labor system of capitalism, many middle-class white Americans found the opportunity to survive economically outside of the nuclear family. Because the family was no longer needed for survival, the ideology of a capitalist society enshrined the family as the "source of love, affection, and emotional security."[7] Similarly, braceros while on contract could survive economically outside of family structures, and both nations made efforts to configure familial affective ties in ways that would ensure the return of these workers.

This amplification of affective bonds resonated loudly with Mexican families. But, in what was surely an unintended consequence, the Bracero Program ended up expanding social relationships and practices of sexuality that, in some instances, redefined notions of gender, the family, and masculinity. Braceros' contracting journey and camp life provide a counternarrative to what Lionel Cantú describes as "heteronormative assumptions that not only deny the existence of nonheterosexual subjects but also cloak the ways in which sexuality itself influences migratory processes."[8] Discourses of family were deployed in service to the program. Following the scholarship of Richard T. Rodríguez, I turn to "various constructions of family that do not adhere to heteropatriarchal demands that in turn establish critical attachments that fall outside the boundaries of normative kinship models."[9] While the Mexican agricultural family did not always exist in the idealized nuclear schema to begin with, I argue that the program gave men an opportunity to sell their labor and survive away from their families, as well as to experience distinct sexual freedoms within camps.

When a bracero departed for the program, it affected his entire community. Braceros were apart from their families for prolonged periods of time, leaving many women to manage on their own and find ways to support their children when promised remittances never arrived. Other women took to the road in search of better economic opportunities. Family units became rearranged, and braceros built new community networks in a predominantly homosocial space in the United States. Labor camps became spaces where braceros could enjoy vices, including prostitution, gambling, and drinking, away from the watchful eye of family or friends who might call attention to or reprimand their behavior. Additionally, men from small towns and villages also found opportunities to engage in nonnormative sexual relationships. They thus contested normative forms of masculinity through expressions of sexual desire, physical violence, and bravado. These practices took on new meanings as braceros reclaimed their bodies, used for disciplined labor production, and reconditioned them to also engage in pleasure and recreation, even if temporarily. Experiences of laboring in the United States went beyond shaping racial and ethnic identity, but also became fertile ground for sexual and intimate practices impacted by the transnational structure of the program.

Migrant men played out a myriad of masculinities throughout the contracting process, not all of which were tied to performing respectable manhood predicated on having nuclear families. In an effort to perform the appropriate form of masculinity that would ensure a contract, they might play up family narratives, though not all rigorously subscribed to these ideals. The countless letters written by aspiring braceros pleading for contracts did not always reflect their actions when immersed in camp life. They entered a highly charged scene in the United States where GIs, zoot suiters, and documented and undocumented workers contested and negotiated modes of Mexican and Mexican American masculinities.[10] To make matters worse, the growing attention to the untempered sexuality of zoot suiters alarmed the general public.[11] The anxieties around the sexual desires of Mexican men thus shaped the contracting process and their camp lives. Furthermore, their actions while on contract demonstrated that they understood the illusion the Mexican government created about respectable domesticity even as they acted against it.

For the Good of the Family

The first wave of braceros entered the United States from a nation-state that had in the previous decade attempted to reconfigure Mexican extended family structures into more tightly bound nuclear units through agrarian reform and popular culture. As Mary Kay Vaughan explains, "With its emphasis on ejidal plots for male heads of household, agrarian policy aimed theoretically at destroying this extended family and replacing it with the nuclear farming family."[12] The Bracero Program, then, would supposedly help cement configurations of the mestizo heteronormative nuclear family life, even as those families were dispersed in transnational circuits. Masculinity came to be understood through frameworks that emphasized labor and its benefit to families. The justification, then, for entering an exploitative program was couched in terms of family advancement and modernization, or familial economics.[13] These discourses naturalized a masculinity tied to the nuclear family. However, as Regina Kunzel explains, "Naturalization does not happen naturally; it requires cultural work."[14] The Mexican state took on the cultural work of promulgating romanticized scenes of domesticity as one way to pressure braceros to return to Mexico and, more important, to send remittances. Growers and other proponents of the program reified these ideas in order to gain acceptance for the program and also ensure that guest workers returned home eventually. Those traveling men who felt no obligation to replicate these particular visions of Mexican domesticity were often vilified as traitors to the nation.

Anthropologist Matthew Gutmann notes, "It follows that if Mexican male sexuality, especially in the guise of man-as-progenitor, has long been romantically linked to a cultural nationalist version of *Mexicanidad*, then changes in male sexuality will necessarily be involved in defining transformations in the modern Mexican nation."[15] Braceros did not stand outside this nationalist vision; instead, they complicated normative masculinities. Architects of the program never allowed braceros to fully practice respectable domesticity; instead, they were given the opportunity to participate in a perverse capitalist vision of respectable transnational domesticity, where remittances took the place of everyday presence, and long-distance intimacy was presented as "temporary." Like transnational Puerto Rican workers in Eileen J. Suárez Findlay's work, remittances would "enable their wives to create properly domestic homes," and in this way family could be "stretched thousands of miles in order to be reconstituted in an acceptable form."[16] While braceros could aspire to create some type of respectable domesticity in Mexico, in the United States while on guest-worker contracts this was much more challenging.[17] Bracero sexuality could not exist in parameters of respectable domesticity.

Because both the United States and Mexico invested in reifying heteronormative "familial bonds," a queer subject or someone who otherwise deviated from heteronormative ideals was a potentially dangerous figure whose deviance might also cause them to stay in the United States. Clearly the desires and the sexual life of braceros needed to be tempered and controlled between new freedoms offered by the program and the system of rigid management of bracero bodies. Ironically, the everyday practices that the program produced existed somewhere in between. For example, marriage in Mexico might not function as a constraint for some men working in the United States. And homosocial relations often led to queer domesticities, where one man, for example, might be charged with the domestic work for several men. Like the Chinese bachelor communities Nayan Shah examines, bracero communities also engaged in "queer domesticity," emphasizing "the variety of erotic ties and social affiliations that counter normative expectations."[18] Unlike in the case of the Chinese workers, the Mexican government endorsed a program that by design placed these men in a homosocial world and created a chimera of aspirational domesticity for their homes in Mexico.

While some men distanced themselves from their social networks and heteronormative family expectations, others strengthened them by moving their families to border towns.[19] Relocation facilitated more frequent visits during and between labor contracts for men working near the U.S.-Mexico border in processing hubs, such as Empalme, Sonora; Mexicali, Baja California; and Ciudad Juarez, Chihuahua. Other families faced long-term separation with very little hope that their bracero family members would send remittances and return home. For some families, the Bracero Program brought about the undeniable fracturing of familial bonds and relations. This opened up opportunities for distinct social configurations of kinship to take place in American fields *and* in Mexican hometowns.

In addition to placing men in situations not conducive to gender normativity, the program did the same for women. Even their demands for normativity show how elusive it was. Many wives and other women who stayed in Mexico were far from passive. Despite all the attention paid to men, women played vital roles within the bracero economy. Many women, for example, fought to keep their families intact and to meet their needs while the men were away. They worked to keep underage sons from joining the program and called attention to the lack of remittances. Women made efforts to decrease prostitution on the border and to make braceros accountable to their families. Even though the government did not implement formal public policies to protect the best interests of the families, many women attempted to claim alimony and child support, and even divorced husbands who, they argued, had "abandoned" the family. Through oral histories, some guest workers acknowledged their unsavory past in the United States and shared information about their intimate experiences during the program that cannot be found in traditional archives.

In the media, narratives of abandonment surfaced as ways to frame the desire of some braceros to stay in the United States. These narratives expressed two types of abandonment: first, of the "patria" or fatherland, and, second, of the family. Writers made sense of these intersections by utilizing racially charged terms explaining the "outrage" the Mexican public felt that "braceros who are now citizens of another country, laugh at their skinny and ugly indian wives from afar."[20] The assumption here devalues Mexican women because of their indigeneity and utilizes their perceived unattractiveness as a reason for their abandonment. Furthermore, the author claimed that the braceros had "new families," and that the Mexican consul of Sacramento was well aware of the problem, saying that the consul knew of over 1,000 Mexican women searching for their husbands who had left as braceros. Elites expressed perspectives in which braceros abandoned much more than their families. They turned their back on their home country, which was embodied by the "skinny and ugly indian" wife. Narratives of family uplift could not coexist with those of abandonment, because together they exposed the contradictions of the program.

A Gendered Struggle to Regulate Family

During the Bracero Program, many men and women followed the bracero routes and made their way to border towns. For *aspirantes*, residing in border towns could potentially ease their transition to the United States. Women, on the other hand, moved to the border for work opportunities and to stay closer to their bracero relatives. Family bonds were strengthened or maintained when braceros could make short visits across the border. This was particularly true for families living in Mexicali, whose braceros worked in Southern California. Other women moved to these border towns in hopes of eventually working in the United States. In this way, women played active roles within the bracero economies of labor, family, and sexuality. While much of the historical focus has been on whether men paid remittances or truly intended to return to their families in Mexico, Ana Rosas's research demonstrates that women did not wait idly at home.[21] Some women subverted ideas of domesticity and family that stressed village ties and proximity to extended kin networks by migrating toward the United States and exerting their influence over the men who had traveled abroad.

Across Mexico, many women wanted new work prospects. They too sought new opportunities to contribute to the family income. On January 26, 1959, Isidora Botello from Matamoros, Tamaulipas, wrote to then-president Adolfo López Mateos: "Allow me to inform you of my necessities. . . . Although I do not know you, I hope you will dignify me with a favor. . . . Perhaps you can give me permission to work in the United States, because I have a lot of family and what I earn here is not enough to support my children."[22] She wrote to the president believing that he could give her access to the migratory avenues available to men across Mexico. She requested an opportunity to work in the United States so she could provide additional income to her household. Indeed, many women petitioned Mexican presidents for permits and visas to enter the U.S. labor pool.[23] Like many braceros, they hoped that through remittances they could dramatically improve their children's quality of life.

Many women saw migration as a realistic solution to their economic problems and felt that they were qualified to enter the migrant labor market. Single women without children also wanted an opportunity to assist their families. In 1962, María Consuelo Miranda Luna of Irapuato, Guanajuato, formally requested a similar permit to enter the United States. The report states, "She asked that she be given a passport to move to the United States of America and help support her household that consists of her mother and nine young siblings."[24] Despite the distance and the social ostracism, Miranda Luna and Isidora Botello were driven to follow in the footsteps of those heading north.

Although these women viewed working in the United States in a positive light, other women felt that the Bracero Program negatively affected their families and marriages. For some families, the program meant enduring the long-term hardship of family separation. Mothers of underage children reported that their children enlisted as braceros despite the fact that they were not old enough. Young people also reported that authorities allowed them to enter the program despite their age.[25] In May 1944, a government inspector noted: "Regularly every train that leaves has around 850 braceros and lately many under-aged [men] (17 to 19 years) have left, until the Federal Forces lately intervened and removed from the train two of them who could not prove their age. . . . The parents of the families are . . . protesting, because there are various under-aged students that are enrolling as braceros, and they say they will go to the competent authority to avoid this."[26] Families felt that authorities were not doing enough to enforce the prohibition of underage men. They asked for assistance and worked to prevent their young sons from leaving. Rather than empowering male breadwinners, the program disempowered parents, especially mothers, who could no longer exert control over their fleeing sons.

Women not only "lost" their sons to the program, but some also felt that they had "lost" their husbands, too. Letters in the Archivo General de la Nación offer evidence of women who wrote to government agencies in search of their husbands.[27] Women, such as Maria Concepción Rosales, were experiencing the pain of abandonment and financial neglect. In August 1947, Rosales's husband left along with four other laborers to try to secure a bracero contract. Five months passed and he still had not communicated with her. She felt deserted and concerned about her children's future. Unlike families who developed transnational strategies to deal with the long-term separation, women like Rosales identified the Bracero Program as the cause of much of their misfortune. In her letter to Mexican president Miguel

Alemán Valdés, Rosales asserted: "Before you, with the respect you deserve, even though I am no one, consider my motives. Because of the contracting and the wetback passes [guest-worker contracts], which both benefit and ruin many homes, in the community where I live five of us women cry oceans of tears because we have been abandoned and our children have no bread. You can help our situation [by] demanding the marriage certificates of wetbacks and those contracted, and hopefully make them return to their homes when they have finished their contracts and I will have some comfort."[28] While wives of braceros wrote Mexican consuls across the United States, Rosales calls attention to the position of wives of undocumented workers, ultimately pushing the state to compel both guest workers and undocumented laborers to return to their families. Rosales went on to declare that the program created an underclass of illiterate workers, because without financial support from her husband, her children could not attend school.[29] In her eyes, the Bracero Program perpetuated a cycle of poverty that she hoped would be broken. While guest workers might have felt the stern control of the program, many wives in Mexico called for even higher levels of state control and regulation in both the movement of guest workers and their remittances.

Although the program was supposed to provide Mexican families with better sources of temporary income, Rosales pointed to a lived reality in which many women had no other choice than to send their children to work rather than to school. Many families hoped that the program would help them break free from abject poverty, but instead women like Rosales faced a deep disillusionment with a national system that could not hold braceros accountable. Rosales understood that she, along with many other women, suffered the repercussions of a state-sponsored program that encouraged men to work away from their families. The social networks, extended family, and communities that could work toward pressuring some braceros to become responsible fathers and husbands were fractured and had little legal recourse.

Rosales was ultimately frustrated in her multiple requests for assistance. When she asked the Mexican consul to help her locate her husband, she was told that many braceros used false names to obtain contracts, making it more difficult to find these men.[30] Since the consul could not help, she thought that the Mexican president should ask those men to return to their country and work the lands left fallow since their departure.[31] Because the nationwide program was causing the problems that many women like Rosales faced, she wondered if there could be a solution at the national public-policy level. She wanted some assurance that her family could reap the benefits of the program without permanently losing her husband.

Other women sought help because they believed that their husbands should be forced to send back earnings. Señora Concepción Bejarán de Múñoz worked with both the Alianza de Braceros Nacionales de México en los Estados Unidos (Alianza) and the Mexican consul to pressure her husband into fulfilling his economic obligations to the family.[32] These wives attempted to claim remittances as child support and alimony. Though no official channels existed for financially abandoned women to claim remittances, women like Bejarán de Múñoz fought to make their concerns heard. Alianza and the Mexican consul collaborated in an effort to locate Bejarán de Múñoz's husband and call his attention to his family's needs, but it remains unknown if he actually responded with money.

Mexican consuls in the United States recognized the growing problem of braceros who neglected their families' financial needs back home. Bracero Asterio López León described the consul's attitude toward braceros who were considered to be irresponsible. León traveled to Blythe as an undocumented laborer, but then his employer helped him secure a guest-worker contract. On one occasion, the Mexican consul went to Blythe to tell the braceros with whom López León worked that "he [the Mexican president] had ordered that all of the braceros be thrown out because there were many who did not send back money to their families, nothing, they spent everything here. [The president wanted] to throw everyone out and send new braceros."[33] The consul attempted to remedy this growing problem by pressuring braceros to send remittances.

The experiences of the women left behind finally received national attention when they started finding new partners or asked for a divorce. The Mexican newspaper *El Universal* published a story titled, "It Went Bad for the Bracero: Many Who Return from the United States Find Their Homes Destroyed." Although these men found their way home with money in the pockets of their fine clothes, the report stated that their wives had run off with other men and taken the children with them, while others wanted to divorce.[34] The article attempted to cast these women in a negative light, but what became apparent was that not every family configuration stayed intact during the program, and some women were not devotedly awaiting their husbands' return or were not invested in keeping their nuclear family together. While sensationalist, this article revealed that some women strategically used their husbands' departures to claim "abandonment," secure formal divorces, and create blended families with new partners.

Many men worried that their wives would engage in extramarital affairs in their absence. This distrust led men like Hilario Martínez Cortez to make sure he left his wife pregnant before he departed for the United States, meaning his participation in the Bracero Program deeply shaped his wife's reproduction patterns. Martínez Cortez explained, "When I left, I left her covered . . . that's why no one won her over, the trap was already occupied." In other words, she was pregnant every time he left Mexico.[35] He acted on two assumptions: that men in their town found her less sexually appealing when she was pregnant, and that women with many children would find it more difficult to forge long-lasting relationships with other suitors. They would be seen as a financial liability. Pregnancy gave him the peace of mind he needed to feel comfortable leaving her in Mexico, confident that she would be there when he returned. He also believed that even if she cheated, there would be no concrete repercussions in terms of illegitimate children.

According to Martínez Cortez, jokes about infidelity were common in the bracero community. Men who returned to their communities showed off new clothes and gadgets like radios and shared stories of adventure. Such gloating sometimes earned them the ridicule of men who stayed behind. Non-braceros would often joke about the ways in which they sexually comforted the wives, mothers, and daughters of braceros.[36] For some braceros, these jokes fueled fears of infidelity and apprehension that women left behind in Mexico would encounter new opportunities for sexual liaisons while the males in their families—be they fathers, brothers, or husbands—worked in the United States.

Although women who stayed behind often felt the judging eyes of extended family and community members, the threat of extramarital affairs in Mexico demonstrated that women also held a sexual power within these long-distance relationships, even as the bracero and non-bracero men might have bragged about their sexual prowess. As women reimagined their lives through the structure of the Bracero Program, gendered power relationships within the transnational households were negotiated and renegotiated. While men were portrayed as potential breadwinners by the program's proponents, women also made attempts to participate in the bracero economy as laborers. Moreover, women pressured men to spend money in ways that benefited those still living in Mexico. These intimate economies of exchange held the potential to reconfigure the very workings of the family unit in complex ways across national boundaries. Even so, men found alternative avenues of intimacy while on their labor journeys through the United States.

Extramarital Encounters

Whereas Martínez Cortez articulated braceros' fears about their wives' fidelity, other braceros, such as Roberto Guardado Montelongo and José Torres Gracian, openly discussed the opportunities that the Bracero Program provided for sexual liaisons and affairs. For some men, the program gave them the freedom to engage in nonmonogamous behavior away from family and social networks; many braceros experienced a sense of sexual freedom. Some men purposely separated from their hometown networks or created social contracts of secrecy with their fellow braceros in order to play out sexual desires in the United States. Their ability to travel far from home and maintain separate family spheres, knowing that the structure of their work might call them away at the end of a contract, meant that expectations for stable families were limited for both the braceros and the women they courted. Wives of braceros felt the repercussions of the sexual lives of guest workers when they took on the economic burden of raising families alone and potentially contracting sexually transmitted diseases (STDs) from their returning husbands.

While cultivating cucumbers in 1957 in Shelby, Michigan, Roberto Guardado Montelongo began to date a young Native American woman. They met while he was working in the fields that her father owned. Many men had courted her, thinking that a relationship with her could lead to a better position on the farm and perhaps to a permanent status in the United States. Guardado Montelongo felt conflicted about the pregnant wife he had left behind and worried about their future if he continued his affair, but he also wondered if marrying the farm owner's daughter would give him the opportunity to run the farm as well as secure residency. Eventually, before the wedding, other braceros started asking him about what would happen to his wife in Mexico. He realized that other men were thinking about exposing him so they could court his girlfriend. They threatened him and a fight broke out. After the altercation, he realized that he needed to leave the farm and return to his wife in Mexico.[37] He told me that the infidelity did not affect his wife because, in the end, he chose his marriage and she never knew about it. Guardado Montelongo felt free to begin an extramarital affair, indicating the separateness of his two lives, but for other braceros these intimate worlds were never truly separate.

Bracero José Torres Gracian also had romantic liaisons and affairs during his stay in the United States. His story exemplifies the freedoms and limits of sexual and intimate practices in the camps. Born in Michoacán, Torres Gracian came to the United States multiple times, as both an undocumented worker and as a bracero. During his first experience in the United States, his employer in McAllen, Texas, helped him obtain a three-month bracero contract, and then Torres Gracian stayed in town after the contract ended. While there, he met a young Tejana, with whom he lived and who became the mother of his first daughter. They separated in 1951 and he became a long-distance father. That same year, he moved to Oklahoma and began dating a different Tejana, Hortencia. After two months of dating, her family thought that if they married he could become a permanent resident. Despite that possibility, he decided to go back to Michoacán, promising to return. She suspected otherwise, telling him before he left, "You're going to leave and you're not coming back."[38] He replied, "Look, if you want I will leave my clothes . . . so you will see I will come back."[39] Hortencia responded, "No, take your clothes because I know you're not coming back."[40] She began to cry when he got on the truck to leave. He remembers, "I even wanted to get down [from the truck] but I made up my mind that I was going to come to Michoacán."[41] He left her that day and did not feel compelled to tell her the truth, which was that she would never see him again.

Hortencia held out hope that he would return and sent letters to him in Mexico. In the beginning, Torres Gracian replied, but on New Year's Day in 1952, he married María Chávez Flores in his hometown. After he married, his family refused to give him any further correspondence from Hortencia, and they sent a note to tell her that he had gone back to the United States to work again. They thought this would stop her from continuing to look for him in Michoacán. Eventually, Torres Gracian did want to go back to the United States to work as a bracero. Although the work under bracero contracts was arduous, he felt a freedom in engaging in extramarital relationships that he could not have in his hometown.

The watchful eyes of neighbors and the people in his social networks seemed distant when he worked in the United States. He felt free of the moral judgment that friends and family in Mexico might pass. While on contract, he explained that, in his free time, he "went to the cantinas and the parties."[42] As a married man, he continued to date, and said, "Women wanted to rope me in and fix my papers."[43] He continued, "In reality one [woman] there in Los Angeles wanted me to marry her. . . . I said, 'Look I cannot marry you because,' I said, 'because I am married in Mexico, and you know I am married in Mexico.' 'It doesn't matter,' she said, 'look we can marry, and, well, your wife and your family will not do without anything,' she said. 'We will be sending [money].' She said, 'Every fifteen days, every month, whatever you decide. They will not go without anything.'"[44] The offer to help him obtain residency did not entice Torres Gracian. He chose to stay with his wife, who never found out about his affair. Like Roberto Guardado Montelongo, he thought that his extramarital affairs did not affect his wife because he always ended the other relationships. Unlike Guardado Montelongo, though, he left a partner and child in Texas for whom he provided no economic support or parental guidance.[45]

Such stories expose the ways that the Bracero Program helped to structure the sexual practices of men who participated in the program and the women they encountered. Thus, while the program was primarily designed to structure labor relations, it also shaped sexuality and family ties. Even as men experienced new sexual opportunities while traveling, their choices still had to be negotiated through family ties on both sides of the border. This constant struggle among family members could limit the degrees of freedom they felt.

Mujeres Alegres

As opportunities for men changed the landscape of sexual practice, women's sexuality also underwent shifts and challenges. The specter of sex work, for example, pointed to women's changing sexual roles in the Bracero Program. As men moved back and forth across the border, separated from their former communities, prostitution became a sexual outlet. By 1953, border patrol officials claimed that "destitute females from Mexico" were following in the footsteps of migrants into California, threatening "the homes and health of communities along the border."[46] This part of the emerging bracero economy marked challenges for both men and women who questioned the morality of sex work while understanding that, for some, it was a necessary form of survival. The Bracero Program did motivate many women to move to the border to be closer to their bracero family members working in the United States, but they also sought out better work opportunities. Service industries based on the needs and desires of the guest workers immediately started cropping up in border towns like Mexicali, Baja California, and Empalme, Sonora, where *aspirantes* went in search of contracts. These cities also became sites of weekend recreation for braceros who worked on nearby farms. Many women went to work in these industries, providing services to both braceros and *aspirantes* as cooks, laundry women, and prostitutes.

On November 6, 1956, two groups in Baja California came together to write a collective letter to the then-president Adolfo Ruíz Cortínez asking that he address the growing problem of prostitution on the border. The Grupo de San Luís and La Unión de Inquilinos del Estado de Baja California wrote,[47] "We [respectfully] inform you that we are aware of the difficult economic situation that is pushing thousands upon thousands of women, the majority with children, to enter prostitution, creating a grave social problem."[48] The Grupo de San Luís and La Unión de Inquilinos del Estado de Baja California viewed prostitution as a social ill, coming from outside the state. The group wanted local and national governments to address this issue by allowing women to work in the United States. They explained, "We are asking you in the most attentive and respectful way that you dictate orders to allow these women to work honorably as domestic workers in the United States of America, with a local passport. In this [way] we believe that they could by night, tend to their homes, tend to their children, and in this way resolve their economic problems, putting an end to this foreign ill."[49] Their proposal assumed that all sex workers had children to support and that they would welcome the opportunity to work "honorably" as maids. Children here represent for these more conservative women the only reason why a woman would enter sex work. The groups were perhaps inspired by braceros who worked in Southern California and settled their families in Tijuana.[50] Although not ideal, the proximity allowed for more frequent visits. Despite the fact that the idea never received serious consideration, women of these Baja California organizations appealed to dominant constructions of a cohesive nuclear family unit and respectable work opportunities for these prostitutes. Domestic work in the United States also represented the possibility of family reunification, where all adult family members could find work opportunities in the United States while creating a family life in Mexico.

To be sure, sex work flourished along the border long before the braceros passed through. It was intrinsically tied to the Southwest's image as the "Wild West" and was later pushed out onto the border, along with alcohol, by the temperance movement.[51] It boomed during World War II in cities such as Juárez and Tijuana because of their proximity to U.S. military bases.[52] Along with servicemen, braceros would form part of the clientele, who were not always contained to the Mexican side of the border. Sex workers could be found at various points of the migrant journey. Daniel Martínez, who conducted research on braceros in the 1950s in Southern California, argued that the large majority of sex workers provided services to these guest workers in social places like cantinas. He claimed that local women who had been betrayed by braceros with false promises of marriage looked for work in these cantinas. Martínez's narrative supported perceptions that guest workers were fracturing Mexican American communities, leaving Mexican American women with illegitimate children and thus forcing some women to enter the arena of sex work to provide for their families.[53] The inability of some braceros to economically support their children could have also contributed to the growing problem of prostitution in Baja California, which the Grupo de San Luís and La Unión de Inquilinos overlooked, choosing to focus on the sex workers instead of the braceros who chose not to send remittances.

In reality, some women entered sex work because of the limited choices that Mexican women had at the time. Women also had the desire to go north in search of better economic opportunities, but they had fewer options and no support from the state. Ex-bracero Juan Topete told me the story of one woman's journey. Topete was born in Mascota, Jalisco, and raised by his single mother. As a teenager, he decided to leave his hometown to look for work in several places, ranging from small ranches to larger cities, like Puerto Vallarta. A young girl, Margarita, from his hometown accompanied him. "Yes, I stole her,"[54] he said, meaning he convinced her to join him and leave her home without her parent's consent. "Well we were boyfriend/girlfriend for some time. I had told her that I needed to [go] . . . and she said, 'Don't leave.' . . . Then I said, 'Well,' I said, 'We can get married if you want and if you don't,' I said 'we can see what happens.' She said, 'That's fine.'"[55] She willingly left her home, without her mother's consent and without marrying, to travel with Topete as he looked for steady work. His promise of marriage seemed to be enough for her to leave her home and begin an adventure with him.

Topete made his way to Amatlán de Cañas, Jalisco, where his father was residing. That night, he and Margarita stayed with his father's extended family. He explained to his father that he intended on traveling to Tepic, Nayarit, to look for work and stay with his uncle on his maternal side. His father disliked the idea and asked, "Well, and what about this girl?"[56] As they talked, Topete explained, "Well, she's coming with me." His father responded, "What do you mean she's coming with you? . . . I wanted to send you to the United States . . . but you have to take this woman back to where you got her from. You have to take her back to her father or her mother." Topete replied, "No," and explained further: "Then that night I talked with her."

"I will go [home] if you want," she said. "As long as once you get there [the United States]," she said, "you write me." "Yes," Topete responded, "that's fine." He went on to say: "Well, I went back to my hometown to take her back [to] her mother. [She] liked me a lot, her mother, because she didn't have a husband."[57] His father did not want Topete to bring the young woman along, only to abandon her en route to the contracting station. Topete explained, "Well he [Topete's father] told me that . . . he did not want me to leave her some place where she didn't know anyone."[58] If Topete abandoned her at the border, Margarita would have been absolutely alone. His father believed that Topete had acted inappropriately in taking her without her mother's consent and then not marrying her. He understood that Topete had not considered Margarita's best interests. If Topete married Margarita, he might feel a moral obligation to care for her and send her remittances. Although Mexico created no institutional guarantee that the wives of braceros would receive remittances or child support, unmarried partners of braceros held an even weaker claim to economic support.

Topete took Margarita back to Mascota and then met his father in Amatlán de las Cañas to begin their long journey to Mexicali. Years passed as he went through several bracero contracts and also labored as an undocumented worker; however, he eventually saw Margarita again:

> You see, you see when I left [the United States] in 1949, I went out to Mexicali and I saw her. I saw her in a place they called the Patio, where I went, lots of braceros went there. . . . Lots of people went there to dance, and I heard [the DJ] say, "This song is dedicated to Margarita. . . . " I said, "Well, what is she doing here?" Yes she was, she was [there]. . . . Yes, she took to life, to the *happy life* and, well, that was it. I was sitting there drinking a beer when she came over and she looked at me. . . . She sat down with me and she gave me a hug and well no, . . . she and I, we didn't continue, because, because no, well no. Not anymore.[59]

He softened his description of her sex work by saying that she took to "*la vida alegre* [the happy life]." Margarita made her way to Mexicali, just as Topete had, from Mascota, Jalisco. It is not clear whether she was trying to follow or find Topete, or whether she believed she could find work opportunities in Mexicali that she did not have in Mascota. Women, like Margarita, who returned to their families after leaving their home with their boyfriends or partners were often viewed unfavorably in their communities, because of the assumption that they had engaged in premarital sex.

New suitors and potential employers were usually dissuaded from engaging with these women, whose reputations were marred. Without much support, Margarita's options were limited.

Some Mexican American women in the United States who had been abandoned by braceros also made the same decision as Margarita.[60] The experiences of these women colored the perspectives of Mexican American parents, who wanted to guard their daughters from braceros. There was a general distrust that these men were not faithful, and rumors proliferated that they had left families in Mexico.[61] Mexican American communities also believed that many of these braceros married Mexican American women in order to obtain legal residency in the United States, and that they would leave their wives once they received citizenship.[62]

Topete acknowledged that the prostitution at El Patio affected not only the women there, but also the wives and families left behind: "Many completed their contract . . . and left the same way they entered, with nothing."[63] According to Topete, these men spent any surplus income on gambling, prostitution, and liquor. "It was wrong, because they didn't save anything. But they did have fun, sure, but they didn't save anything. . . . Well, many, many at that time left their families because . . . everything seemed easy here, and they didn't send anything."[64] The work braceros carried out was extremely difficult, and some men felt entitled to use their income for diversion, even if their families in Mexico would suffer. Away from their home communities, they faced less social pressure to take care of their families and provide for their children. These narratives about pleasure also illuminate the argument of some critics of the program that these men were "slaves" and experienced abject poverty and dehumanization. Clearly, these men experienced regimes of capitalist exploitation. However, within the limits of the program, men found ways to enter and in some cases create economies of pleasure. Although oral histories such as Topete's do not provide hard numbers for how much of their income braceros spent on sex workers, other histories can give us an idea. Dawn Bohulano Mabalon found that Filipino workers in the 1930s in California spent half of their earnings on gambling and prostitution — $2 million alone in the agricultural town of Stockton.[65]

Peripheral systems of sex work developed along the bracero journey, from Mexican contracting and processing centers to American fields. Authorities in both Mexico and the United States either turned a blind eye to these illicit economies or found them difficult to regulate. The Bracero Program also sparked an increase in sex work in border cities like Tijuana. As Dr. Richard Barbour described the situation, "There are thousands of prostitutes. Every male is importuned by them and by their hangers-on. American girls and women may be importuned by male prostitutes. So called sex circuses are available for those who wish to attend them or participate in them. Every perversion is provided. If such sex activity is a sin and I believe it is, Tijuana is probably the most sinful city in the Western World."[66] Tourist economies of sex work grew alongside industries that catered to Mexican workers coming back from the United States with American dollars. From 1940 to 1950, the population in Tijuana more than tripled, from 16,486 to 59,962, as braceros, undocumented workers, and others settled in the bustling metropolis.[67]

Sex workers were present throughout the bracero journey into agricultural and railroad camps, but police officers found camp sex workers particularly difficult to track down and detain. Officials explained to a journalist from the *Santa Cruz Sentinel*, "By this system girls, usually from out of the country, are dropped off in labor camps by their procurers, and are usually gone the same night or the next day. This is combated by camp informants, information from labor-camp operators and constant, unannounced routine checks by sheriff's office detectives."[68] Labor-camp sex workers would often enter agricultural camps on payday and on the weekends, and in California they could earn from thirty-nine to forty dollars a night in 1959.[69] While braceros such as Guadalupe Cano Quiroz made from forty to fifty dollars for two weeks of work, prostitutes could make that salary in one night.[70] Officials explained, "Actual arrest of a prostitute in a labor camp is difficult, because by the time an officer gets past the front door, the woman is usually half way across a Brussels sprout field."[71] A journalist described this process in 1957: "What happens in these cases is that the prostitutes instead of going into the camp, simply drive around to the back—maybe they park in the middle of a nearby orchard—and go about their trade. I have seen them in great big old Packards, which have the back converted into a sort of bed. They are really whore houses on wheels."[72]

Braceros shared many stories about illicit economies with oral historians in the Bracero History Project. Born in Michoacán in 1926, José Baltazar Sánchez worked in agriculture in his youth. His father's abuse prompted him to run away at the age of thirteen. He eventually enrolled in the Mexican Army, but then he decided to go to the United States as an undocumented worker. In 1953, he returned to Mexico for the opportunity to obtain a bracero contract, which then sent him to Yuma, Arizona. On one occasion, the U.S. immigration authorities and police came to his work site, which employed approximately 200 braceros. He explained, "There was a report that there were men taking women to the camps . . . that's why they went.

Because men were taking women to the camp and to dance. . . . The immigration and the police went . . . but I am not aware if they took anyone."[73] The police were looking for sex workers who immigration services believed might be undocumented. Sánchez could not recall anyone being apprehended, but it did cause a stir and commotion. Sánchez also described the gambling and drinking that went on in the labor camps. "The patrón had a cantina . . . it wasn't the patrón it was one of the supervisors, it was called el Café Sonora, and it was a cantina and we went there to drink beer. They didn't charge us [to cash our checks], but we spent our paycheck there."[74] Supervisors made extra money by catering to bracero desires for liquor. Indeed, bar owners, vendors of American products, and sex workers were eager to fulfill the needs of Mexican guest workers on payday.

According to Henry P. Anderson of the University of California, Berkeley, who studied bracero health, this may have had something to do with the fact that, although the presence of sex workers violated contract stipulations, few employers were willing to put an end to labor-camp sex work: "The Standard Work Contract provides that employers of braceros shall 'take all reasonable steps to keep professional gamblers, vendors of intoxication liquors and other persons engaged in immoral and illegal activities away from the Mexican Worker's place of employment.' Few such steps are taken. Prostitutes ply their trade openly around many camps, and occasionally within camps."[75] He saw the presence of sex workers as a grave issue that affected not only braceros' morals but also their health, and, in some cases, the health of their families.

Priests and clergy followed suit and contended that the Bracero Program promoted vice and immorality among Mexican migrant workers.[76] Catholic activists and priests began calling for reforms or for an end to the Bracero Program, not to enact economic justice but as a moral imperative.[77] These views were expressed by Father Alan McCoy of Stockton, California, in a 1958 newsletter of the Bishop's Committee of the Spanish Speaking: "The vice of gambling, which is prevalent in the camps, has led to the impoverishment of the family of the braceros in many instances. In his personal life, the bracero is subject to a great pressure in regards to drinking. There is continual danger from the widespread prostitution in the camps, along with other vices which arise when men are unnaturally separated from their families."[78] The heteronormative family is at the center of this debate, as Catholic clergy believed it was "unnatural" to separate families, and this separation caused immorality. Catholic clergy believed that the root cause of camp sex work was the practice of recruiting Mexican men only, and that without their families they would engage in illicit economies.

Catholic clergy believed that the Mexican nuclear family found itself in peril as long-term separation within the Bracero Program caused guest workers to turn to vice. Father McCoy explained, "Tastes and habits are cultivated here which cannot possibly be continued in Mexico without divorces from the homes surrounding. The consequent breaking up of the family has been perhaps the greatest evil in the moral life of the bracero."[79] He went on, "These nationals are denied a family life. Conjugal rights and responsibilities are abanded [abandoned] for the time of their bracero program."[80] Father McCoy believed that without nuclear families, "immoral" intimacy would arise among braceros.

Susan González, a Mexican American resident of Ripley, California, first observed braceros interacting with prostitutes when she was twelve years old. Her family lived on the east side of Ripley near the Talamantes Bar. As a child, she played with her friends in the tall weeds near the bar. She prefaced her observations by explaining, "I'm going to tell you the secrets here," and went on to say, "They had a bar and a restaurant and on the side, they had the outside showers, and we were always playing in the weeds and we would discover that there was mattresses out there in the weeds. . . . And this is where the braceros took some of their ladies and they had their beds there because there wasn't a hotel, there was no rooms that they could go to."[81] Historian José Alamillo's work on saloons in Corona, California, in the first decades of the twentieth century points to the role of spaces of vice within working-class communities. He explains, "Within the walls of this homosocial environment, group solidarity was reinforced by ritual drinking practices," which also "created problems for the community and threatened marital relations."[82] González also acknowledged that sex workers frequented the Talamantes Bar: "We were out there jumping on the mattresses and playing around and we had discovered something big and we would see them coming out. We would see the ladies coming out with the guys." As a child she thought, "Oh, there's another one that went to the mattress."[83] When González came of age, she washed and ironed for braceros because, as she observed, "Some of them wanted to look nice when they went out here on the weekend to see the ladies."[84] González asserted that sex work was quite common in Blythe.

Americans who worked closely with braceros also noted the abundance of sex workers. Employed in the office of Public Health at the Rio Vista

Processing Center in Texas, Julius Lowenberg noted the intertwined nature of the bracero journey and illicit economies. He recalled that other employees at Rio Vista worked with prostitutes who provided services on site. "I remember the guards. I remember they used to have . . . prostitutes coming out [at night]."[85] The guards opened the chain link fence that surrounded the center in order to let in prostitutes who, Lowenberg believed, came from Juarez, Mexico.

Like Lowenberg, Sebastian Martínez provides the perspective of those who worked closely with braceros and witnessed the sexual economies in which they participated. As Tejanos, the Martínez family developed a close relationship with local growers and Mexican guest workers.

> I worked in some of those farms along side some of the braceros;
> we commuted back and forth to the farms. . . . My dad did odd jobs
> and I also chopped cotton and that kind of thing during the '50s. . . .
> I was fourteen or fifteen when we started working with the brace-
> ros. . . . Some of the things that were bad was when they went into
> the town to Pecos; they were more or less herded over to the east side
> where the Mexican population of Pecos was because the town was
> very rigidly segregated. The east side was the Mexican community
> and the west side was the Anglo community. So they were mostly
> bussed to that area of town.[86]

Braceros abided by the segregation enforced in the cities and towns they lived in, and racial segregation shaped both their social lives and their sexual lives.

Race also came to shape which sex workers were deemed suitable for Mexican guest workers. Joseph Hellmer described the relations he observed while working as a supervisor at the Pennsylvania railroad camp in Bush River, Maryland, from July to November 1944.[87] That September he was called as an interpreter to a "disciplinary case" in Havre de Grace, Maryland, where several braceros were "accused of harboring a woman in their bunkhouse." The mayor of the town was present and focused on Mexican and African American relations, stating that Mexicans "were not permitted to associate with the Negroes in the community." A spokesman within the group of workers explained, "The case was simply that the few Mexicans in the group who were of Negro origin, naturally sought out Negro girls and men for companionship in the town." The representative went on to explain that they worked alongside "Negroes" and that they were "forced at times to frequent restaurants and other public places where Negroes went, because 'white' places ostracized them."[88] It was also explained that the woman in question was "a whore of Latin American or Spanish birth, from Washington, D.C., and that she came to the camp 'soliciting business.'"[89]

This case raised a series of questions for town officials about the sexual contours of race relations. They were less concerned with the presence of the sex worker in the camp than with her racial identity. In this context, it is also interesting to note that some braceros identified themselves racially as "negro," indicating that Afro-Mestizos from Mexico also found their way into the program.[90] This example is indicative of complicated modes of racialization, whereby highlighting Mexican blackness versus a mestizo racial identity could be a strategy to normalize intimate relations with black women in the eyes of town officials. Clearly, braceros understood their social place in a segregated racial landscape. In this case, the braceros were identified as "negro," while the sex worker's identity is purposely recorded as black and Latin American or Spanish in order to mediate a more acceptable sexual relationship between them. The meeting concluded without a resolution. Hellmer writes that nothing was accomplished except "the complete bewilderment of Mexicans at the behavior of the town."[91]

Although railroad braceros in Maryland experienced race relations that were distinct from the agricultural workers in Texas, braceros could easily solicit sex workers in both. As a young teenager, Sebastian Martínez became aware of the relationship between braceros and sex workers in Pecos, Texas:

> Most of them took time to go into town on Saturday nights and either went to the bars, the cantinas and the whore houses. . . . Yeah, most of them of course went into town for recreation and there were a lot of cantinas. I recall there were some blocks, some city blocks that had anywhere from four to five cantinas. It reminded me of Juarez here in the 60s where the red light district [was located]. Pecos turned into that, at least the east side of town turned into a red light district. Because Pecos had basically a population of six to ten thousand, then the population would swell to as much as fifty thousand because all [the] men [came]. They filled the cantinas, and they had to get their recreation somewhere, and there were a lot of women who serviced the men in the cantinas. Sometimes these recreational activities became well organized, where you had a man who would buy a van, would take two or three women, and would go from farm to farm soliciting the business. Some of them did very well.

I recall . . . several women who were very poor but eventually they
ended up with good convertibles.[92]

Sex work had many venues, from cantinas to camps to automobiles. In
Lubbock, Texas, prostitution followed the cycles of cotton cultivation; as
migratory labor increased during the fall, so did prostitution. In the 1950s,
if sex workers were found and pleaded guilty, they faced a fine of fifteen
dollars.[93] Those who catered to braceros in this area supported themselves
economically, but they also suffered from and spread STDs at alarming
rates.

Guest worker Rosendo Alarcón Carrera was aware of this when he worked
in Pecos, Texas, during the final years of the Bracero Program. When asked
if representatives of the Mexican Consul or immigration authorities ever
showed up in the camp, he responded that the only individuals to visit the
camp were camper trucks with two or three prostitutes. They would show
up "on the weekend" when they knew braceros would be paid. "They would
arrive at twelve or one in the morning, because they never arrived early."[94]
He described the women as diverse, remembering in particular the African
American women who charged five dollars. Alarcón Carrera felt apprehen-
sive about sleeping with the prostitutes, explaining, "Lord knows how many
illnesses they had."[95]

Dr. Pedro A. Ortega noted the abundance of guest workers infected with
STDs. Raised and trained as a doctor in Cuba, Ortega provided medical
examinations to braceros at the Rio Vista Contracting Station in 1961. He
took the job because he did not speak English and wanted to work near the
beach because it reminded him of the water surrounding Cuba. He looked
at a map and thought it would suit his needs because it seemed close to the
Gulf and the Rio Grande. Fourteen days after he arrived, Dr. Ortega began
working in the U.S. Public Health Service with braceros. Because he spoke
Spanish, he replaced the army doctors who had been processing braceros
for three- to six-month periods. The station could process a little over 3,000
men a day.[96]

One of the most common tests Dr. Ortega administered was for STDs,
and he contributed to research on the implementation of new systems for
detecting syphilis in braceros. He always checked for hernias, deformities,
tuberculosis, and syphilis, as well as other sexually transmitted diseases, during his medical examinations. At Rio Vista Contracting Station, he rejected
any bracero who tested positive for any infectious or contagious disease
that doctors could not control. He noted, "I remember one time we started

getting people positive for syphilis . . . more than usual. All of them were coming from one small place in the state of Guerrero. . . . They were Indians, almost all of them were relatives, they didn't speak Spanish, there was one interpreter. . . . More than fifteen [came from] the same place with syphilis."[97]

Dr. Ortega's observation indicates that indigenous populations also participated in sexual economies in the fields and hired prostitutes. STDs spread through camps and tightly knit communities, making clusters of monolingual indigenous language speakers more susceptible. And while language barriers did not hinder their participation in sexual economies, it did impact their ability to access medical attention for STDs. Medical problems could be exacerbated by ineffective communication with doctors and nurses. Although the most common illness that Dr. Ortega diagnosed was syphilis, he still approved infected men for contracts because he could give them a treatment that lasted several months and hope that they would return to Mexico by the time they became contagious again. Dr. Ortega's decision to allow these men to enter after receiving treatment demonstrates what historian John Mckiernan-González argues is the power of the "political authority of the medical border" to control people's mobility.[98]

Journalists who covered the health concerns of Mexican agricultural labor often focused on STDs and framed their sexuality as a potential danger to the public's health. Nate Haseltine of the *Washington Post* wrote, "So needed were their farm services that they were readily hired without question. The ready reception was perpetuating self imported contagions of syphilis, gonorrhea and other venereal diseases."[99] Concerns around braceros as potential STD carriers, along with the growing need for these laborers, led to a focus on faster STD testing. Prior to same-day detection tests, "even when specimens were air-mailed to laboratory testing facilities, and the results wired back to the reception centers, the migrants had been entered and were at work in the fields. They had to be rounded up, whenever possible, and taken back to the centers or to clinics or private physicians for penicillin treatment."[100] Although Mexico wanted the United States to administer the same test to braceros returning home, the United States would not invest in those resources, since officials believed that Mexico had already benefited from the first round of testing: "Since the names and addresses of the VD-infected and their home community sex contacts are supplied to the appropriate Mexican local health departments . . . they are able to stop the further spread of infections in the homeland."[101] This issue caught national attention as the Centers for Disease Control spent six months developing the test that health care providers, such as Dr. Ortega, would later administer.

The potential of contracting an STD could deter braceros from hiring sex workers. Guest worker Juan Virgen Díaz explained that while working in Southern California, he was offered the services of women he described as *"mujeres alegres"* and *"mujeres que andan vendiendo su amor,"* happy women and women who sell their love. He tells of his first encounter with a sex worker at the camp by saying, "They [the pimp] had her laying on a mattress there, and well all of a sudden I felt like I wanted to get with her."[102] The pimp told Virgen Díaz that it would cost him three dollars, and when he finally decided that he would pay, a fellow bracero told him, "Are you going to go with that woman? Don't go there."[103] The bracero described the woman as a "mess" and a "pig sty," meaning that he saw a higher potential of contracting an STD because she had already had sex with many men. After providing her services to about fifteen to twenty men, braceros found her to be undesirable because in their minds the potential for contracting an STD had risen. The next time around the pimp would bring in other women, and men would wait around to be the first in line.

As sexual economies expanded along the border and in labor camps, gender and sexual relations were reimagined by braceros who found themselves in homosocial spaces. While sex work provided an economy of pleasure that catered to migrant workers, interpretations of prostitution varied. Despite the fact that some believed that prostitution was a scourge on society, some communities in the United States understood sexual encounters as a basic necessity for these men, and sex workers provided services that could ensure the protection of a wider spectrum of "respectable" American women who might otherwise fall "prey" to these men's advances.

Queer Desire

In the process of valorizing the bracero contributions as a source of national pride, complicated stories of nonmarital sexual desire were pushed to the margins by a Mexican government awaiting their return and remittances. As a result, a stoic image of the noble laborer emerged. And while the narrative played down stories of heterosexual relations outside of marriage, it completely silenced sexual encounters that were not based on heterosexual desire. Braceros lived in homosocial spaces, and some could engage in queer sexual encounters with relative ease. This is not to say that sexual identities were not contested in Mexico.[104] As seen in the previous examples, gender and sexual roles were in a state of flux because of the ways the Bracero Program restructured families. This meant that men had opportunities not only for heterosexual dalliances, but also for queer sex acts. As Lionel Cantú notes, "We must move away from one-dimensional cultural models and examine these sexualities from a more complex and materialist perspective that recognizes that culture, social relations, and identities are embedded in global processes."[105] These transnational labor networks, then, provide a space to investigate how changing material conditions also shaped negotiations over queer masculinities. Antigay violence did not prevent some queer laborers from coming out in public areas.

Bracero Gustavo Eloy Reyes Rodríguez, who boldly stated *"Yo le digo* [I will tell you]," when I asked about queer encounters during the Bracero Program, openly described what he witnessed as other braceros sat and listened to his oral history. A Oaxacan bracero, he received his first contract to work in Blythe, California.

> Look, in [19]60 when I was in Blythe, in that time, you heard very little talk about, about those people. . . . Before you could see very few, or maybe there were very few. But in the camp, in the barrack where I was, where I slept, there was one, one kid that also lived in the same barrack, by the entrance to the barrack. . . . One day the light was cut off, but we didn't know why until there was a discussion, an argument among some guys near the door, and the next day they clarified why it happened. That kid was named Porfirio, he was from the state of Oaxaca and . . . and they figured out that he was, like they say now, the gays, or homosexual, or like that. Then that kid clarified that he was like that . . . he had turned off the light because he was in a relationship with a man. And then we called his attention to it in the . . . fields where we worked. And then he said yes, that he was of that . . . that he was gay.[106]

Rodríguez explained that everyone assumed that Porfirio had a love affair with another bracero, and to keep his lover's identity anonymous he cut the wire that led to the light switch. They would fix the wire, and then find that it had been cut again. At night, they could hear noises, which Rodríguez assumed came from the two lovers; however, since the bunk was pitch-black at night they could not be sure.[107] The other men in the barracks started getting annoyed with the blackouts, to the point that one confronted and intimidated Porfirio. According to Rodríguez,

> He performed the mannerism as if to declare it publicly that, that he was, because he was very public, he had the mannerism, even the way

he walked, no? . . . And he never denied it; he never said no, he said yes. . . . Someone from Michoacán asked him to please leave. With strong words he said, "You are going to go someplace far, far away." And then [Porfirio] . . . said okay. But he was a worker, how was he going to leave? So he didn't leave, he continued on. But he didn't commit the error of cutting off the light again. But yes, it was then that it became clear, that it was the kid [Porfirio]. But he didn't deny it, he said yes.[108]

The Bracero Program limited Porfirio's mobility, and he, like many workers, had only two choices: skip out on his contract and become an undocumented laborer or fulfill his contractual obligations. Despite the hostility that Porfirio faced in the labor camp, he continued to work and remained open about his sexual preferences. Ironically, Rodríguez never knew who Porfirio's lover was, meaning that he never faced any of the bullying Porfirio had to deal with. Perhaps he was not marked as queer in the same way that Porfirio was. The lack of interest in tracking down the lover underscores Rodríguez's claims that a large majority of the men at that camp did not care much about Porfirio's sexual preferences and chose not to make a big deal about it.[109] To most of the braceros, men like Porfirio did not seem so out of the ordinary in these migrant labor spaces.

Some men in the camp pursued social encounters, not only with Porfirio, but also with other individuals who expanded their sense of nonheteronormative desire. Rodríguez remembered how a transgender group would often come to the camps.[110] They traveled up from Mexicali to visit the Southern California farm where he labored with over 300 other workers. Rodríguez explained that these were "men dressed as women," and that there was no way they would be confused for braceros. Despite this, these transgender sex workers felt comfortable enough to introduce themselves and to take part in the leisure spaces of bracero camp life. Rodríguez never witnessed threats of violence against these sex workers, and the frequency of their visits suggests their popularity.

While interviewing elderly braceros in 2012, anthropologist Juan Miguel Sarricolea Torres documented the experience of a man named Santos who worked during the final years of the Bracero Program. While awaiting a contract in Empalme, Sonora, he and his godfather attended a dance, where his godfather sent Santos a "*monota*," a large "doll" to dance with. Santos was taken aback by her beauty, especially her sexy "legs" and "small waist." She was a transgender prostitute, and Santos noted in their intimate acts that "hers was even bigger than mine." Santos in no way felt deceived. Before she won him over, he felt a bit of stubble on her face and pulled out his knife and explained that he did not like her stubble.[111] He used words like "*monota*" and "*muchachona*" to describe her large and feminine physique. Neither Santos nor his godfather expressed that she was unwelcome or out of place in this setting; instead Santos articulated an admiration for her beauty.

As the sexual economy changed for women, it also changed for queer men, transgender sex workers, and men who engaged in queer sex acts. Significantly, these stories have been largely left out of bracero histories. When we listen to and make space for them, however, a fuller picture of gender and sexual negotiations becomes visible. They both humanize the braceros and demonstrate the limits to the sexual freedoms that border crossings permitted. The rearrangement of material practices that constituted the shifting boundaries of sexuality again provided opportunities for men and transgender people to explore sexual relations, even as the program placed limits on this "freedom."

Reinterpreting Deviance

In 1948, film director Alfonso Patiño Gómez released *Pito Perez Se Va De Bracero*, based on a script he co-wrote with Leopoldo Baeza y Aceves. They centered the script on a popular character, Pito Perez, introduced nearly a decade earlier in a novel by José Rubén Romero. Some critics argued that all of the charm, freshness, and social satire that made this character so popular was lost in this movie.[112] According to film historian Emilio García Riera, the film failed to capture the audience's attention.[113] Although some scholars describe the film as a "'tragicomedy' without social critique,"[114] I believe that the character of Pito Perez has long been misunderstood. Pito Perez depicts a bracero deviance that was not rooted in the Mexican nation-building project that held the transnational heteronormative family as central. He is not married and has no children, and he does not see the need to work. Although these facts mark him as deviant, what is more important is that he defiantly has no desire to embody masculinity through tropes of family or labor.

The opening scene of the film introduces us to Pito as an antihero jailed for drunken misconduct. On his journey to the United States, he exposes an ironic nationalism: "Mexico is a great country that produces; it even produces braceros for the United States."[115] Pito haphazardly obtains a bracero contract and goes through the medical exams. When asked about his work history, he explains, "I consider work such an awful thing that they have to pay one to do it."[116] Despite his meager work history peddling knickknacks, he gets a contract picking and packing citrus in Pomona, California. There his attitudes are juxtaposed with those of his co-workers, who have adopted American work habits and make comments such as "Time is money." Pito is unhappy with the fast pace of work in the citrus industry and decides to walk off the job; he becomes undocumented before our eyes.

Pito then stumbles upon work on the railroad and joins a group of braceros. The monotonous pace of labor drives him to spike the workers' water with alcohol. He realizes that although he has very little power while he is working, he does have the power to quit, noting, "At least I can leave them when I feel like it."[117] The conflict in the film plays out in his visits to a club, where he goes to see a performer he has become enamored with, and with a group of men who want him to serve as a coyote for Mexican undocumented workers. He refuses and decides to return to Mexico. Although the film was envisioned as a picaresque comedy, Pito presented the public with images of the bracero contracting process and of laboring Mexican bodies in the United States. As a tragic antihero, Pito also provides a critique of American labor practices. He understands that his value lies in his ability to work as quickly as possible, but he pushes back and repeatedly chooses to fulfill his desires instead of his obligations as a worker. He reclaims carnal pleasures by drinking alcohol, dancing, singing, and enjoying the company of an American woman. And he does all of this solely for his own gratification. Throughout the film, Pito stands in contradistinction to hardworking braceros, and it is perhaps his disdain for labor that made him unpopular with both Mexican and American audiences. Or perhaps it was the fact that the Bracero Program was no joke. In the Mexican state's narrative, these men endured exploitation in order to achieve family uplift. The goal was not supposed to be taken lightly. Pito's character suggested a deviance from that expectation that purposely defied the state's narrative.

The Bracero Program shaped the family lives and intimate encounters of bracero communities. These alternate histories, and Pito Perez himself, present a more complex and less idealized vision of masculinity, family, and labor. They challenge the heroic narrative created to legitimize the national contributions of these men and present a more diverse vision of bracero sexual economies. Nonnormative intimate encounters did exist in these communities prior to the program, but the program provided additional anonymity, distance from family, and potentially expendable income to practice them more freely. Some men engaged in extramarital affairs outside of the watchful eyes and social pressures of their home communities. In comparison to women, men faced less severe ostracism, and many chose to place their own needs for leisure and vice above the economic needs of their families. Parents worked to keep their children from enrolling in the Bracero Program, and women fought to claim back wages as alimony and child support. Some women restructured their family lives by moving closer to the border in order to visit male kin on the weekends. Economies of pleasure and vice emerged to cater to the needs of these guest workers. In addition, braceros created their own spheres of vice through practices such as gambling.

The patriarchal narratives about these guest workers as husbands, fathers, sons, and noble laborers obscures the complicated family interactions, economies of pleasure, and sexual encounters shaped during this period. Supporters of the program cast deviant and defiant individuals in the shadows, as if their acts brought shame on the entire group. Bringing these men out of the shadows of the camp and highlighting their actions based on pleasure, adventure, and desire might seem like a marring of their historical contribution, but I argue that what surfaces is a more complicated picture of the program. These men are not simply victims or heroes. They were unique combinations of these two archetypes, and their aspirations and actions challenged both American and Mexican state power. Braceros understood how to demonstrate respectable masculinity in order to overcome government obstacles to secure contracts, and they also learned how to use these narratives of fatherhood and breadwinning to confront multiple levels of exploitation that took place as soon as they began their journey through Mexico and onto their work sites.

The character of Pito Perez must have been seared into labor organizer Ernesto Galarza's mind, as it became the namesake for a composite bracero in *Strangers in Our Fields*, Galarza's exposé of exploitative practices within the Bracero Program. Galarza's well-researched publication brought national attention to the plight of Mexican guest workers. Galarza gives Pito Perez a new story as "a typical example of the men who work in U.S. fields. . . . Pito lives with his wife and four children in Rancho de la Mojonera, Michoacán. He has at times vaguely thought of trying to get on as a bracero."[118] Galarza reimagines the character in opposition to the film, placing Pito back into a nuclear family where he is the patriarch. He normalizes Pito's relationship to family, the state, and labor by evoking the Mexican and U.S. narratives about the program. Galarza emphasizes family and offers up the states' logic for Pito's entrance into an exploitative system of labor. In *Strangers in*

Our Fields, Galarza creates a version of Pito designed to move his audience toward a harsher critique of the program, knowing that the deviant and defiant Pito would not move people to action but would instead justify the harsh management of guest workers. Despite the imprint this film leaves in the mind of Galarza and labor history, Pito Perez as characterized in the film continues to occupy a liminal space, as he embodies many of the characteristics that are written out of contemporary accounts of bracero experiences.

INTERLUDE Documenting

During a public call for local communities to collaborate with the
Bracero History Project in Southern California, Luis Estrada, the son of
a deceased bracero, decided to share his oral history. He recalled that as
a child his mother, grandparents, and siblings accompanied his father
on a three-hour walk to the nearest town in which his father could catch
a bus to head to the nearest contracting station.[1] He also decided to
bring in his father's worn identification from the Alliance of National
Workers of Mexico in the United States of America (Alianza de Braceros
Nacionales de México en los Estados Unidos). One corner was stamped
with a Mexican union seal and the other with the American Federation
of Labor seal, whose design incorporated the word "Alianza." "What an
intriguing organization," I thought. From that moment on, I scoured
collecting sites in search of more ex-braceros that could tell me about
this seemingly mysterious organization, but to no avail. The following
summer, I encountered an identification card for the second time; this
time close to my family's hometown in Manuel Doblado, Guanajuato.
An ex-bracero had kept his guest-worker identification pressed together
with his Alliance of National Workers of Mexico card for over forty years.
To my dismay, the worker could not recall details about the organization,
except that he originally believed affiliation with this organization would
allow him to obtain a contract more easily. I listened to many recordings
of oral histories collected by others, and finally I found one recording
that referenced this organization. The bracero, José Santos Guevara
Rodríguez, did not remember very much about the organization, except
for his experience with one organizer of Alianza, Pedro Cerón. Cerón
helped Guevara Rodríguez and others from Oaxaca, Jalisco, and

Guanajuato obtain contracts. Guevara Rodríguez described the dues he paid. "We didn't pay him much," and "later [Cerón told us] we were in an Alianza."[2] Although it seemed that braceros' memories could not provide more about Alianza, I thought that traditional archives might have recorded what memory had not.

THREE UNIONIZING THE IMPOSSIBLE

Alianza de Braceros Nacionales de México en los Estados Unidos

Ganamos la Guerra—Ganemos La Paz. (We Won the
War—Let Us Win Peace.)
—Alianza de Braceros Nacionales de México en los
  Estados Unidos slogan, 1946 to 1954

Por el Triunfo de las Democracias. (For the Triumph
of the Democracies.)
—Alianza de Braceros Nacionales de México en los
  Estados Unidos slogan, 1943 to 1945 and again
  in 1955

A carefully guarded captive, he is unorganized and
yet unorganizable.
—TED LE BERTHON

One year after the first braceros set foot in Stockton, California, a group
of Mexican citrus workers in Fullerton, California, gathered around to discuss the potential of creating a bracero organization. At 10:00 A.M. on
Saturday, October 2, 1943, over three dozen men constituted the Alianza
de Braceros Nacionales de México en los Estados Unidos (Alianza) under
the leadership of braceros José Lara Jimenez and José Hernández Serrano.
The members elected Hernández Serrano to be head of the organization,
a position he held for over twenty years. Little biographical information is
known about him except that several of his family members held key positions in the organization and that they were from the town Tepotzotlán,
Estado de México, which lies outside of Mexico City.[1] More important, what
is known about Hernández Serrano is revealed in correspondence with
labor leaders, such as Ernesto Galarza, and in letters to Mexican presidents
that made their way into the Mexican national archive. These letters also
shed light on the sophisticated outlook of a group of braceros who dared

to challenge the status quo and whose aspirations for a transnational labor union deviated from the visions of growers and the Mexican and American governments alike.

As an organization created for and by Mexican guest workers, Alianza made many pleas on behalf of these guest workers for the Mexican government to intervene and protect the interests of its citizens abroad. It began as a group that espoused patriotic principles, but as worker abuses rose it took on a more radical stance and aligned itself with labor unions, purposely defying state power. Alianza used normative narratives tied to nation, masculinity, and family in order to create an image of the respectable guest worker. Its goal was to secure contracts for *aspirantes* and to advocate for their reincorporation into the Mexican economy through redistribution of land and wealth.

These revolutionary ideals, however, reached their zenith under Mexican president Lázaro Cárdenas (1934–40). The 1940s ushered in a more conservative turn within the government, embodied by the rise of the Partido Revolucionario Institucional (PRI), the party that would come to rule Mexico for seventy-one years. Mexican president Manuel Ávila Camacho transitioned the government from focusing on fulfilling revolutionary promises to catering to capital under the guise of modernization. *Life* magazine described him as the "mild" candidate and predicted that "if elected, he is almost certain" to tone down the "so-called 'Revolution.'"[2] In an odd twist, "Leftist Ávila Camacho is very conservative" and the right was described as very liberal. Ávila Camacho was the first in a series of leaders under the PRI regime to quell labor unions and protect capitalists; his corruption would become synonymous with the party. Under these conditions, members of Alianza invested in images of mestizo normativity as entry points into the Mexican nation-building project. But their frustration grew when, despite their normative stance, the government failed to protect guest workers and began to characterize the organization's activism as deviant, dangerous, and communist. The Mexican government then went further and placed many of the members of Alianza under surveillance, in addition to prosecuting leaders for a number of issues related to their activism.

Ernesto Galarza rested many hopes of organizing workers transnationally on Alianza, and much of what is known about Alianza is contained in his correspondence with the group. While Galarza is widely recognized as a strong critic of guest-worker labor who fought tirelessly to help bring an end to the program, his involvement with Alianza exposes an understudied side of his labor activism. In a time before the successful efforts of Cesar

Chavez, Galarza attempted to organize farm laborers. Unlike those of Chavez, Galarza's initial attempts focused on finding a place for Mexican migrants within larger American labor movements. Galarza's early efforts toward unionizing braceros while at the National Farm Labor Union (NFLU) are considered by historian Stephen Pitti as one of the most creative turns in ethnic Mexican efforts to think transnationally about pressing political efforts in labor organizing.[3]

As a child, Galarza was familiar with Mexican political turmoil; he and his family fled during the Mexican Revolution and made their way to Sacramento, California, where they became farmworkers. Based on his experience as a migrant and as an agricultural laborer, Galarza sympathized with the plight of guest workers. His educational background allowed him to go one step further and intellectualize the economic relationship between Mexico and the United States. Galarza did well in school and received a scholarship to attend Occidental College. While completing his undergraduate degree, he would return home during summers and continue working as a farm laborer. His interest in Latin America and labor led him to complete a master's degree at Stanford University and later a Ph.D. in economics at Columbia University. Both his educational and his personal background ignited his desire for social change in the area of labor reform. After completing his doctorate, Galarza worked for Pan American Union in Washington, D.C., and then became the director of Research and Education for the NFLU. During this period of his career, he worked closely with braceros employed in fields that were reminiscent of those in which Galarza had labored during his youth.

Alianza came to Ernesto Galarza's attention in the late 1940s, and he began to view many of the prospects of unionizing braceros as resting on this organization. During his many trips to meet with Mexican unions and Mexican officials about the plight of Mexican migrant workers, he talked with the leadership of Alianza. By January 1951, he felt confident that he could incorporate braceros into his unionizing efforts through the mounting labor strikes in the Imperial Valley of California. The challenge set before him was to organize braceros alongside American agricultural laborers in order to place pressure on growers. According to historian Dionicio Nodín Valdés, Galarza considered this moment the most favorable for agricultural unionism in the Imperial Valley in generations.[4] Galarza had garnered support from domestic workers, from Mexican pro-union allies, and from sympathetic American reporters.[5] Several months later, his aims shifted as he became increasingly frustrated with the Mexican government's repressive treatment of Alianza and had to face the failures of the 1951 labor strike in the Imperial Valley. From then on, he stopped trying to organize guest workers and instead focused on collecting data that would eventually be used in congressional hearings to help terminate the Bracero Program. He also swayed public opinion against the program through his groundbreaking exposé, *Strangers in Our Fields*. At this point, his relationship with Alianza members went from working with them for unionization to using them to gather information for additional research and publications.

What was the political vision of men like Hernández Serrano and the leadership of Alianza? Although they defiantly believed that guest workers could be organized into a transnational union, they stood apart from most braceros because they were highly literate and had access to organizing tools, such as typewriters, mimeographs, and office space. Their efforts also demonstrate intra-ethnic tensions, as they drew divisions between Mexican migrant laborers and fought hard to distinguish themselves from "wetbacks." Rooted in a mestizo subjectivity, many Alianza members invoked patriotic narratives that chastised the undocumented and looked down on indigenous braceros, as they believed their "primitive" outlook limited their organizing potential.[6] The Alianza leadership wrapped itself in the mantle of normativity rooted in patriotism, legal status, hard work, and masculinity to advance their own interests, only to find that Mexican officials would not support their cause.

Despite the limits to their radicalism, they levied strong critiques against the Mexican government for painting them as deviants, communists, and racketeers. They also accused the Mexican government of purposely creating conditions that would allow for bracero exploitation and marginalization. Furthermore, their story reveals longer histories of Mexican exploitation of migrants and interrogates formulations of state power in which Mexican labor exploitation stems from uneven power relations. Lastly, Alianza illustrated that the lives of Mexican guest workers were preconditioned by exploitation, rooted in racialized colonial relations that were then mapped onto the agricultural labor system. Ultimately, their aim was to connect these histories with emerging systems of managing bracerismo, that is, Public Law 78, which further curtailed their potential to organize.

The Patriotic Alianza

Recruited with the guarantee of a decent wage and the promise of serving the greater good during a time of war, many braceros left Mexico City in 1942. False rumors spread that the U.S. government was making plans to send braceros off to war; however, many men decided to enroll in the program despite feelings of hesitation and skepticism.[7] The U.S. government quelled these rumors by evoking Roosevelt's Good Neighbor Policy and insisting that it was the patriotic duty of Mexicans to assist the United States in war efforts. Braceros internalized the "good neighbor" spirit as they eventually decided to take part in the program.[8] Many guest workers who took part during those first years told positive stories of cheerful, welcoming committees and decent treatment, despite the difficulty of their work. Early propaganda about the Bracero Program highlighted its patriotic efforts, encouraging American communities to understand the role of these workers as essential to securing the prosperity of the home front. Many guest workers reinforced such interpretations by asserting: "We fed America during the war."[9] Alianza worked within these parameters of patriotic duty to address concerns raised by aspiring braceros who knew little about the program. These patriotic discourses served to make sense of the status of these guest workers in the United States, and in this context, their rights as workers were made to seem less important.

Scholars have claimed that Alianza started in Mexico City during the late 1940s, but the organization has a slightly longer transnational history.[10] During the first meeting in California, Lara Jimenez said, "The meeting's objective is to form an organization that is considered necessary in light of the fact that many braceros do not understand the responsibility we have here in the United States of North America, in these transcendental global moments, in which all countries fight for liberty."[11] He believed that many braceros did not comprehend their role in global politics and did not complete the terms of the contract.[12] He went on to argue that braceros who did not want to work became a source of national embarrassment and shame for those who did work hard. The organizers wanted to protect the image of braceros in order to attain a higher status for them vis-à-vis undocumented workers.

During this brief one-hour meeting, the members created and filled seven positions within the organization by unanimous votes. By October 18, 1943, Alianza leadership mailed off a statement on their newly acquired letterhead to the president of Mexico, Manuel Ávila Camacho, to inform him of the organization's creation. The head of Alianza expressed that the goal of the organization was to provide an orientation for its members, ensuring that these representatives of Mexico honored their mother country.[13] The early slogan articulated the perceived role of the bracero in the United States: "For the Triumph of the Democracies."[14] Inspired by Roosevelt's Good Neighbor Policy, their labor would aid American efforts in the war and the worldwide effort for democracy. According to Alianza, the braceros were not merely stoop labor. Additionally, Alianza saw itself as an organization that followed patriotic principles. It wanted to make sure that the violent, drunk, and lazy men of Mexico did not secure contracts and thus disgrace Mexico abroad.[15] The leadership went so far as to print a notice about the organization in the widely circulated Mexican newspaper *La Prensa*, stating that its aim was to ensure that braceros saw to their obligations abroad so that democracy would prevail.[16] Alianza proposed accessing state power through labor enforcement.

Alianza wanted to accomplish these goals by becoming part of the Mexican contracting process. Leaders of the organization proposed that its members could work to orient braceros so they knew what to expect, and thus potentially decrease the number of braceros who "skipped out" on their contracts. For a bracero to "skip out" meant that he abandoned his work to seek new job opportunities outside the parameters of his contract, automatically changing his status to undocumented. Braceros who broke their contracts became a major problem for employers, who sometimes quickly lost their workforce. The problem of desertion surged within one month after the first arrival of braceros in 1942, as 15 percent of workers skipped out of their contracts.[17] The organization viewed this problem as a consequence of contracting unreliable men and felt that the organization could work toward improving this embarrassing situation nationwide.[18]

Alianza's indictment of undocumented workers furthered its claims that braceros were worthy of entering the United States on guest-worker contracts. Through these discourses, the organization highlighted the aspiring braceros' sense of ethics, their understanding of the law, and, over all, their patriotism—all of which served their self-interests in securing contracts amid the large stream of documented and undocumented workers competing in the same labor market. In order to further advance the interests of its members, Alianza also wanted contract preference given to braceros who completed the terms of their previous contracts. Alianza argued that men with experience as guest workers in the United States knew what the work entailed and were less likely to skip out on their new contracts. As these first groups of men returned home, they dispelled the myth that braceros were sent to the front lines of the war. They also spoke about their experiences and wages in the United States, generating more interest in the program. Soon thousands of *aspirantes* lined up in areas around the national stadium in Mexico City. Writer Jesús Topete described this area as a "Bracerópolis," as hungry men far from their hometowns slept on streets.[19] Potential guest workers took on debt to get to Mexico City, where many were continuously taken advantage of by people who made empty promises to get these *aspirantes* on bracero lists for small bribes commonly known as *mordidas*. The local and national governments turned a blind eye to the injustices committed against guest workers. Historian Stephen Niblo agues that "Mexico's participation in World War II became absolutely critical in the process of shifting the revolution away from Cárdenas's populism and onto a more conservative course."[20] Mexican president Manuel Ávila Camacho would usher in a conservative turn that would strengthen ties with the United States and court U.S. investments. Alianza's activism, in turn, increased with the unjust treatment of braceros and the Mexican government's reluctance to work on their behalf.

The Criminalized Alianza

After the war ended, the organization recognized that the crimes against braceros extended beyond the Mexican border. As the exploitative practices of American growers increased, Alianza put energy into calling national and international attention to them. Although they previously mediated guest-worker conflicts within the contracting system and with American growers, the level of attention placed on these exploitative practices grew dramatically. No longer centrally concerned with sending the best workers of Mexico to represent the nation abroad, they focused on protecting the men against both U.S. and Mexican exploitation. Alianza believed one of the major hurdles put before it was the rising number of undocumented workers. This made it particularly difficult to advocate for bracero worker rights because some employers could easily replace guest workers with undocumented labor. In this struggle, Alianza leaders sought to advance their own self-interests, not those of all Mexican workers in the United States.

Their strategy for advancing bracero interests was to seek alliances with other organized workers. The leadership of Alianza grew concerned with finding a place for braceros within larger labor movements despite the Mexican labor movement's waning power under Ávila Camacho's conservative regime. Ávila Camacho adamantly opposed organized labor, saying, "You know, I could easily crush these labour leaders with a strong hand, but I don't wish to use force unnecessarily."[21] The Mexican government was creating a more unfavorable political environment for labor organizing. Although the braceros were clearly viewed as workers, their rights were limited within the Bracero Program. While organizing to meet their new aims, Alianza faced heavy surveillance by Mexican officials, and the leaders of the organization suffered state repression in Mexico in the form of legal prosecution, blacklisting, and even imprisonment.[22]

These shifts within the organization began by the mid-1940s, a time when Alianza saw itself as a bracero-advocacy and social-service organization. As members' contracts ended and they returned to Mexico, activists in the organization moved the headquarters from Fullerton, California, to Mexico City.[23] Perhaps this was because several key leaders lived in and around Mexico City, or because the nature of the guest-worker contracts gave braceros very little power to choose where they worked. They could not build the long-term, year-round stability needed to strengthen the organization from California. In an investigation of the organization, Manuel Rio Thivol, a government agent, reported, "Upon their return to their home country, they were in agreement to reorganize because here too in this country they are victims of the same economic exploitations that because of evident poverty they cannot solve."[24] Leadership of the organization recognized that the exploitation of braceros began with the deplorable work conditions and economic hardship in their hometowns, which motivated them to leave. On the long road to acquiring a bracero contract, many *aspirantes* went into debt and experienced swindling at the hands of unscrupulous individuals with false promises of work in the United States. Leadership in Alianza argued that *aspirantes* could easily fall into conditions that in their eyes closely resembled a type of "slavery" through the work of American contractors that aimed at delivering undocumented workers with few rights and recourses.[25] They opened an office in Mexico City in order to more effectively work on decreasing *aspirante* abuses and to create politicized groups of braceros who could call attention to guest-worker abuses as well.

The organization also created new positions to reflect these aims. The board of Alianza created and appointed a Commission of Justice and Honor, legal advisors, a secretary of Education and Athletics, a secretary for Conflicts, and secretary aids who focused on enhancing the quality of life of braceros in the fields. From 1943 to 1945, Alianza began to speak on behalf of braceros and their families to try to resolve contracting, transportation, salary, and domestic conflicts. In 1944, it wrote to the Mexican consul in an attempt to mediate salary disputes between braceros of Chula Vista and their employer.[26] In 1945, it supported Concepción Bejarán de Muñóz's claim that she had a right to receive remittances from her bracero husband. The organization worked with the Mexican consul to put pressure on her husband, Francisco Muñoz Barrera, to address his wife's concerns.[27] These mediations represented efforts to address the needs of the bracero family in Mexico.

Interventions of this kind came to a drastic halt in 1946, when the state placed the executive board of Alianza on trial. Mexican officials argued that the organization was attempting to function as a union. Although the stipulations within the bi-national agreement allowed braceros to choose a representative from their own group to represent their interests in the fields, it prohibited them from joining unions and striking. The office of the Secretary of Labor publicly denied that its aim was to dissolve Alianza, even though it stated that the organization's activities seemed unlawful.[28] This contradiction continued as the organization saw itself lambasted by the government in articles printed in Mexican newspapers that toed the government line—titles like "An Alliance That Only Exploits Braceros," which argued that the enrollment fee Alianza members paid was exploitative.[29] The subtext often drew parallels between enrollment fees and the *mordidas* that *aspirantes* paid for a chance at a contract. For the next two years, the organization remained relatively inactive, until September 22, 1948, when it was ruled that Alianza did not commit any crimes and that the organization acted within the legal boundaries of a civic association, not a union. Officials found that the executive board did not act criminally or exhibit inappropriate behavior.[30] Because of this, Alianza's board had to work to restore its image with members of various regional chapters of the organization. José Hernández Serrano, head of the organization, stated that after the trial he had to clear the air and do away with suspicion and inaccurate portrayals of Alianza.[31] Despite the trial's outcome, the federal government continued to investigate Alianza.[32] When Mexico's new president, Manuel Alemán Valdés, was sworn in to power, on December 1, 1946, he not only solidified Mexico's shift to the right under the PRI, he also took a hard line against Mexican communists, as the Truman administration intensified the Cold War.[33]

Even as leaders of Alianza embraced their identity as a civic association to avoid being suppressed, they were still eager to find a place within larger unions. In order to protect the organization, they shifted the language used in many of the flyers they printed and circulated. A flyer that was obtained by government agent Manuel Rios Thivol described the organization's membership as "totally composed of aspirantes, and ex-braceros."[34] Alianza failed to include current braceros in this document because its leaders did not want to be perceived as an entity that organized workers in the United States. These public statements often hid their attempts to reach guest workers in the American fields. Alianza suggested that *aspirantes* and ex-braceros residing in Mexico pay a three-peso registration fee and one-peso monthly dues and that braceros working in the United States pay a one-dollar registration fee and fifty-cent monthly dues. According to Rios Thivol, "I became aware that the founding members of this organization in the United States of America are those that are part of the Executive Committee, having C. José Hernández Serrano as the General Secretary. . . . They are committed to pay the expenditures that originate from supporting the organization, for example in respect to managing, paper, ink, and other desk supplies that every office needs in order to avoid additional costs to their members, the majority of whom find themselves in lamentable economic conditions."[35] Aware that many of its members found themselves in deplorable economic conditions, the leadership found ways to cut back on the expenses of the organization. The leaders paid for office supplies, and they secured a rent-free office space by sharing an office with the Fraternity of Waiters of Mexico City.[36]

Alianza felt slighted by the administration of Mexican president Miguel Alemán Valdés because it had supported his presidential campaign believing that he, in turn, would support labor organizations. In a letter to President Alemán Valdés, Hernández Serrano protested, "Our organization is not unknown to you and it is impossible for you to continue to act like it."[37] The president ignored Alianza's pleas, and the organization felt a deep betrayal as it faced repressive actions by the government. Like several other labor organizations, Alianza believed that Alemán Valdés would push for the same labor rights that he had worked toward as a young lawyer. It became disillusioned with his presidency, however, because he did not do more to address the exploitation of braceros and actively undermined larger labor-movement efforts in Mexico. Although publicly Alianza projected itself as a civic organization, it was clear that it was still searching for a place within labor movements, as it signed letters, "Always standing within the Mexican National Labor and Campesino Movement."[38]

During the next year, the leaders of Alianza decided to return to their public alignment within labor movements, marked by their participation in the 1949 Confederación Proletaria Nacional (CPN, National Proletariat Confederation) convention. Established in 1942, the CPN was considered a moderate union.[39] After the convention, Alianza became part of the CPN, and by 1950 it had developed a formal relationship with Galarza's Sindicato Nacional de Trabajadores Agrícolas (SANTA, National Syndicate of Agricultural Workers), which came under the National Agricultural Workers

Union, part of the American Farm Labor Union (AFL).[40] Through correspondence, Galarza and Alianza charted strategies that benefited both braceros and American labor. Alianza agreed with the CPN and SANTA that one of the major challenges to organizing braceros was the increasing number of undocumented Mexican laborers in American fields; however, they disagreed on the solution to this problem. SANTA supported legalizing undocumented Mexican workers in the United States, while Alianza believed that the legalization of undocumented workers would exacerbate the problem in the United States. All the while, many American unions identified the Bracero Program as the problem because undocumented laborers followed in the shadows of braceros.

The lines between documented and undocumented migrants became incredibly tangled as braceros could easily go between authorized and unauthorized by simply leaving or breaking their contracts and finding unsanctioned work. On December 19, 1949, in a letter to H. L. Mitchell of the NFLU, José Hernández Serrano, the head of Alianza, wrote that if the NFLU stood against the continued contracting of braceros, the ultimate effect would be an increase in undocumented Mexican workers in the United States. Hernández Serrano argued that braceros could find undocumented labor in the fields better than the Mexican or American officials could, because braceros were put into situations in which they labored alongside undocumented workers. Alianza leadership suggested that members could report undocumented workers to local U.S. authorities. Hernández Serrano believed that 30,000 to 40,000 bracero contracts would greatly remedy their common interest in addressing the problems that undocumented labor posed to their organizing efforts.[41] These men could fill the need for agricultural workers while also reporting undocumented workers to American authorities.

Alianza Works against Undocumented Labor

Alianza made suggestions to the CPN and the Mexican government on ways to decrease undocumented migration to the United States. Throughout the first phases of the program, the Mexican government placed the major contracting stations in its central states, but eventually it moved them closer to the border. The leadership of Alianza argued that moving these sites to the border provided temptation for Mexicans to cross as undocumented workers. As *aspirantes* grew frustrated waiting for bracero contracts, *coyotes*[42] offered to help them cross the border, and working as undocumented laborers seemed more attractive. As Hernández Serrano commented, the site change "foments their [*aspirantes*] irresponsibility and lack of patriotism."[43] In December 1949, Hernández Serrano told Manuel Garcia from the CPN that it was easy to cross the border since security was only there between 8:00 A.M. and 9:00 P.M. Beyond these hours, *enganchadores*[44] delivered men and their families by van to the United States. The Mexicans paid ten pesos per person, and American growers gave these contractors an additional two dollars.[45] The majority of these illegal work contractors delivered braceros to growers in Texas. Additionally, crossing the border as undocumented labor was one of the few ways Mexican families could remain united in the shadows of the Bracero Program. Alianza tried to call the president's attention to the fraudulent pay stubs growers provided to undocumented laborers in order to work them into the Bracero Program and thus decrease their responsibility to pay for transportation costs of the guest worker. A key site of struggle for Alianza at this time was Texas.

From 1943 to 1947, the Mexican government barred Texas growers from participating in the Bracero Program because of the intense racial discrimination against Mexicans in the state.[46] Texas growers in places like Crystal City and Harlingen circumvented this by working with *enganchadores* to secure undocumented Mexican labor. Alianza felt that Texas growers represented one of the biggest threats to their organizing efforts and to the livelihood of guest workers, especially if this model that encouraged undocumented labor was replicated in other states.[47] Moving contracting centers from central states in Mexico to the U.S.-Mexico border made it much easier to recruit undocumented workers, even after Texas started receiving braceros in 1948.[48] With these issues in mind, Alianza insisted that it was unfair that growers could access avenues to legalize their undocumented labor because it rewarded a lack of discipline and encouraged unruliness.[49] In this way, the undocumented became criminalized and then were absolved of their unlawful entry at the mercy of growers. This further marginalized both American labor and bracero workers, as it placed more power in the hands of growers.

Alianza believed that if the Mexican government did not step in to regulate Mexican immigration to the United States, the numbers of undocumented workers would undoubtedly double within one year.[50] The Mexican government attempted to regulate immigration internally by allowing residents of some Mexican states to participate in larger numbers than others. But Alianza argued that as some states were favored over others, undocumented Mexican labor coming from those unfavored states increased. Hernández

Serrano suggested that the Mexican government work more diligently to determine who was in real need of bracero contracts. He suggested that the government should work with industries and conduct research on the background of *aspirantes* in order to exclude those who had other avenues of work. He also wanted the government to give preference to agricultural workers who did not own land in Mexico to protect the interest of the most exploitable labor in the country, the "landless." Ultimately, Hernández Serrano argued that both industry and agriculture in Mexico were negatively affected by the flight of Mexican workers to the United States and that Mexico needed to control the exodus of labor more carefully.[51]

In 1950, Alianza began a national campaign against *aspirantes* moving toward the border and crossing as undocumented labor. They made tangible gains as the Mexican government agreed that it would authorize 2,000 Alianza members to receive bracero contracts.[52] In order to prepare these members for their temporary work contracts, Alianza looked to H. L. Mitchell and SANTA for information on the going wage for various agricultural jobs, in the hopes that their members would tell authorities if they were paid less.[53] In addition, Alianza requested that Galarza send a sample contract growers used to employ U.S. citizens. Galarza responded that the wages fluctuated and that there was no set standard that growers paid. Furthermore, unlike braceros, American-born agricultural workers had no contracts, as growers were not forced to sign individual contracts with them.[54]

Galarza felt that the system for making growers accountable often failed, as neither the U.S. government nor the Mexican government forced growers to abide by all of the standards and regulations set forth in the bi-national agreement that had established the program. He was convinced that the only way to establish accountability was to allow braceros to join SANTA, and thus collectively bargain in such a way that both American-born workers and braceros would be treated equally. Alianza proceeded to formalize its relationship with Galarza's NFLU. Alianza decided that when braceros joined either the NFLU or Alianza, they would automatically become members of both. However, Galarza was frustrated with this arrangement because the organization often took months to respond to his letters. Perhaps this was because Alianza leadership found itself working away from Mexico City and instead near bracero recruitment centers to carry out bracero orientations. Through these orientations, they encouraged the men to complete the terms of their contracts, be vigilant about protecting their rights as workers, and understand the system in order to report injustices committed against them. Alianza also urged *aspirantes* to denounce undocumented laborers, and in this way be good allies to American labor unions.

The effectiveness of these orientations is unclear since the gains were often accompanied by setbacks. In the recruitment and contracting process of April 21, 1950, Alianza provided an orientation for braceros in Monterrey, Nuevo Leon.[55] It also created a Pro-Bracero Regional Committee in Monterrey, which was in charge of future orientations. Though economic limitations kept members of Alianza from traveling to the processing centers of Sonora or Chihuahua in order to organize those braceros, it seemed that at least the men in Monterrey would go to the United States organized and aware that they had a concrete relationship with SANTA. With great disappointment, however, Alianza informed SANTA that the men who were given the orientation in Monterrey were meant to travel to California to pick oranges, but contracting had been suspended because the growers did not need more workers. Additional financial hardships compounded these problems. During the next contracting period, Alianza reported to SANTA, on September 6, 1950, that it was unable to give men an orientation because it lacked the funds. Even so, it repeatedly tried to assure Ernesto Galarza that they were strong allies and that the Bracero Program was the only solution to combating the rising numbers of *espaldas mojadas* (wetbacks).[56]

Despite these problems, Galarza continued to work with Alianza in an effort to integrate braceros into SANTA. On October 21, 1950, Galarza explained to Alianza that the main problem was that "the contracts written and ratified by the governments are not complied with because the bracero lacks the collective power to make them comply."[57] He went on to state, "I continue to think that the only way to protect both the contracted bracero and American farm worker is the integration of braceros to the rank and file of the Union."[58] He explained that this was the only means to achieve the collective bargaining needed to ensure that every worker received an adequate salary and work conditions. In May 1950, Galarza mailed materials to Alianza, and in turn, Hernández Serrano immediately forwarded them on to various chapters. However, there were not enough copies, and Hernández Serrano asked Galarza for more. These flyers were meant to deter *aspirantes* from becoming undocumented workers in the United States and to expose them to the reality of the exploitation awaiting them if they chose to do so.[59] By November 28, 1950, Alianza was using its resources to translate pamphlets and materials sent by SANTA.[60] Because the cost of travel prevented Alianza from meeting with each individual chapter, its leaders hoped that, through these pamphlets, members would understand their new role in the United States and their relationship with SANTA.

Alianza went a step further in attempting to advocate for a place for SANTA within the Bracero Program. Hernández Serrano urged the Labor Commission to invite representatives from SANTA to the next discussion of the Bracero Program. He argued that SANTA could offer up its opinion on controlling the numbers of braceros needed in the United States, and thus braceros would cause less strife for domestic workers. Due to Alianza's public alignment with labor movements, the Mexican government constantly red-baited them. Hernández Serrano deflected criticism of Alianza by stating that it was other braceros outside of the organization that supported communism and anti-Americanism, not Alianza. The Mexican government's anti-communist campaign aimed at pleasing the United States, demonstrating that Mexico was an effective ally and curtailing the Mexican left, showing that there was "no future in bucking the PRI."[61] Hernández Serrano also wanted to convince the Labor Commission that Alianza could serve another necessary role in the Bracero Program: weeding out communist cells that attempted to infiltrate the United States as braceros.[62] Alianza argued that individuals often had "anti-yanqui" sentiments that were harmful once inside the United States. Hernández Serrano wrote that these measures were necessary in order to avoid situations such as that of Puerto Rican nationalists Oscar Collazo's and Griselio Torresola's attempts to assassinate President Harry Truman.[63] Growing anticommunist sentiments led Hernández Serrano to declare that Alianza's members could potentially help both governments deal with communist threats.

1951: The Alliance Is Put to the Test

In many ways, Galarza did not understand the full potential of the organization until January 1951. During this period, Galarza traveled to Mexico City in an effort to represent the interests of American agricultural laborers in negotiations to extend the Bracero Program. This was not the first time he thought about traveling to Mexico to advocate for American labor interests. In January 1949, Alianza and Galarza felt slighted by both the U.S. and the Mexican governments, as neither was invited to Mexico City to participate in any significant manner in the negotiations on the program extension. Before that meeting Galarza wrote,

As to my going to Mexico City, I have misgivings what good it will do. I'll have no status, no team. . . . I'll be surrounded and cut off from the press and government contacts. Even this would not dissuade me if I could see where we could have a practical effect on the outcomes. . . . The negotiations are to be held in Mexico City. This is a smart move. In Mexico City the USES [U.S. Employment Service] and the State Department will be as far away from the heat as they can possibly get. The AFL can have no effect whatever through publicity of contact with Federal officials in order to influence the conversations that will go on in Mexico City.[64]

He believed that the U.S. government held meetings to extend the guest-worker program as far away as possible from the turmoil in the American fields as domestic agricultural workers clamored for an end to the program. In Mexico, on the other hand, by 1951 the PRI had placed the largest Mexican labor unions under its thumb.[65] The repressive climate toward labor unions made Mexico City the natural choice for hosting these meetings.

The 1951 meetings between the leadership of Alianza and Galarza compelled him to think of creative ways of including guest workers in his organizing strategies. Although the CPN recognized Alianza's efforts, other Mexican labor unions hesitated to incorporate guest workers. Galarza noted, "The labor leadership—all fourteen national confederations—appears to be afraid to take a stand on any big issue, but they are especially afraid of this one."[66] Alianza arose as one of the few risk-takers in favor of collaboration between Mexican labor organizations and the AFL. Several years earlier, Galarza had participated in a three-day meeting organized by the CPN, the Confederación Obrera y Campesina, and the Confederación Interamericana de Trabajadores, "to work out a joint program to combat discrimination against Mexican workers in the United States and to attack the problems arising out of legal and illegal migration between the two countries."[67] The participating organizations concluded that they would pressure their respective governments to make a series of amendments to the guest-worker contracts. As officials discussed the extension of the program in Mexico City, Galarza noted that, other than Alianza, representatives of Mexico's labor unions were nowhere to be found. He felt frustrated that Mexican labor unions had seemingly made earlier efforts to discuss the problems of guest workers, but upon his 1951 visit they did not want to take public action on behalf of braceros.

Although Galarza understood that neither government wanted to allow labor interests to enter into discussions about the Bracero Program, Galarza arrived in Mexico in January 1951 with the conviction that he would learn more about the position of *aspirantes* and explain to them the role of the AFL in the United States. In a meeting with ex-braceros and *aspirantes*, organized by Alianza on Sunday, January 28, Galarza explained, "I spoke in an empty lot humped with garbage and smelling of dry, powdered human excrement. The result is a mass meeting is [*sic*] being planned for Thursday, we expect 10,000 men to come."[68] In addition, that afternoon he engaged in a three-hour planning session with Alianza's board.[69]

Galarza expressed a growing concern with the plight of Mexican labor and the growing class divide. After the meeting with Alianza, he woke up bright and early the next morning to explore Mexican working-class neighborhoods.[70] Joining an upper-middle-class friend for breakfast in Chapultepec, he was impressed by both the extreme poverty and the wealth, comparing it to the United States.[71] He juxtaposed the plight of these working-class populations with middle-class comforts. Under the PRI regime, Mexico continued to increase a class divide and inequality, which by 1950 favored the top 10 percent of the population, which enjoyed 49 percent of the national income, while the bottom 20 percent of citizens shared 6.1 percent of the national income.[72] The PRI had cut most Mexicans out of the nation's wealth and had put in place a system of kickbacks, corruption, and cronyism.[73]

After breakfast, Galarza moved on to the primary concern of his trip: influencing the closed-door discussions he was not invited to. As the day progressed, he met with the first secretary of the U.S. Embassy, whom he found to be supportive of U.S. labor.[74] He wrapped up the day with a meeting of Alianza's twelve district committees. He explained, "The delegates meeting had about 100 men. . . . These men have trade union experience."[75] Although Galarza did not mention what unions they had worked with, it was an important observation for Galarza as he drew lines of commonality with Alianza members. Galarza felt that the previous meetings with Alianza members were so effective that "my estimate is that their enrollment in the area will run to 200,000 by the end of the week."[76] These new members could represent an increase of about one-third or one-half of its current 40,000 to 60,000 members.[77] He spoke to the leadership of these district committees and laid out the AFL organizing approach, which the organization voted to accept.[78] The meeting exceeded Galarza's expectations, and he felt confident that the AFL could continue to formalize its relationship with Alianza.

Surveillance and the "Peculiar Problems"
of Transnational Organizing

As the Monday meeting with Alianza came to a close, a message arrived from the Mexican Department of the Interior, specifically the office of Trade Unions and Associations. The officers asked that the executive board of Alianza report to the police headquarters. Galarza accompanied members of Alianza to the police station. The board members stayed behind for questioning while Galarza headed back to his hotel and waited for an update on the situation. Two hours after his departure from the police station, Galarza received word that officials had charged three members of Alianza with illegal contracting. Galarza explained: "Figuring it was in connection with my appearances I took the boys to headquarters. . . . Three members of the Exibd [Executive Board] of the Alianza presented themselves. They were charged with illegal contracting. They were told they were under arrest. The Alianza was ordered to stop all organizations, including the mass meeting for next Fri. at which I was scheduled to speak. . . . The officer who fla[s]hed the order of arrest on the A[l]ianza told them flatly the govt does not want the Nationals organized, that they must be on their own. This lets the kitty out of the yarn."[79]

The officials suspended the board members' arrest on the condition that Alianza stop organizing immediately. Alianza protested that it had never engaged in illegal contracting and that it made this clear to its potential members by stamping letters and documents "La Alianza de Braceros, Agremia No Contrata [Alianza de Braceros organizes/unionizes, it does not provide contracts]." Alianza explained that authorities told them, "What we should have done, was to stop advising our peers, because we did not care to keep them. We did not have to care whether or not they emigrated to the border, because they were not our brothers, and so they migrated to their own detriment," meaning they emigrated and encountered prejudice of their own accord.[80] What became clear during this event was that Mexican officials were watching and harassing Alianza. Galarza explained, "The mass meeting was called off but it was agreed I would meet with small groups of applicant braceros who gathered daily in the national stadium and some of the public parks."[81] He continued his work with ex-braceros and *aspirantes* and found these smaller meetings productive.

Galarza understood that he too was being closely surveilled and that the Mexican government wanted very little press covering American labor interests in the program. Though Galarza began to suspect he was being followed, he pressed forward with his actions. He wrote H. L. Mitchell and communicated his plan "to get out daily leaflets under the Alianza letterhead, for which the Alianza will take full responsibility. . . . I will sign anything I say. There is a middling chance the govt will try to throw me out of the country."[82] Galarza felt an odd sense of disappointment when the Mexican government did not deport him. Because he was a Mexican-born U.S. citizen, he explained, "I would present the Mexican government with peculiar problems. . . . My deportation would be the best way to call international attention to what was happening in Mexico City."[83] Officials wanted the organization to understand that they disapproved of its efforts to protect braceros. This was not the first time the leadership of Alianza had faced detainment. During past quibbles with the threat of detainment, Alianza had vacillated between publicly embracing an identity as a labor organization and disowning it. Galarza's presence changed that, as they were now invested in claiming membership in the NFLU. Galarza argued that it was a Mexican constitutional right to unionize and that no international agreement could abrogate it.[84] The organization agreed with Galarza but found it difficult to negotiate its stance in the face of imprisonment and detention in Mexico.

Galarza was aware of Alianza's previous issues with the Mexican government, but Monday evening was the first time he witnessed it himself, and he believed that he too could easily fall victim to harassment. Because he was not allowed to participate directly in the conversations about the Mexican guest-worker program, Galarza focused on influencing those allowed to participate and calling media attention to the plight of the bracero and the program's effect on American labor. He found this extremely challenging because "the publicity lid is on tighter then [sic] a tick. This is the policy of both sides."[85] He felt purposely blocked out, as he stated, "since the beginning I have had no documents to work from. Not even the spare rib press releases of the embassy."[86] Galarza continued to grow frustrated when he met with officials included in the discussions. The next day, after meeting with Carl Strom, consul general and head of the U.S. delegation, Galarza wrote, "He gave me the crap about only Mexicans can and like to do stoop labor."[87] In his meeting with the U.S. ambassador, U.S. officials communicated that Mexican officials believed that representatives of U.S. labor unions had no place in Bracero Program negotiations, as many of their issues should be dealt with in the United States.[88] Galarza felt unhappy that the negotiations were proceeding in "secret and great dither."[89] Ultimately, what upset him the most was that the representatives of growers' associations participated in the negotiations while organized labor was excluded.

Galarza was not shaken by the Mexican government's repressive strate-gies, and he continued to press forward, organizing a massive press confer-ence on Thursday, February 1, 1951. He thought, "Our friends here needed the protection that publicity can give," adding that the "main theme was the AFL battling for Mexican and U.S. peasants. Up to this aim we have over 200 inches of column space. I belive [sic] this is about 199 more than the delegation got. It's still coming in."[90] Years later, when writing *Farm Workers and Agri-Business in California, 1947–1960*, he did not mention Alianza by name and described the press conference more pragmatically: "At the press conference a room full of correspondents received copies of documents I had brought concerning wages and working conditions concerning braceros who had returned from California and asked the NFLU to assist them in pressing grievances."[91] He presented this information to the press knowing that the press would not be privy to the conversations behind closed doors and that the Mexican and U.S. governments would put a positive spin on the extension of the program.

During the negotiations for the extension of the program, Alianza fol-lowed Galarza's lead and strategically clamored for press coverage in an effort to gain visibility and perhaps potential protection. They carried out a collection drive among members to fund a full-page manifesto that was published that Saturday in the newspaper *La Prensa*. Galarza explained, "In the same issue there was a full account of my press conference. 'AFL defends the peasants of Mexico and the US. Breaks grower-controlled U.S. delegation.' I consider the language mild but then, I guess we can't have the moon."[92] Ultimately he reports, "The members of the X-bd [Executive Board] of the Alianza came through magnificently. They operate our way. If we can develop them they will be the only solid contact the AFandL [AFL] will have here."[93] Alianza and Galarza set common goals and Alianza "authorized a circular [letter] which will be distributed to all the braceros urging them to act in solidarity with the Union in all our activities." He recorded his final thoughts about the matter before returning to the United States: "We had very unpleasant incidents. The Government of Mexico wanted to prevent the working class public assemblies in the capital. The delegation of the United States tried to suffocate us in silence. The comrades of La Alianza were threatened with prison for their activities. Despite these maneuvers, the workers' representatives succeeded in clearing the smokescreen around the negotiations. . . . There is only one way forward—to organize and continue fighting."[94] Despite the Mexican government's pressure to end their activities,

Alianza and Galarza pressed forward with their cause. Both organizations agreed that they would work closely to organize guest workers.

After the passing of Public Law 78, Alianza attempted to continue its recruitment of members and orientations on the border, but it quickly experienced recurring issues with funding. All of the members labored as guest workers, and the leadership viewed the body of the organization as working class and often as working poor. The leadership helped subsidize many costs of organizing. Alianza faced these economic hardships alongside increasing public accusations of communism. Red-baiting impacted its recruitment efforts as potential members felt a deep hesitation to join. José Hernández Serrano sent an urgent telegram to Galarza on February 25, 1951, asking why Mexican and U.S. newspapers printed articles associating communist infiltration with Alianza.[95] In the past, U.S. growers crippled strikes by claiming that union members and their supporters were communists.[96] The Mexican press also printed articles on a communist presence in the Bracero Program. Hernández Serrano wrote several letters about press efforts to red-bait braceros. On May 17, *Excélsior* printed an article titled, "With the Braceros the Communist Virus Is Injected."[97] Leadership in Alianza feared that these accusations detracted attention from the exploitation of braceros.

In a press release on March 14, 1951, Galarza wrote, "The Mexican Government is preparing legal action to make it a crime for Mexican workers to cooperate with the American Federation of Labor in the struggle to maintain and raise the living standards in this hemisphere." He went on to say, "The immediate target of this move to intimidate the friends of United States labor is the Alianza Nacional de Braceros de Mexico."[98] During the January negotiations concerning the Bracero Program, Alianza supported the AFL and the Railway Brotherhood in opposing the use of braceros to bring down working standards. Galarza explained: "Now the Ministry of the Interior of the Mexican Government has announced that it will file criminal charges against officials of Alianza because they are allegedly running an international headhunting racket, and because they are working closely with United States labor."[99] Galarza believed that these charges were an attempt to cover up what was happening within the program and the fact that many stipulations in bracero contracts were not being met.

Galarza knew that the Mexican government's Ministry of the Interior planned to harass and jail the executive board of Alianza, and he wanted to rally American union support for the members. Galarza wrote, "While United States and Mexican negotiators conferred in secret in the Mexico

City negotiations of last January, the Alianza did not hesitate to support the AFL in its successful effort to break through the curtain of censorship. It was the Alianza, alone of all the Mexican labor confederations, that stood with the AFL and the Railway Brotherhoods in opposing the present inter-government drive to lower working standards in every trade and craft."[100] He further explained, "Without the support of the Alianza we could not have broadened out our support and eventually broken the censorship on the press which the Mexican and American delegations set up."[101] Galarza wanted American labor unions to step in and defend Alianza. He felt that the Mexican government would decrease its persecution of these activists if other organizations rallied around Alianza.

Strangers Enter the Fields

Upon his return from Mexico, Galarza was swiftly made aware of the question of whether braceros could organize when they entered the California fields during an NFLU strike in the Imperial Valley. He felt that organizations, such as Alianza and La Unión de Trabajadores Agrícolas de Méxicali, could provide the vehicle to politicize guest workers and support broader visions of transnational labor organizing. Would Galarza's strategy work during this pivotal moment of agricultural labor organizing? Could the NFLU effectively organize all agricultural labors, and would the strikes find success?

To keep its side of the agreement, Alianza once again began its work enlisting braceros into the organization and providing orientations at the border. Many of its own leadership hoped — along with general members — to obtain a contract. They became Galarza's eyes and ears on the border as they provided reports on recruitment conditions. In May, Pedro Cerón González, the internal secretary of Alianza, traveled to Mexicali, Hermosillo, in a failed attempt to secure a guest-worker contract. He informed Galarza on contracting conditions as he traveled with a group of thirty-eight Alianza members.[102] Besides Cerón González's group, other Alianza members attempted to come to the United States as braceros. That same month, 500 members made it to Soledad, and a dozen of these men attended the meetings of Local 284. Although the agreement between Alianza and Galarza recognized them as members of the NFLU, their contracts prohibited them from formal labor organizing in the United States, and the local union leaders did not know what to do. They reached out to Galarza and wrote, "We are reluctant to advise the boys [braceros] on what to do without first getting information and instructions from you."[103] They were confused by Galarza's organizing strategies and unsure of whether or not braceros could be legally incorporated into the union.

As Alianza members attempted to secure guest-worker contracts, Galarza focused much of his attention on the NFLU strike in the Imperial Valley. U.S.-born agricultural workers from Calexico, El Centro, and Brawley led the activities, which would initially attempt to incorporate braceros and undocumented workers. Galarza explained, "In each of the three locals there was a team of volunteers altogether twenty-five men and women, to mobilize a labor force of fifteen thousand domestics [American workers], braceros and illegals."[104] Galarza understood this as a triangular relationship and attempted to address the problems of all three constituencies. This became the biggest challenge for union leadership and domestic workers because growers used guest workers and undocumented workers as strikebreakers.[105] Growers dictated the extension of the Bracero Program under Public Law 78, which was intended to create an environment where domestic workers were not pitted against braceros but growers quickly found ways to work around this. According to Public Law 78, growers needed official certification from the Department of Labor to verify that there was a shortage of domestic labor, thereby granting the use of guest workers. These guest workers were to be paid the prevailing wage, but often growers held the final say on determining that wage. When domestic workers would not work for this wage, growers could establish a shortage of domestic workers and thus employ braceros. It was not until 1955 that an amendment was added that domestic workers had to be consulted in establishing prevailing wages.[106] In addition, according to this law, growers who employed undocumented workers could not be certified to receive braceros. Their punishment for breaking the agreement was that they would not receive guest workers. Galarza thought this particularly problematic during the Imperial Valley strike because this rule was not enforced.[107] Furthermore, he believed that growers had finally been able to shape the program enough that they could manipulate it in ways that most benefited them.[108]

On May 31, 1,000 braceros were brought into the valley by growers, who attempted to isolate the men and keep them away from organizers. The NFLU worked hard to find ways to come into contact with these men and inform them about the conditions that local agricultural labor faced. "In June forty braceros in different locales had signed authorization cards. They became the source of detailed knowledge of the operations of the bracero program in the Valley, as well as current information on the conditions inside the ranches."[109] It is likely that some of these forty men were originally Alianza members, as José Hernández Serrano sent a list from Mexico City of several members who had recently obtained contracts. Alianza members, such as Alberto Cardenas Corona, Joel A. Cabrera, and Doroteo Reyes Sánchez among others, obtained contracts in the Imperial Valley.[110] They arrived in the valley with some understanding of their affiliation to the NFLU and their rights as guest workers. Sadly, as these Alianza members entered California, the AFL pulled major support for the Imperial Valley union activities.[111] As historian Dionicio Valdés explains, the AFL was never fully supportive of the Imperial Valley strikes because it was comfortable with the business-like relations with growers as they were.[112]

During the labor strikes in California, SANTA passed out flyers asking braceros not to work, furthermore pointing out that guest-worker contracts stipulated that braceros were entitled to pay for 75 percent of the duration of their contract in the event that they could not work in the fields due to either climate or strikes. One flyer stated, "If local workers are able to obtain fair contracts, the Union will invite Mexican braceros to join their ranks and the Union will ensure that the contracts are strictly enforced, as the contracts have been violated so shamelessly by bosses [employers] in the past."[113] The leaflet stated that SANTA was affiliated with Alianza and La Unión de Trabajadores Agrícolas de Méxicali. Through the agreement, Alianza and La Unión de Trabajadores Agrícolas de Méxicali would charge a two-dollar initiation fee for membership in SANTA.[114] Although Pedro Cerón González encountered contracting problems, he would eventually continue his work and organizing efforts in the fields. Laboring as a guest worker in Anaheim, he registered new members for SANTA and mailed off these registration forms to Galarza.[115] One of the men in his group was José Hernández Serrano's brother, Benito, along with several other men from Patamban, Mexico.

On June 13, José Hernández Serrano wrote to Galarza from Mexico City to inform him that twenty-five members and key leaders had obtained contracts. These leaders were to fulfill the goal of the partnership between Alianza and SANTA, which was to organize braceros in the fields. They estimated that because of efforts in Mexico, the organization would be able to send approximately fifty members to the United States every week.[116] Hernández Serrano also included the addresses of the members working in American fields in order to aid Galarza's research efforts. All but one member of his group received contracts to work in California.

Even as many Alianza leaders felt that they were finally making gains, government repression and continued economic problems severely affected Hernández Serrano's morale. On June 8, 1951, Alianza asked SANTA for a loan of $200. Hernández Serrano faced a dire situation and felt that many of the gains Alianza had made were being lost. Despite some of his membership obtaining contracts, others were unable to secure them, and rumors of assassination attempts against his life circulated. Word spread that the price on his head was 5,000 pesos.[117] Hernández Serrano was not the only Alianza member facing intense repercussions for labor-organizing efforts. By the end of the month, some of the leadership of Alianza felt it necessary to leave Mexico City and attempt to travel to the United States as braceros. Pedro Cerón González, Alianza's internal secretary, informed Galarza on June 30, 1951, that some of the Alianza organizers were finding it difficult to secure guest-worker contracts. Hernández Serrano was able to obtain a contract, but Cerón González was not. In attempting to secure a contract, Cerón González got as far as crossing the Nogales border but was detained by U.S. immigration authorities because he was found to be blacklisted as a communist agitator. He believed that individuals who were protecting and compelling *aspirantes* to cross over as undocumented workers stood behind his detention because they wanted to scare those in the movement to organize braceros. Two other men who collaborated with Cerón González were also rejected for bracero contracts in Nogales.[118] The head of immigration asked Cerón González to denounce his participation in Alianza and to promise in writing that he would never participate in any labor organization, including Alianza. Cerón González needed the income he earned from his work as a bracero. He eventually received a contract working for the Growers Farm Labor Association, in Salinas, California.[119]

Galarza also negotiated a formal arrangement between SANTA, Alianza, and La Unión de Trabajadores Agrícolas de Méxicali. All of these organizations agreed that they would function separately but hold affiliations with each other in order to address the plight of the braceros.[120] He met with the head of Alianza, José Hernández Serrano, Pedro Cerón González, the internal secretary, and Jacinto Cerón Aguillon, the secretary of Conflict, who signed a ten-point agreement on the terms of the affiliation.

Despite Galarza's attempts to represent the grievances of braceros to the Department of Labor, he made very few gains because their contracts could easily be terminated and they could be deported. This led the union to set up shop along the border, "where the union hung on the wire fence

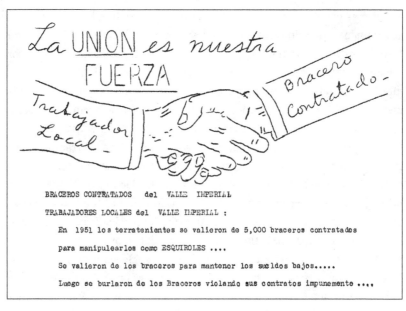

ILLUSTRATION 6 La Union Es Nuestra Fuerza. Ernesto Galarza Papers, M0224, Department of Special Collections, Stanford University Libraries, Stanford, California.

that separated the two countries a sign that said: Consultas-La Unión."[121] The overwhelming use of braceros and the lack of support from the AFL caused the NFLU to call off the strike on June 25.

In the summer of 1951, SANTA also organized meetings for braceros in various agricultural towns of Northern California, including Salinas, Castroville, and Soledad. The purpose of these meetings was to inform braceros about their workers' rights that were ensured by their contracts. Despite his problems returning to the United States as a bracero, by the end of July, José Hernández Serrano held a contract that placed him in the Salinas Valley. Galarza and Hernández Serrano met to discuss future organizing plans, but Hernández Serrano expressed disappointment that he could not bring more Alianza members and leadership with him to work in the United States as braceros. They developed their partnership further by agreeing that Alianza would receive fifty cents of enrollment dues and take care of the publicity in Mexico. Finally, materials geared toward braceros would be developed and circulated separately from those of domestic workers. One such flyer, titled "La Union Es Nuestra Fuerza [The Union Is Our Strength]," depicted the hand of a domestic worker shaking that of a bracero (ill. 6).[122] The content encouraged braceros to organize with domestic workers so that together they could work against low wages, displacements, and contract violations.[123]

In order to organize farmworkers, both domestic and guest workers, effectively, Galarza and Hernández Serrano wanted to set up an undercover delegation in each camp that would report back to them. Alianza would have to make sure that their members were encouraged not to skip out on their contracts and not to work as strikebreakers.[124] Galarza went further and asked Hernández Serrano to join a group that would visit labor camps in an attempt to broaden their guest-worker membership. Guest workers could find both Galarza and Hernández Serrano on Sundays from 10:00 A.M. to 3:00 P.M. at the Labor Temple in Salinas, where Galarza would play Mexican records on a Victrola.[125] Hernández Serrano reported directly to Galarza, but he also took concerns directly to the Mexican consul in Fresno.[126] Their work in Salinas included a large meeting of agricultural workers, to which both local workers and braceros were invited.[127] While SANTA and Alianza worked toward organizing braceros, some NFLU locales fought to get rid of these guest workers in the fields.

During the fall of 1951, Galarza received reports from Alianza members from fields across California. Jesus Hernández Uresti reported on the living conditions in Stockton, where the grower did not provide braceros with enough food. When the braceros brought it to the attention of growers, they were told that if they were not full, they should buy their own food in order to eat more.[128] Galarza and Alianza needed to devise a system to make guest workers aware of their rights. In September, Leopoldo Hernández Serrano led the board in writing an orientation document. In it, they expressed five points, the first one being that if problems should arise, braceros could seek assistance with the Mexican consul or SANTA; they should be aware that they had health insurance; they should be attentive to their wages; they should not be scared to speak up; and they should be aware that they were members of SANTA.[129] The flyer also stated: "Bracero compañero, organize and fight your exploiters, don't let them mislead you; because the governments of United States and Mexico demand our collaboration, and no one can deny you the right to organize; since the right to organize is your unique heritage granted to you by the Constitution of Mexico, and the labor law of the United States of America."[130] The leadership of Alianza deployed Galarza's discourse of Mexican constitutional rights to remind these men that although they were transnational laborers, they still held labor rights.[131]

Despite Alianza's lofty goals, the organization continued to be plagued by divisive tendencies, as some leaders within the organization continued to blame the "primitive" bracero for Alianza's inability to more effectively organize. While in Anaheim, California, Benito Hernández described his co-workers as ignorant of social movements and "the benefits of organizing."[132] He went on: "The great majority are illiterate" and were preferred by the bosses. Most could not write numbers and instead used symbols to mark the boxes of oranges they had picked. Benito duplicated some of these symbols in his letter to his brother. He lamented, "I am on the same level as these poor *compañeros*.... I have never found a more primitive element."[133] Here "primitive" is again used as a euphemism to describe indigeneity. While Benito would have liked to organize these workers, he blamed them for not understanding the value of organizing. Ultimately, Benito demonstrated that although Alianza wrapped itself in the mantle of mestizo normativity, it positioned itself above these "primitive" classes.

By October, Galarza felt frustrated with his lack of progress organizing braceros in the United States. Not only did the organizing efforts in the Imperial Valley fail, but his views on the organizing potential of guest workers shifted as he began to see Mexican guest-worker organizations as vehicles for academic research and not as union members. Reflecting on a research trip, he wrote to José Hernández Serrano and outlined the major hurdles for organizing braceros. The first was that the members of Alianza in the United States did not want to engage for fear of contract termination. Second, the members did not want to authorize SANTA to speak on their behalf about labor disputes in the fields. Last, he argued that there was a fundamental problem with the way in which braceros were chosen, conveying that growers preferred Mexicans who were the most socially disadvantaged. Echoing Benito Hernández's perspective, Galarza wrote, "The vast majority of the braceros have been selected by the bosses based on illiteracy, social inexperience and ideological backwardness, conditions which, coupled with the absence of leadership capacity within the group's core, completely nullifies the possibility of collective action."[134] Through this statement, Galarza coded his feelings about rural folks and indigenous workers by using terms such as "social inexperience" and "backwardness." Indigenous communities, such as those presented in Chapter 1, were perceived as a hurdle for organizers. Galarza believed they were purposely chosen because they did not hold the potential for collective action. This statement served as a sort of challenge to Hernández Serrano, who perhaps agreed with Galarza and his brother Benito that it was the laborers who were perceived as socially "backward" who were also an impediment to their organizing.

To be sure, the materials produced by the NFLU played on these intra-ethnic tensions by alluding to braceros' relationship with indigeneity. One flyer, titled "Los Encomenderos de 1951," depicts braceros stooped over the fields. One figure, the Encomendero, stands upright staring at the men working.[135] The flyer explains that braceros entrusted to growers by the U.S. and Mexican governments were similar to the *encomiendas*, indigenous groups entrusted to particular men, called *encomenderos*, by the Spanish crown during the colonial period.[136] The purpose of the flyer was to make mestizo braceros uncomfortable, and it worked as a call to fight against a reimagined colonial relationship that cast them as indigenous. On one level, the flyer critiqued American exploitation; but on another level, it strongly criticized a Mexican government that created social hierarchies in which certain citizens could be easily exploited.

To compound the problems, Galarza and Hernández Serrano held drastically different positions on contract renewals. While Hernández Serrano pushed for contract renewals for Alianza's membership, Galarza did not think it would actually benefit their mutual goal of organizing. Galarza stated, "I think that a campaign for the renewal would not bring any syndical benefit, in view that braceros of all categories are willing to suffer unconditionally the capricious treatment of employers. Resentment exists but it does not lead to social consciousness or much less in organized resistance."[137] Galarza believed that many of the members of Alianza were not concerned with fighting for their labor rights but instead wanted the organization to assist them with contract renewal. The statements in this letter begin to demonstrate Galarza's move away from braceros as potential union members.

Some Alianza members believed that their paid dues entitled them to representation and preference for contract renewals. Braceros such as José Frias Briones wrote from Anaheim, California, to José Hernández Serrano claiming that he had paid his registration fee to Benito Hernández Serrano, José's brother, and in return he wanted help securing another contract.[138] While on a contract in Atwood, California, Joaquin Gutierres also wrote Hernández Serrano, claiming that on average he worked four hours a day and that he desperately needed help obtaining another contract.[139] Like José Frias Briones, he pointed out that he was an active dues-paying member of Alianza. Although members like Frias Briones and Gutierres assumed that the organization would help them with contract renewals, affiliation with Alianza had in fact made contract renewal more difficult for some members.[140] Many braceros who were members but not part of the leadership of Alianza were unaware that the government had blacklisted some core members of Alianza.[141]

The optimistic visions of a transnational labor organization were slowly being pulled apart for Galarza and the Alianza leadership, while the few braceros entering the union ranks encountered problems with local union leadership. Despite all of the NFLU flyers and leaflets created to encourage braceros to join the union efforts, some locals did not agree. In November 1951, AFL Local 272 of Porterville, California, printed a flyer that read: "Emergency Mass Meeting! The Mexican Nationals and Wetbacks Must Go!"[142] These announcements stated, "There are legal ways to prevent further importation of nationals and legal ways to get the wetbacks picked up. A few of us cannot do this. It takes cooperation from all. . . . We cannot wait till the area is flooded with wets and nationals. The President of Local 272 has fought the nationals and the wetbacks for a long time."[143] One of the biggest obstacles Galarza faced was convincing the leadership at the local level that the guest worker was not the enemy and that in fact the bracero could be organized. The insurmountable problem was in no way resolved. How could Galarza tell the leadership of Alianza that their members were part of the NFLU, and that if braceros encountered problems they should contact local NFLU officials, and then have Hugh C. Williams of Local 272 state that the local was fighting the Mexican National, or bracero?[144]

The attitudes of local organizers contributed to the larger problems Galarza faced in attempting to organize guest workers. Under Public Law 78, the Mexican government and the Department of Labor seemingly yielded more control over the program and were unable to create stable positions for braceros. Dissenting braceros held even less power than under the previous incarnations of the Bracero Program. Although Galarza and Alianza at times attributed it to the contracted preference of less-politicized and less-educated braceros, repression in Mexico often caused braceros to vocalize less dissent there. Years later, reflecting on this period, Galarza wrote, "The promise[d] land of collective bargaining rights that trade unionism was striving for held the promise of more income for fewer workers, the effects of technology, integration, higher wages and better fringe benefits for those who survived the attrition. To protect it the border would have to become an unbreachable line of containment behind which a diminishing number of American workers could rest secure."[145] The failures of the 1951 strike in the Imperial Valley, the limited power of Alianza, and the repressive strategies of the U.S. and Mexican governments contributed to this unbreachable border in which domestic labor could not be organized alongside guest workers and undocumented workers. Galarza would conclude, "By the end of 1952, it had become clear, however, that the corporate farmers against whom most of the action had been directed had organized a formidable deterrent to unionization, the 'bracero' system."[146] Braceros, along with undocumented labor, would continue to be seen as an impediment to agricultural organizing by U.S. trade unionists. After the termination of the Bracero Program, the successful efforts of the United Farm Workers Union would reinforce this divide and focus solely on "American citizens and resident aliens."[147]

The Broken Alliance

Hernández Serrano feared that Mexican labor organizations would not build lasting relationships of mutual support with Alianza. They aligned for a brief period with the CPN, but then dropped that relationship because leaders of Alianza felt that the CPN did not address their concerns and did not offer them protection within the union. Invited to join the Confederación General de Trabajadores de México (CGT, General Confederation of Workers in Mexico), their faith in the Mexican labor movement was renewed, and leaders of Alianza felt they could find a place within the movement through the CGT.[148] During the next decade, they attempted to work closely with labor organizations and made countless gestures toward the Mexican federal government in an effort to address the rising reports of exploitation.

At a conference in May 1953, Fidel Velasquez, head of the Confederación de Trabajadores de México (CTM, Confederation of Workers in Mexico), spoke about the possibilities of organizing braceros well enough so that they could protect their own interests and not allow themselves to be used against other labor organizations. In the presence of Mexican president Adolfo Ruíz Cortínes, Velasquez supported Alianza's initiatives and argued that braceros needed representation in the United States. The CTM was in an awkward position because it was the government-backed labor federation, but when the Bracero Program began, the Mexican government greatly limited CTM's work with Mexican labor in the United States.[149] In the 1940s, Mexican president Ávila Camacho had maneuvered Fidel Velasquez to replace the previous, more left-leaning president of the CTM, and in the war years the CTM had lost much of its membership and power.[150] Although Fidel Velasquez spoke in favor of organizing guest workers, the CTM did nothing concrete to carry this out.

The Mexican government continued to aggressively target the head organizers of Alianza. On March 2, 1953, Hernández Serrano was detained in Jalisco, and he asked José T. Rocha to write to Galarza.[151] Hernández Serrano explained to Galarza that in March he went to visit a member of the organization who was held on charges of fraud by municipal police in the town of Tula, Jalisco.[152] The local government targeted and imprisoned Hernández Serrano because Alianza spoke out against municipal authorities who took advantage of braceros in that area.[153] He and another member of Alianza were incarcerated for three months and charged a total of 4,000 pesos, and he asked Galarza for monetary support. Hernández Serrano was eventually released on bail and ordered to report to authorities in Tula every eight days. His members could no longer help him economically because they feared detention in doing so. He was heavily in debt and knew that every day that he was away from home his debt grew.[154] While on parole, Hernández Serrano asked why Galarza did not answer his letters from jail. He wrote, "Your distance is odd, *compañero* Galarza, I don't know if you are thinking of retiring from the fight, or you might see that our relationship is too insignificant to help reach your goal; but if it is this I am sure that you will not find another compañero, that on principle alone will constantly step in the dungeons of a prison."[155] Hernández Serrano also explained that there were individuals interested in distancing them from each other.

By late 1953, Hernández Serrano believed Alianza was falling out of favor with labor organizations, such as the CGT, because braceros were controversial figures among labor union members.[156] Many of these Mexican unions did not know what to do with braceros because they worked outside of Mexico and thus outside of the legal frameworks that protected Mexican workers in Mexico. In addition, they fell outside of organizing strategies used by popular labor unions in Mexico. Alianza recognized that braceros were often used as scapegoats within larger labor issues. Defending braceros as workers was seen as condoning the use of guest workers, and many labor organizations did not want to support the use of Mexican guest workers in the United States. These attitudes made Hernández Serrano fear that Alianza would soon find itself alone.[157]

In an effort to fortify the bonds between Alianza and Mexican and American labor organizations, in 1954, Alianza suggested that they work together to pressure the U.S. and Mexican governments to create a Comisión Mixta. Through a Mixed Bracero Commission, the parties involved could represent their interests. Hernández Serrano pointed out that official Bracero Program commissions were made up of individuals who did not have much experience with the program. He suggested that the Comisión Mixta be made up of a representative each from the AFL, the CIO, the CGT, and Alianza, and with two representatives from growers' associations, who preferably resided in Los Angeles.[158] Hernández Serrano believed that this committee could address several issues. It could work out ways to prevent contract skipping and thus alleviate undocumented worker issues. It would also be vigilant about the use of Mexican labor to bring down the salaries of domestic labor. Finally, it could solve disputes between growers and braceros.[159] During this same year, President Eisenhower appointed a Migratory Labor Committee to investigate problems within the Bracero Program and advise on legislation. Again, Alianza saw itself outside of official conversations about the future of the Bracero Program.

The next year, Alianza contributed legislative suggestions to the Mexican government for altering the Bracero Program to protect workers' rights. It urged the government to establish "pro-bracero defense offices" in the United States in areas with large concentrations of bracero workforces.[160] These pro-bracero defense offices would work independently from the consulate bureaucracy. Alianza deemed the consul system inadequate because it was unable to enforce the rules and regulations of the Bracero Program. It also asked the Mexican government for approval to build one contracting center in a central state. This contracting center would have the medical capabilities to examine *aspirantes* before they crossed over to the United States. The aim was to reduce the numbers of *aspirantes* rejected in American territory. Alianza requested that this contracting center have dormitories, bathrooms, kitchens, and recreation facilities. These facilities would also reduce the abuses against *aspirantes* and the rampant vice and alcoholism associated with the *aspirantes*' long waiting periods in contracting centers. Alianza did not ask the government for funding. Instead, it asked for approval because its leaders anticipated that this structure could be built with mandatory bracero contributions within three years' time. Although Alianza acknowledged that the Bracero Program facilities would not be as permanent as a new contracting building, it believed that this building could be used as a school, hospital, or government offices once the Bracero Program was terminated. It argued that the current system was like a cattle call, in which the cattle that are chosen are destined for the slaughterhouse and the only ones to blame are those that allow this to continue.[161] These demands for alterations in the program were not addressed, but Alianza continued to propose solutions to the problems of the Bracero Program.

Galarza had clearly moved away from organizing braceros and instead worked with Alianza to gather information on corruption, abuses, and scandals within the Bracero Program. He continued a correspondence with Alianza to these ends. In May 1955, Galarza requested that Hernández Serrano ask his members to submit any evidence of corruption and wrongdoing to SANTA.[162] Galarza began collecting survey information from braceros working in the

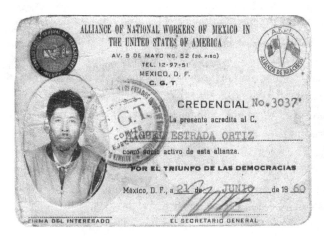

ILLUSTRATION 7
Miguel Estrada Ortiz's Alliance of National Workers of Mexico in the United States of America identification, June 21, 1960. Bracero History Archive.

United States and Mexico.[163] He had received a grant to study problems related to the Bracero Program in California. Galarza researched issues facing guest workers from the perspective of those working in American fields, but he felt it valuable to include the experience of ex-braceros residing in Mexico and asked Hernández Serrano for assistance with survey information. He included fifty dollars for any cost incurred while assisting in the survey and finally added that perhaps they could continue this type of cooperation.[164] The next year, Galarza published *Strangers in Our Fields*, an exposé concerning the labor exploitation and deplorable living conditions of braceros, which, in historian Matthew Garcia's words, "initiated a quiet reassessment of the policy by the department of labor."[165] This publication became central to shaping the discourses around the rights of guest workers. In addition to providing resources for the research and dissemination of *Strangers in Our Fields*, the Fund for the Republic also hired photojournalist Leonard Nadel to document the plight of the braceros.[166] Leonard Nadel followed in Galarza's research footsteps in order to capture the guest-worker journey. These photographs appeared in *Jubilee* and *Pageant* and opened American eyes to bracero exploitation.[167]

As Galarza distanced himself from Alianza, representatives of the AFL investigated Alianza's affiliation with this organization in 1957.[168] The agreements with Galarza and SANTA led Alianza leadership to assert that it had been affiliated with the AFL since 1951. In fact, its leaders felt confident enough about this agreement that they used a circular emblem with the American and Mexican flags at the center and with "AFL" printed at the top on their membership identifications. During this AFL investigation, Alianza asked if it was against American laws to print "AFL" on its emblem. It is not clear if this issue was ever resolved, but it continued to use the same emblem.[169] After the publication of *Strangers in Our Fields*, Galarza corresponded with Alianza less frequently, and the communication dwindled considerably in the early 1960s.[170] The already-strained relationship between Alianza and labor organizations further weakened, despite Alianza's efforts to find a place for guest workers within the labor movements of the time. It continued to organize until the end of the program, and although its correspondence with Galarza dwindled dramatically, the organization continued to issue identification cards. Galarza's optimism concerning the potential of organizing braceros also dissipated. From 1952 until 1964, Galarza became increasingly convinced that the Bracero Program must end. The losses in the Imperial Valley and state repression of Alianza convinced him that braceros could not be unionized. His waning interest also caused Alianza to focus efforts on the reincorporation of braceros into the Mexican economy, as it viewed the experience of many guest workers as part of a larger history of Mexican exploitation of landless agricultural workers.

In order to promote the economic reincorporation of braceros, Alianza also proposed a large-scale land redistribution project, Granjas Agrícolas para ex-Braceros (Agricultural Farms for Ex-Braceros), favoring ex–guest workers. This project began as early as 1948 requesting land, which they continued to push for throughout its trajectory.[171] In their early requests, Alianza leaders asked to meet with the secretary of Agriculture and Livestock in order to begin working toward finding national land that could be bought at low prices by braceros.[172] They preferred that land be set up and sold as private property rather than as ejidos, because of the restrictive limitation on the use and sale of ejidos. Ultimately, Alianza was unable to organize the program for Granjas Agrícolas para ex-Braceros, but the debates around the project shed light on the aspirations of braceros to be reincorporated into the Mexican economy and to redefine their relationship to agricultural labor.

By 1958, Alianza organized Regional Bracero Committees in several states, including Guanajuato, Puebla, Oaxaca, Michoacán, Tlaxcala, and Jalisco, and in towns, such as Chilacachapa, Guerrero. In a letter to the Mexican president, the organization based in Chilacachapa argued that it had formed the organization to ensure that its members would receive "the fruits of the revolution."[173] In the organization's constitution, over 100 members of the regional organization expressed that they had no land and no work and that they needed to support their wives and children. Its secondary objective was to ensure that braceros would acquire land when the Bracero Program ended. The Regional Committee of Chilacachapa, Guerrero, believed that the program, Granjas Agricolas para ex-Braceros, was a real means to ending their participation in the Bracero Program, and, furthermore, that "it is the only way to liberate ourselves and to stop being eternal immigrant slaves."[174] The members of this chapter rejected the Bracero Program as the best long-term solution to their economic hardship. Many ex-braceros could not see themselves as landless *campesinos* at the mercy of *hacendados*. To be true modern mestizos, they needed to control their own land and do away with the *campesino/hacendado* relationship that harked back to colonial relations. They drew parallels between this relationship and that of patrón/bracero in the United States and decided to use the opportunity in the United States to do away with the exploitation in Mexico.

Toward Bracero Politics

After the termination of the program, Alianza attempted to reconfigure the organization and focus on ex-braceros. It believed that the United States had become dependent on Mexican labor and that formal guest-worker programs were the only way to protect these laborers. The need for cheap agricultural labor was not limited to the United States and would spill over to Canada, where Mexicans would be seen as the ideal stoop worker. Hernández Serrano supported efforts to send Mexican workers to Canada: "We know the Canadian farmers are interested in getting braceros. . . . But whether an agreement will be reached so that our men can go . . . well, that's another matter."[175] Alianza never again came to represent guest workers. Although it is difficult to assess the lasting accomplishments of Alianza, its existence points toward Mexicans' efforts to construct transnational labor movements in Mexico and the United States, despite the inability to claim rights afforded to American citizens.

While some braceros defiantly held on to their racial identity, and others defiantly took control of their bodies through acts of pleasure, Alianza members challenged the U.S. state imagination of the docile workforce by actively trying to create a transnational union and defying those state parameters, even if unsuccessful. Furthermore, they addressed this relationship and recognized that many braceros did not want to return to the harsh economic realities and exploitation waiting for them in their hometowns. These organizers stood against the policies that did not allow braceros to form unions and instead articulated a sophisticated political understanding of American dependency on Mexican labor.

The relationship between the leadership of Alianza and Galarza also reveals a side of Galarza that is distinct from the popular perception of the man who fought vigorously to terminate the Bracero Program. In the 1940s, Galarza felt optimistic about finding a place for braceros with his labor-organizing efforts. He had a commitment to organizing these men into his vision of a hemispheric transnational union. By the end of 1951, this vision dissipated because of the Mexican government's criminalization of Alianza and the failures of the strikes in the Imperial Valley. He spoke against the persecution of Alianza and rallied efforts to protect activists within the organization. Despite his hard work, he was unable to defend his allies, and his relationship with Alianza became severely strained.

As an organization representing guest workers, Alianza struggled to find a place within Galarza's labor-organizing efforts and within labor movements in Mexico. Labor organizations on both sides of the border could not find a significant place for braceros within their movement. Alianza realized their marginal position, but even within it, they drew distinctions between themselves and undocumented laborers, indigenous workers, and illiterate classes. Leaders of Alianza sought to distinguish their members from undocumented, indigenous, and illiterate workers, as they considered themselves a highly literate class of men that often clashed with the undocumented and those whom they viewed as "primitive" and apolitical. Their contradictions show the complicated nature of bracero subjectivity, as their class background did not shield them from the exploitative work in the fields. They struggled against repression at home and abroad and found themselves articulating the paradigmatic shifts within citizenship, labor rights, and national belonging of a class of workers that by design were exploitable and expendable. The actions of these men contradict the all-too-popular representations of Mexican workers holding short-handle hoes with smiles and working toward family uplift. While they evoke discourses of patriotism, family, and national progress, they also critiqued a government that continued to deliver Mexican workers to the United States without representation. Their harsh indictment of the collusion between the Mexican and U.S. governments would be echoed decades later by another Alianza representing guest workers. This time the activism would not center on young able-bodied men, but instead on bodies weathered by time and harsh labor entering the twilight of their years demanding justice for ex-braceros.

INTERLUDE Ten Percent

On December 14, 2007, Alma Carrillo, an oral historian with the Bracero History Project, and I arrived in a small town in the state of Tabasco. An organizer with the Bracero Justice Movement had arranged for us to meet a chapter composed of many indigenous braceros. We walked into the living room of a small house that resonated with the sounds of Spanish, Chontal Maya, and a mixture of the two languages. The men immediately spoke collectively about the need to receive their back wages and asked what we could do for them. This was not the first time I was presented with this question; many bracero community members had asked me about it, from the very first collecting site to the last. Over and over I told them, "I can record your story and make sure that it's safe, so that no one will forget." This was reason enough for some bracero communities to participate, as they wanted to tell their stories and gain visibility. In this particular room, a couple of men requested to be recorded in their indigenous language. "We will not be able to understand," I explained, "but we will record your story however you want." In a noisy room, Alma and I took turns carrying out interviews, many shorter than we wanted them to be, since there were so many men waiting and this was just one stop of many that we had scheduled. As I looked on during Alma's interview with Felipe Hernández Cruz, he said to her, "This issue . . . has been going on for years. We have had enough, because we are people of the fields, we are *campesinos*."[1] He paused, looked directly at Alma, and said, "I will translate for you." Then he switched to Chontal Maya. After he finished his statement, he said, "Now I will tell you [in Spanish] what I said. It has been a while since we raised this issue and we still haven't achieved anything. Hopefully the president of the republic, or the governor, will pay attention to us because we are people in need."[2] Hernández Cruz reminded us that his views of the past are firmly planted in the politics of the present, and that indigenous and mestizo campesinos continue to occupy liminal spaces where their needs are not met and their voices fall on politicians' deaf ears.

FOUR *LA POLÍTICA DE LA DIGNIDAD*

Creating the Bracero Justice Movement

> Revivimos un muerto . . . porque esto ya estaba
> sepultado. (We revived the dead . . . because this
> [case] was already buried.)
> —ALBA NIDIA RUBIO LEYVA, Bracero Proa Activist
>   and daughter of a bracero

> Por Dignidad, Por Vergüenza. (For Dignity,
> Because of Shame.)
> —FELIPE MUÑOZ PAVÓN, ex-bracero

Nearly half a century after the first braceros entered the United States, ex-braceros and their families are reclaiming their historic contributions and bringing attention to government corruption, abuse, and wage theft. Written into the bracero contract was a stipulation that employers would deposit 10 percent of a bracero's wages into individual savings accounts, which were subsequently aggregated into a single pool in Mexico, to be paid out to braceros once they returned. Initiated as part of the international agreement to provide braceros with savings and economic capital upon fulfilling their contracts, the account served as an incentive for braceros to "go home" to Mexico.[1] The Mexican government, however, failed to establish a bureaucratic mechanism to distribute these funds effectively. Estimates put the amount of money that the Mexican government collected from bracero-held wages at over $32 million.[2] Although the Mexican government asserts that there were no deductions of wages after 1948, the Bracero Justice Movement rejects the claim and is fighting for what it believes was a 10 percent deduction taken from every bracero paycheck throughout the life of the program.

As early as 1942, a small number of braceros began to demand their saved or back wages.[3] This continued throughout the duration of the program. On January 19, 1950, José Martínez Valtierra from Guadalajara, Jalisco, wrote to Mexican president Miguel Alemán Valdés requesting his savings, which a citrus association had deducted per his guest-worker contracts that spanned 1947–48.[4] Antonio Vasquez de Casas from Juchipila, Zacatecas, wrote to Mexican president Adolfo López Mateos on December 8, 1958, requesting assistance in obtaining his savings from the Banco Nacional de Ahorro, collected while he was working as a bracero on the railroads in Baltimore and Ohio.[5] Braceros residing in or near the Mexican capital who made inquiries to government officials were often given the runaround. For braceros who lived in rural villages, the additional travel to Mexico City to petition government officials for their wages made the process both costly and frustrating. Others were not aware of the 10 percent deduction from their paychecks, confessing they could not read proficiently enough to fully understand the contract.[6]

Although Mexico's national archives, the Archivo General de la Nación, contain hundreds of letters from braceros asking about their savings, there are very few records indicating that guest workers received payment. One of those was a railroad worker residing in Mexico City, Juan Vega Olvera, who in May 1944 wrote to President Manuel Ávila Camacho and explained that he had received $331.69 of the $635.21 owed to him.[7] He asked for assistance in order to resolve the matter. Similarly, Altagracia Estrada Flores from Uruapan, Michoacán, asked the president to issue her a copy of her deceased husband's contract so that she could petition to receive his savings, six weeks after his death. He entered the United States in December 1943 and passed away March 4, 1944, in Santa Barbara, California, leaving behind his wife and seven children. It is not clear whether his widow was ever able to obtain his savings, but her letter demonstrates that women also worked to recuperate these back wages at the time.[8]

In the 1990s, the widow of a former bracero living in Puruándiro, Michoacán, asked her grandson, a migrant-labor organizer based out of Coachella, California, to make inquiries about what she called her husband's "Social Security" entitlement, referring to the American federal insurance program.[9] She believed that her husband was entitled to these payments through his contract as a guest worker in the United States. Armed with his grandfather's original contract as a railroad bracero, Ventura Gutiérrez discovered that his grandmother was not entitled to Social Security benefits, but instead to 10 percent of his grandfather's collected wages. It quickly dawned on him that 10 percent of over 4.5 million contracts amounted to billions of dollars of back wages owed.[10] Gutiérrez also recognized that many present-day transnational workers felt a deep connection to the role their parents and grandparents had played as guest workers, as he did. And many of these bracero families lived in conditions that could be greatly improved with the payment of these back wages. But beyond whether they "needed" the back wages, the money was rightfully theirs. Gutiérrez was left with two questions: Where did this money go, and, more important, how could ex-bracero families claim their back wages?

Gutiérrez became a leading figure in a handful of transnational organizations that make up what historian Stephen Pitti has termed the Bracero Justice Movement (BJM).[11] Through the BJM, ex-braceros, activists, and their families began to articulate what I call a *política de la dignidad*, a politics of dignity that calls on the state to protect migrant workers beyond the physical boundaries of Mexico. Rooted in radical indigenous movements, the *política de la dignidad* exposes the unwillingness of Mexico to truly work toward the protection of its migrant citizens and, furthermore, calls into question the legitimacy of government regimes that further the marginalization of migrant workers by stealing their wages. As ex-bracero Rosendo Alarcón Carrera asserted, "We knew perfectly well that they were renting us [out] like animals." On the missing wages, he quipped, "And savings funds, for whom? Well, for the Mexican government I think."[12] Many of these elderly men felt that the Mexican government not only failed to protect them but also repeatedly exploited their circumstances. The movement was a response not only to wage theft but also to a collective Mexican historic "amnesia" about the program.[13]

The shifting position of emigrants into prodigal sons of a country eager to reincorporate their dollars into the national economy, along with the Zapatista indigenous movement uprising, the passage of the North American Free Trade Act (NAFTA), and the 1994 economic crisis signaled by the devaluation of the Mexican peso, set the stage for the rise of the BJM. Facing tremendous economic challenges, the Mexican government worked hard to connect migrant communities residing in the United States to the Mexican state. It went from portraying migrants as unpatriotic citizens to portraying them as "national heroes," as the remittances from these communities not only maintained families left behind in Mexico but also financed roads, schools, and community centers there.[14] Ex-braceros knew they represented the historical roots of state-sanctioned migration, and they began demanding recognition. They saw the hypocrisy in the government's rhetoric and how it was still leaning on migrants instead of supporting them. Following the Zapatistas, leaders of the BJM launched strong critiques against a class of Mexican elites and politicians they believed had never served the interests of the working poor, rural populations, or indigenous communities of Mexico.

On January 1, 1994, the day that NAFTA took effect, the Ejército Zapatista de Liberación Nacional (EZLN, Zapatista Army of National Liberation), made up of indigenous communities throughout the highlands and jungle of eastern Chiapas in Mexico, "carried out coordinated attacks" in an effort to use "the legacy of Emiliano Zapata and the Mexican Revolution to stake a claim against NAFTA and the kind of Mexico associated with the political and economic elite supporting [it]."[15] Throughout the 1990s and 2000s, the Zapatistas pushed a national discussion about mestizo and indígena campesinos, indigenous rights, and "mal gobierno," a government that continually fails its citizens. Calling for autonomy for indigenous and marginalized communities, their visions of social change shaped the discourses deployed by the BJM. Ex-braceros would come to see themselves as a historical product of the "mal gobierno" and utilized Zapatista ideals of "dignity" to frame their political struggle, which went beyond money. Both mestizo and indigenous braceros tied their struggles to those of indigenous populations in the Zapatista movement, agreeing that they both understood state marginalization and state violence.[16] However, the BJM diverged from the Zapatistas' orientation toward social change for future generations by instead focusing on an aging population that needed and deserved recognition through reparations.

Activist and ex-bracero Antonio Aragón explained: "They are waiting for us to die, so that this issue will be forgotten."[17] Ex-braceros argued that the humiliation and exploitation did not end with the Bracero Program, but that migrant workers in general were only seen as laboring bodies; now, because of their age, they had become invisible, and government officials no longer viewed them as valuable citizens. For many within these communities, reparations would also expose the corruption of the Mexican government and the U.S. exploitation of migrant workers. Ex-braceros, such as José Trinidad Heras, launched strong critiques against the Mexican government by stating, "Do you know who had the good fortune of spending that money, without suffering, without working over there, and without being fumigated? The enemy . . . our enemy, the Mexican government."[18]

Ex-braceros are claiming back wages and protections through rhetoric that blames the Mexican government for allowing their exploitation. They have brought to public light important stories and images of dehumanizing aspects of the bracero experience. Through a política de la dignidad, the movement strategically deploys these narratives to shame the government into restoring what it believes was taken away from braceros: back wages and dignity. In this effort, the BJM has been one of the major catalysts for creating a public memory about the program. Sociologist Ronald Mize noted in his own research that prior to the movement, braceros confirmed details about their experience but stayed "silent" on certain aspects of the program. As the BJM grew, respondents in his research "spoke at length" about "some of the more unfavorable and humiliating aspects of the program," because the movement had created a space for sharing these experiences.[19] These "humiliating" elements of the program became touchstones for the public and formed collective memory of the program. Documentary photographs that depict seminal moments of the bracero experience, including images of processing stations, medical exams, and labor contracts, gained popularity within ex-bracero communities. The collective memory being built around these testimonies and images, however, silences stories of deviance and pleasure because they do not fit within a narrative that seeks restitution, and they cannot be collectively deployed to incriminate a nation-state that failed to protect them. In this schema, narratives of bracero deviance based in pleasure and adventure cannot coexist with government shaming. Difference rooted in race and ethnicity, on the other hand, could be useful for calling attention to the government's exploitation of mestizo and indigenous populations. Like Galarza's early attempts to organize braceros, narratives about the long historical labor exploitation of mestizo and indigenous campesinos could be used to incriminate nation-states that allowed for their continual marginalization. Along with their calls for back wages, ex-braceros within the BJM reveal the failures of the mestizo project in truly integrating the rural poor into the national economy, showing that the majority within these communities still faces glaring inequality. The BJM placed mestizos' and indigenous guest workers' shared identity as braceros at the fore.

The fight to recover back wages was a catalyst for a larger discussion about the Mexican state taking responsibility for a class of workers—the ex-bracero—that it had helped create. Ex-braceros and their families began fighting to have these workers recognized as a type of "protected class." But this meant hardening the lines between documented and undocumented workers, which, as some of the stories in this book have already shown, were quite fluid. Because undocumented workers had no legal claim to back wages, the movement has had to distinguish between those who at any point were official guest workers and those who never held this status. Through this logic, the BJM excluded undocumented workers who labored in the United States during the period of the program and relied on a logic that obscured the Mexican government's hand in shaping historical undocumented migration. Despite this, the BJM connected the program to contemporary undocumented migrants, as these migrants were viewed as the real and metaphoric children and grandchildren of guest workers. For the purposes of recovering reparations and back wages, communities' ex-braceros sought documents that could establish a bracero identity. In lieu of documents, many ex–guest workers have relied on their memories in order to "prove" they were braceros. The BJM has utilized their testimonies not only to move the general public to action but to shame public officials for their inability to act on behalf of this aging population. By some measures, shaming and attracting media attention through direct actions, such as occupying President Vicente Fox's family ranch or holding peaceful protests, have been successful BJM tactics. In this sense, the BJM continually embraces defiance in its *política de la dignidad*.

The movement caught national attention as journalists disseminated compelling images of protests in Mexico that featured elderly men and women peacefully marching, as well as the government's response to these protests in the form of police brutality. The public cringed at the sight of these elders facing billy clubs, and disturbing images emerged that juxtaposed the menacing figures of police in riot gear clashing with elderly men and women holding up picket signs stating: "I am the widow of an ex-bracero," "Humiliation and Exploitation," "No More Lies," "There Is No Justice," "We Are Ex-braceros, Not Beggars," and "The Dead Also Demand Justice." Ex-braceros also caught the attention of American journalist Randal C. Archibold from the *New York Times*, who described these men as relics of a distant past in American history with "skin leathery and bronzed from decades of work in the fields."[20] Using imagery that evoked a sense of imminent disappearance, he wrote, "These braceros are fading fast, some pushing or over 90 . . . ever reliant on family and friends to get by."[21]

In the United States, the movement found expression in ex-bracero meetings in places ranging from small agricultural towns such as Salinas, California, to larger cities like Chicago. Through these meetings, bracero communities discussed strategies to secure the back wages owed to them. These meetings also served as platforms for ex-braceros to reconnect with one another and to gain recognition for braceros' underacknowledged contributions to U.S. histories of labor and migration. These became critical sites that shaped the public memory of the program as men retold stories in their communities that helped separate their narrative from those of the undocumented workers.

This chapter explores the bi-national trajectory of the BJM and begins by focusing on the repressive strategies the Mexican state used to obfuscate the

ILLUSTRATION 8 Ventura Gutiérrez holding a microphone protesting with ex-braceros, Mexico City, April 7, 2003. Bracero History Archive.

history of Mexican guest workers and their back wages. Ex-braceros understood this, and they also recognized that their experiences fit within a larger trajectory of state oppression and exploitation by the Mexican state. They took action through the BJM to demand that the Mexican state recognize ex-braceros as a protected class of citizens that had suffered the most heinous type of disenfranchisement. As such, they demanded not only back wages but also social services for the ex-bracero community. The part of the story I examine here focuses on the period between 1998, when one of the first organizations of the movement, Bracero Proa, was formed, to December 2009, when ex-braceros residing in the United States received the first and only compensation for their back wages.

Bracero Proa and the Bracero Justice Movement

Bracero Proa is the largest, and often considered the first, of the contemporary bracero organizations.[22] The group was founded in 2000 by Ventura Gutiérrez, whose experiences in the Chicano Movement and in labor organizing informed the BJM's early strategies. As the head of Bracero Proa, Gutiérrez often served as the spokesperson of the BJM and negotiated directly with Mexican officials for bracero back wages and additional social services. Many bracero families, in both the United States and Mexico, knew him personally and regarded him as the leading voice in the BJM.

Ventura Gutiérrez was born in 1948 in Puruándiro, Michoacán, but his American-born father brought him and his mother to live in a trailer in Coachella Valley, California. As agricultural workers, they earned their living in the fields, harvesting crops such as onions, carrots, tomatoes, okra, and grapes. Eventually the family moved into a one-bedroom home in a Mexican neighborhood of Coachella, commonly known as Coachellita Number I. In 1969, Gutiérrez made his way to community college before being drafted for the Vietnam War. As a conscientious objector he applied for a discharge, later withdrawing his application in exchange for being stationed in Germany for over one year. Upon reflection, he had changed his mind about military service, concluding that, as he told me, "I had to swallow the same medicine, independently of whether I was in agreement of the war … and I pulled my application and let the dice roll."[23] When he returned to Coachella, Gutiérrez continued to pursue an education through the GI Bill, eventually enrolling in the University of California, Riverside, and earning a bachelor's degree in sociology. He then enrolled in a master's program in education and Chicano studies, but he stopped shortly before completing the requirements for graduation.

Throughout the late 1970s and 1980s, Gutiérrez worked in higher education because he believed that teaching provided a means to promote social change. Initially, he had a difficult time landing a teaching position because of his public activism within the Chicano Movement and community organizing. He, like many young residents of the Coachella Valley, participated in groups like the United Mexican American Student Organization (UMAS), Movimiento Estudiantil Chicano de Aztlan (MEChA), Mexican American Political Association (MAPA), and the United Farm Workers of America (UFW). Gutiérrez began as an active member and supporter of many of these organizations, but by the mid-1980s he had become disillusioned with the strategies deployed by these groups and sought more transnational approaches to social justice.[24] He started looking to Mexican social movements that challenged state power for new models of activism.

During the late 1980s and early 1990s, Gutiérrez turned to full-time union organizing of date-palm workers in Southern California. By 1996, convinced that these transnational workers could be more effectively organized from their sending communities, Gutiérrez helped to establish Unión Sin Fronteras. This organization created its first service center in Puruándiro, Michoacán. In many ways, the transnational labor-organizing strategies are reminiscent of the work of the Alianza de Braceros Nacionales de México en los Estados Unidos (Alianza) and Ernesto Galarza. Gutiérrez was also inspired by the political work of prominent politician Cuauhtémoc Cárdenas, who in 1998 helped found the Partido de la Revolución Democrática (PRD), a political party that would challenge the Partido Revolucionario Institucional's (PRI) authoritarian rule of Mexico. Gutiérrez invited Cárdenas to cut the ribbon to inaugurate the service center.[25] It was during this event that Gutiérrez's grandmother gave him his grandfather's bracero identification card and asked that he investigate whether she had a right to compensation.

On a research trip to El Paso, Gutiérrez stopped in to visit a friend and long-time local activist, Carlos Marentes. At the time, Marentes was focused on creating a bracero memorial and writing a book on the Bracero Program. In a room at Marentes's center, Gutiérrez noticed that he had collected boxes of bracero IDs and contracts, organized in alphabetical order by states from Aguascalientes to Zacatecas.[26] Marentes had convinced thousands of braceros to hand over their documentation for a potential museum, something that later proved to hamper the BJM's efforts. During this visit, Marentes gave Gutiérrez a copy of the labor agreement, where he came across the section concerning a 10 percent savings fund. Gutiérrez asked Marentes to join him in organizing braceros, but Marentes declined, stating that his only interest was in writing a historical account of the program and building a memorial for braceros in El Paso, Texas.[27] This refusal proved to be fortuitous. It turned out later that Marentes repeatedly failed to respond to the community's call to return the original bracero IDs and documents to their owners, so the fact that Marentes was not involved in Bracero Proa made it easier for movement activists to gain the trust of local communities.

On May 5, 1998, Gutiérrez brought together four ex-braceros as an initiative of Unión Sin Fronteras to determine what should be done about the 10 percent savings that had been withheld. They unanimously voted to resolve what in their minds was "fraud" committed more than fifty years earlier. In the first phase of organizing, they held many meetings and press conferences in Guanajuato, Michoacán, and Jalisco. Gutiérrez felt the movement had a chance to succeed if he could organize these states effectively, as they had been the largest sending states to the program.

Gutiérrez made generational connections between braceros and current waves of workers that shaped his organizing strategies. In the early 1990s, while organizing a mushroom workers' strike in Pennsylvania with migrants from Moroleón, Guanajuato, Gutiérrez noticed that many of the strikers were the children or grandchildren of braceros. He believed that these relationships would be a successful building block for the movement. Because of his close relationship to these workers, he chose their hometown to hold a meeting for braceros from Guanajuato in November 1998. The family members of the mushroom-strike workers became central participants, but many more families joined the struggle to claim back wages.

He built on these transnational labor connections, always recognizing that if the movement was to be successful it needed to focus on these communities across borders. Momentum grew for the movement, and the next year, 5,000 ex-braceros attended his meeting in Irapuato, Guanajuato. These high rates of attendance demonstrated to the leadership that there was a desire to organize around the back wages, and the families of these guest workers were just as interested in the movement as the braceros themselves. Ultimately, Gutiérrez realized that bracero families needed an organization solely focused on ex-bracero issues. To address that need, Gutiérrez and his supporters created Alianza Bracero Proa on February 5, 2000. Gutiérrez named it after the Mexican government's bailout of the banking sector, the Fondo Bancario de Protección al Ahorro, commonly known as Fobaproa, five years earlier.[28] Gutiérrez stated that the name helped people quickly comprehend what many people of Mexico considered a "fraud" because Fobaproa represented government bailouts for the rich on the backs of the poor and working class.[29] Thus Alianza Bracero Proa's motto quickly became "The first proa theft was not Fobaproa but Bracero Proa."[30] Through this analogy, Gutiérrez meant to convey that the first large-scale fleecing of the people was not this recent banking fraud, but the withholding of braceros' back wages, which had occurred decades earlier. The popular slogan reminded the bracero community that the banks that held the savings accounts were partly responsible for the fraud.

Through the support of Bracero Proa members and leadership, Gutiérrez traveled from large cities like Monterrey in northern Mexico, to small towns in the south such as Dzoncauich, Yucatán, holding meetings with hundreds of bracero families in an effort to keep these communities informed and connected to the case. Local organizers asked members for donations to pay for Gutiérrez's bus fare. Some families donated two pesos, the equivalent of twenty U.S. cents, while others offered more when they could. Activists pooled these meager funds together for Gutiérrez's basic travel expenses and to cover other members' travel costs to larger meetings. Moving from town to town, often sleeping in bus terminals, Gutiérrez managed to form organizations that covered most of Mexico. Ex-bracero families in regions in which many thought no bracero families resided, such as Campeche, Quintana Roo, and Chiapas, organized their own chapters.

Although ex-braceros composed the broadest constituency, few of them became leaders at the regional level. Those ex-braceros who did, like Antonio Aragón from Oaxaca, had excellent physical health and high literacy skills. Men like Aragón embodied the "ideal ex-bracero" for the movement, as he could travel, write, and even use the latest technology for organizing: the computer. This was a unique and privileged position for an ex-bracero because the program had targeted rural workers with low levels of literacy, and multiple contracts could lead workers' health to decline.[31] Because many ex-braceros had died or were in poor health, the children and grandchildren of braceros also found leadership positions within the movement. They staked claims of belonging to the movement by declaring, "*Soy hijo de bracero* [I am the son of a bracero]." The movement grew because of the intergenerational involvement of bracero families. Regional Coordinator Alba Nidia Rubio Leyva first came in contact with the BJM through her father's activism in the organization. When he became involved, she and her siblings would laugh at him because they thought it was a futile fight. But then he asked her to help him because he could not read or write, and she felt compelled to support her father. In 2000, she committed to joining the movement. In the first phase of her involvement, she organized out of her home and spent much of her own money to keep her chapter of the organization running. Eventually, she and her husband decided that the organization was becoming too much of a financial burden. The long travels to meet with regional coordinators across the state economically drained Rubio Leyva. The bracero community in her region decided to implement monthly dues in order to rent office space and subsidize the travel costs associated with organizing. They rented out a local storefront for clerical work associated with the movement, and Rubio Leyva points out that it also functions as a social space for the ex-bracero community.[32]

It was in these newly configured spaces that ex-braceros more intensely exchanged stories and collectively created public narratives about the history of the Bracero Program. These social spaces became exclusive ex-bracero domains. Those who had entered the United States as undocumented workers and had never held a guest-worker contract were excluded. But among this elderly generation of men it was often difficult to draw lines of separation, as some undocumented workers of the period who labored alongside guest workers claimed a bracero identity prior to the BJM. Until recent years, many migrant workers called themselves "braceros" because the word itself has often generically meant agricultural worker in Mexican popular culture. Through the BJM, official braceros demarcated strong lines between themselves and undocumented workers, which was complicated for those who oscillated between the two. Regardless, for many in the BJM, one guest-worker contract qualified him as a bracero, despite other moments of laboring in the United States as an undocumented worker. While children, grandchildren, and widows became an integral part of the movement, the privileged voice was always that of the ex-bracero, so they remained at the periphery of the collective memory of the program.

As the movement started gaining its footing, competing organizations also emerged; some were created because Bracero Proa had focused attention only on certain geographic areas, while others splintered off because of interpersonal politics and disputes. Such disagreements often came along with accusations of funding mismanagement or that leadership utilized the organization for political gain. These rumors caused some ex-braceros to grow distrustful of the leadership and draw parallels to their experience as guest workers, stating, "Even then people were looking to make money off us, exploit us because we had little education."[33] Their journey to become braceros opened them up to exploitation at the hands of local officials, contracting center employees, and growers, and their fight for recognition and restitution also opened them up to being taken advantage of by unscrupulous people who charged these elderly men exorbitant fees for everything from making copies of their documents to filing paperwork on their behalf.

Tactics and State Repression

Faced with calls to return back wages, Mexican officials argued that the money was never earmarked, so it was "lost" in transition. They also claimed that the Mexican government never kept master lists of all guest workers in the United States. Thus, the burden of locating the funds and proving that individuals participated in the program fell on BJM organizations. In response, the BJM developed three approaches to addressing the recuperation of the back wages: research, law, and protest. In the early phase of the BJM, leadership looked at both local and national archives in Mexico and the United States to research where the funds might be. Braceros also approached law firms in an attempt to resolve the issue through the courts. Finally, BJM organizations began to stage public protests to pressure banks and public officials to return the back wages. All of these approaches carefully separated guest workers from undocumented workers, and "proof" of temporary worker status became a central focus.

Bracero Proa targeted Banrural in Mexico and Wells Fargo in the United States, both of which were thought to have managed or held the original savings funds. Wells Fargo deducted the money from the braceros' paychecks, while the Banco Nacional de Crédito Agrícola received these apportions from the salaries; the latter merged with Banrural, one of Mexico's major banks, which then inherited this thorny legacy. The bank was unwilling to work with activists from the BJM to investigate the disappearance of these funds. Banrural argued that when it merged with the Banco Nacional de Crédito Agrícola, no saving funds were flagged as bracero accounts. Nonetheless, two months after formally establishing Bracero Proa, Gutiérrez led a protest at the corporate offices of Banrural in Mexico City, shutting down the bank.[34] Although the bank again publicly stated that it had no record of ever holding the savings, ex-bracero families responded that they wanted an independent investigation of Banrural.[35] Banrural refused to allow BJM organizers access to their archives and financial records. There was an immediate backlash to Gutiérrez's organizing efforts, as he was harassed and detained by officials.[36]

In 2001, the BJM's efforts to call attention to state and institutional accountability moved to center stage in the United States. While driving bus number 9 in a Zapatista protest caravan to Mexico City, Gutiérrez learned that the Chicago law firm of Hughes, Socol, Piers, Resnick, and Dym had filed a class-action lawsuit against Wells Fargo on behalf of ex–guest workers. The "March for Indigenous Dignity" traveled across several Mexican states and ended in a session at the Mexican Congress, where representatives of the EZLN (Ejército Zapatista de Liberación Nacional) would speak.[37] Although Gutiérrez felt committed to the Zapatista efforts, he left the march and organized a press conference in Morelia, Michoacán, announcing the legal action taken on behalf of the braceros. The case was brought to the law firm's attention early on because of its growing reputation among migrants after they reached an agreement in 2000 with money-transfer companies, such as Western Union, Money Gram, and Orlandi Valuta. The knowledge about migrant communities gained by lawyers and paralegals would be used to examine the wage theft of Mexican guest workers. Along with the law firm's efforts, Bracero Proa continued to place pressure on Banrural, and Gutiérrez worked toward mobilizing transnational communities.

Although Bracero Proa was optimistic about reaching a resolution through the courts, the leadership also viewed legal avenues as lengthy and lethal to a movement based on elderly people who did not have time on their side. They agreed that they needed more media attention in order to pressure officials. On February 5, 2002, Bracero Proa began La Caravana de Las Botas, a protest caravan that started in Yakima, Washington, and toured through bracero communities in the American Southwest and Mexico until reaching its final destination in Mexico City.[38] The name, "Caravan of the Boots," was coined in reference to the infamous exchange of boots between the Mexican and American presidents, Vicente Fox and George W. Bush.[39] The symbol of the boots also resonated with braceros, as many first-time braceros who entered the United States with sandals had returned to Mexico wearing boots. They, like Fox and Bush, could also wear boots. The Bracero Program transformed them into modern boot-wearing workers. The caravan focused on catching the national attention of both leaders and nations by tracing an imagined reverse trajectory of braceros. Through this route, which led back to Mexico City, the organization was also framing bracero exploitations as symbolically emanating from the nation's capital—that is, through Mexican policy makers and officials who approved the Bracero Program and brokered bracero "arms."

In the next year, Bracero Proa managed to capture national attention in Mexico. By October 27, 2003, the Mexican House of Representatives took steps to inaugurate an initiative to compensate braceros. The first phase called for a census to account for citizens who had participated in the program. The second phase focused on monetary compensation, which had not yet been approved, which led Bracero Proa to refuse to participate in the census, because there was no incentive for their members. They also viewed the census as flawed because the onus of proving one had been a bracero fell on the individual and not the government.[40] During this same month, other ex-bracero organizations, such as La Asamblea Nacional de Ex-Braceros (ANB), pressured legislators to pass the second part of the initiative.

Frustrated with the process, the leadership of Bracero Proa decided to adopt a more defiant strategy through confrontational forms of protest. On February 7, 2004, about 1,000 members of Bracero Proa peacefully protested on the private property of Mercedes Quesada Etxaide, the mother of Mexico's President Fox. They demanded to speak to Fox, his family, or a designated representative about the president's inability to work toward the repayment of bracero back wages. Mercedes Fox Quesada, the president's sister, was the first to listen to their concerns, with the Subsecretario de Gobernación (Subsecretary of the Interior) Ramón Martín Huerta continuing the conversation. During the protest, the president's mother fainted and was taken to a hospital in the state capital. Gutiérrez told reporters, "We did not come here with the intention to be violent, but the national security committed a grave error when they laughed in the faces of grandmothers and grandfathers who have been looking for a solution for 55 years."[41] Two days later, President Vicente Fox issued a public statement that he did not have the executive powers to return the braceros' back wages. This, he argued, fell under the jurisdiction of Congress. Simultaneously, the Fox family dropped trespassing charges against the leaders of Bracero Proa.[42]

The protest at the Fox ranch received much-needed media attention that compelled bracero communities in other towns and cities to continue to protest. In the United States, many of these protests took place at local Mexican consulates. In Mexico, they occurred in front of the offices of local officials and the American Embassy. The Secretaría de Gobernación (secretary of the Interior) felt pressured to find some incentive to persuade the bracero community to participate in the census. Bracero Proa finally decided to cooperate with the census, and in exchange, they were offered inclusion in social service programs, such as the Instituto Mexicano de Seguro Social (IMSS) and the Secretaría de Desarrollo Social (SEDESOL). While the first protest at the Fox ranch was relatively successful, winning tangible gains for the BJM, leaders in the movement continued to work toward recovering the back wages.

A month after the first protest, Bracero Proa decided to return to the Fox ranch. Again, the leadership peacefully aired their concerns about the back wages and explained that the social programs offered to ex-braceros were not enough. The second protest received the same level of attention as the first and again resulted in tangible gains, as congressional representatives agreed to create a special commission for braceros. In June 2004, the Cámara de Diputados (Chamber of Deputies, or the lower house) lobbied to pass a special proposal for 2005 that would allow monetary compensation and social programs for additional braceros.[43]

The protests at Banrural and the Fox ranch transformed the image of braceros, as the media showed elderly men with signs and aging widows enduring police violence. Alba Nidia Rubio Leyva admitted that before her involvement with the BJM she had thought her father's efforts to recuperate his back wages were futile. But then she watched television images of police harassing and physically abusing ex-braceros.[44] These images, in addition to her father's request for support, led her to join the movement. Antonio Aragón's children also watched television avidly when he was part of the widely broadcast first protest at the Fox ranch. They sobbed when they saw him being bullied by police.[45]

Elderly women and daughters of ex-braceros began taking a more central role in Bracero Proa's public actions. During the first protest at the Fox ranch, Antonio Aragón did not allow elderly women from his Oaxacan group to participate. Aware of the danger and violence that could erupt during the protests, Aragón believed it was inappropriate to take women. Even though other Bracero Proa groups included women in these actions, Aragón feared that the women in his group could get hurt and thought it was too risky. But Aragón's views on the role of women in the organization changed when they protested at the Oficinas de Gobernación. As usual, he had asked the women in his group, Rufina and Isabel, to wait for them at the bus station. But this time they refused, stating that women joined their husbands during the time of the revolution, and that if the state was going to kill their fellow men, they would have to kill them, too. The women decided to carry the most attention-grabbing banner, proclaiming, *"No Más Atole con El PAN,"* to signal that they would no longer be accepting the rhetoric of PAN (Partido Acción Nacional) and washing it down with *atole*, a traditional Mexican beverage. Rubio Leyva claimed that during one such protest, "Almost all of us in front were women."[46] By proclaiming this, these women were signaling that the PAN was no better than the PRI, the party that had dominated Mexican presidential politics for most of the twentieth century. PAN candidate Vicente Fox was the first to defeat the PRI in a presidential election, but his failure to truly address the concerns of the BJM caused many within the movement to see this transition in political power as not changing anything.

As part of the emerging *política de la dignidad*, these organizations circulated historical images of braceros in an effort to emotionally move people to support the plight of ex-braceros and pressure government officials to answer the call to return the back wages. One of the central images that Bracero Proa reproduced on signs, T-shirts, and calendars was commonly referred to as *"los desnudos* [the nudes]." *"Los desnudos"* became the unofficial logo of the movement. The photograph, taken in Mexico City's National Stadium in 1943, showed doctors examining braceros (ill. 9). In the image, the *aspirantes* are covering their genitals with small pieces of paper as if to preserve some sense of the dignity that is being taken away by this invasive and humiliating process.

Ex-bracero organizations felt compelled to reproduce images that showed braceros as an exploited class of workers at the mercy of doctors and government officials. Whether it was a historical image of officials checking their hands for calluses or spraying braceros with DDT or the most popular image of medical exams, ex-braceros felt that these images captured in metaphor their real position in society. Surprisingly, they wore the *"los desnudos"* T-shirts proudly during protests and meetings. They also repro-

ILLUSTRATION 9 Medical examinations circa 1943. Photo originally published in "Snapshots in a Farm Labor Tradition," by Howard R. Rosenberg, *Labor Management Decisions* 3, no. 1 (1993). University of California Division of Agriculture and Natural Resources.

duced photographs of police abusing the elderly in the movement. One such image was incorporated into a protest poster with the caption "*Ex-braceros exigen su pago a Fox y a garrotazos nos quieren pagar* [Ex-braceros demand Fox pay them and they want to pay us with a beating]."[47] Another slogan reproduced was "*páganos o mátanos* [pay us or kill us]."[48] Bracero Proa also began issuing its own membership identification cards, which took on important symbolism for many ex-braceros who had lost all of their guest-worker documentation, thus giving them something material to connect to their experiences.

Organizations in the BJM also began to copy and enlarge the documents of ex-bracero members who had saved their bracero identifications or contracts. Proof of guest-worker status was shoved in the face of officials, who over and over professed that the state kept no master list of Mexican braceros. The lack of official records listing all workers made some bracero communities feel that the Mexican government wanted a historical amnesia about the program. Some activists scoured Mexican and U.S. archives in search of such records and faced frustration when officials would not legitimize short partial lists of men who left their hometowns as *aspirantes*

ILLUSTRATION 10
Manuel de Jesús Roman
Gaxiola's Alianza Bracero Proa
identification card. Bracero
History Archive.

or men who aired grievances to Mexican consuls across the United States. During protests, the enlarged identification photos that ex-braceros held reminded the general public that bracero salaries were stolen when these workers were able-bodied young men. When children, widows, and siblings held these same enlarged identifications, they reminded officials that braceros were part of a larger community that was not going to forget about their historical contribution or their stolen wages.

Although Bracero Proa was the largest organization in the BJM, other organizations, such as La Asamblea Nacional de Ex-Braceros (ANB), La Unión Binacional de Ex-Braceros (La Unión), and La Alianza de Ex-Braceros del Norte, made substantial contributions and called attention to different aspects of the BJM's demands. La Unión was an organization that broke off from Bracero Proa because of personal disputes within the leadership. On July 1, 2004, members of La Unión protested in front of the Mexican House of Representatives and the delegation of Instituto Nacional para la Atención de Adultos Mayores (INAPAM) to demand that the social service programs Secretaría de Desarrollo Social (SEDESOL) and Instituto Mexicano de Seguro Social (IMSS) provide the social services promised to ex-braceros earlier that year.[49]

Three weeks later, La Unión Binacional de Ex-Braceros led a protest in front of the Mexican Consulate in San Diego, demanding that it pressure Mexican political figures to widen the parameters of the investigation of bracero back wages. In September 27, 2004, La Unión returned to the consul's office to demand he pressure Mexican president Vicente Fox to take action. La Unión wanted the consul to intercede on behalf of Mexican guest workers and pressure officials to answer the movement's calls and carry out a full investigation on the whereabouts of the wages. It also wanted Mexican officials to take note that bracero communities in the United States were also invested in the outcomes of the Mexican policies created to address these issues.

Based on the gains made directly after the first protest on the Fox ranch, the movement's largest action, La Unión Binacional de Ex-Braceros and Bracero Proa understood the need for more international attention. Leaders of the BJM acknowledged that one of the movement's most effective tools was to publicly shame Mexican officials. On November 22, 2004, 5,000 members of Bracero Proa unsuccessfully attempted yet another protest on a ranch belonging to President Fox's family, this time to call attention to the fact that no legislative action had been passed to compensate ex-braceros.[50] Finally, on April 22, 2005, the Mexican House of Representatives approved a law that would establish a trust for ex-braceros, which would be administered by El Fondo de Apoyo Social para Ex Trabajadores Migratorios Mexicanos (Social Support Fund for Mexican Ex–Migrant Workers). This trust would monetarily compensate ex-braceros or their widows and children who participated in the early census, and particularly those who worked from 1942 to 1946. Illegitimate children, domestic partners, and divorced spouses were not considered worthy of inclusion in these discussions over claims to back wages. Seven days later, the Senate went on to approve this law as well. Those registered in the census were entitled to 38,000 pesos per guest worker, roughly $3,500, which was characterized not as back wages but as *compensación social* [social support]—in essence, a social welfare fund. Some activists were offended by the fact that the officials refused to name the fund in a way that would admit that the salaries had been stolen. They wanted the government to publicly acknowledge that it had unlawfully stolen salaries from braceros. The amount also raised concerns among ex-bracero communities because it was a flat sum. Men who worked multiple contracts over several years would receive the same amount as those who had worked only one short contract. The next month, Bracero Proa led the fifth protest march to the Fox family ranch in San Cristobal, Guanajuato. It demanded that more individuals be included on the rosters of those who would receive guest-worker benefits.[51]

Major legal gains were made on May 9, 2007, as the Mexican Supreme Court ruled that all ex-braceros who worked through the official Bracero Program between 1942 and 1964 were entitled to compensation from the Social Support Fund for Mexican Ex–Migrant Workers. They also ruled that in cases in which the ex-bracero was deceased, only the widow or children of that ex-bracero would be able to register for the compensation. Parents and siblings were directly excluded.[52] These new policies not only strengthened, but also legitimized, visions of the bracero nuclear family. The Mexican government would not give reparations to deceased individuals' families if they did not fit this nuclear schema. Additionally, the court ruled that all of those enrolled for the $3,500 during this period and subsequent early periods had to reside in Mexico. There was no avenue for ex-braceros living in the United States to receive this compensation other than a costly registration trip to Mexico.

Thus, as ex-braceros in the United States joined a class-action lawsuit, ex-braceros in Mexico saw a clearer path to compensation. The Mexican government finally responded to the call made by the BJM to award money to all guest workers. In September 2008, the government published the laws that officially established the trust for the Social Support Fund for Mexican Ex–Migrant Workers and opened the registration period for the final payouts. Living ex-braceros, widows, and their children were allowed to register from November 28, 2008, to January 28, 2009, in any of the thirty-six registration centers created across Mexico. Hundreds of ex-braceros, widows, and children of deceased braceros lined up every day in these registration centers.

The lines became so long that ex-braceros felt that they were re-creating scenes from the days when they first joined the program. They slept overnight on sidewalks in order to receive service the next day. They purchased their meals from vendors and often traveled to these reception centers in groups from their villages, towns, and neighborhoods.[53] These groups looked out for one another, holding each other's place in line while others purchased something to eat or visited the restroom. Older individuals who went on their own often had a harder time. Reports of elderly men whose health suffered in these lines became the focus of discussion for members of Bracero Proa. The organization spoke out after news surfaced of an ex-bracero suffering a heart attack while in line.[54] Bracero Proa complained about the conditions and asked the local government to provide water, restrooms, and a larger staff to process registration to speed up the transactions. Their petitions fell on deaf ears as the lines continued to grow throughout January.

I urged my Uncle Juan to register, and he flew from Chicago to León, Guanajuato. He then traveled to his home village of El Sitio de Maravillas. As I discussed his travel arrangements with my cousin Danny, he said, "Isn't it going to cost more to send him than what he will get? This isn't about the money for both of you." My uncle responded, "This is about what is owed to us." He was right. As I sat next to my uncle and talked about what the money meant, we both understood that the payout was not exactly the back wages but reparations. Though it was costly, my Tío Juan reminded me that the

Mexican government was counting on that attitude and hoping ex-braceros and their families would not register. When he came back, he told me that he had waited for over six hours in a line of over 300 people on January 22 and 24 in León, Guanajuato.[55] He also observed that hustlers asked many elderly for *mordidas* (bribes), as had happened when they wanted to apply to become braceros decades ago. Hustlers walked up to men in line and told them that they would speed up the registration process for a small "fee."[56] Those who paid this "fee" reported not only losing their money and their place in line, but also their irreplaceable documents.[57]

For some, the establishment of the Social Support Fund for Mexican Ex–Migrant Workers and the latest registration periods signaled the final chapter of the BJM. However, this was not the end for Bracero Proa; there were still thousands of ex-bracero families that did not have official proof that they or their family members had been braceros. Without the documents, they were left with nothing. These families formed the core of Bracero Proa's fight to broaden the scope of federally recognized bracero documents. They argued that documents such as official correspondence from employers and personal letters sent home by braceros should be recognized as proof. Furthermore, they asked the federal government to find or compile official lists of braceros through archival research in the Archivo General de la Nación, the U.S. National Archives, and the U.S. Agricultural Archives. Activists argued that the Mexican state should accept some of the burden of proof, instead of placing the responsibility solely on guest workers and their families. In the minds of activists in BJM, the state's strategy to refer to back wages as "social compensation" allowed activists to continue to work toward recovering those wages. Bracero Proa argued that since the funds were not recognized officially as back wages, the BJM could still work to recover those while accepting the funds already being offered. Thus, many activists continued the struggle.

Conflicts within the Bracero Justice Movement

As the movement developed, important and sometimes crippling internal conflicts arose. Tensions rooted in acts, and rumors of acts, by activists abusing power and taking advantage of ex-bracero families led to a general distrust in many guest-worker communities. Several groups splintered off from Bracero Proa when accusations of corruption arose, even though Bracero Proa publicly denounced organizers who behaved badly. The Bracero Proa leadership expelled activists for mismanaging funds or using the organization to advance personal political careers. Other activists left Bracero Proa because of interpersonal problems with the organization's leadership. In the first decade of the movement, Bracero Proa implemented a nonpartisan policy in both Mexico and the United States. This policy upset Mexican activists who believed that the BJM stood to benefit from an alignment with the Partido de la Revolución Democrática (PRD). These activists blamed the PAN for the government's inability to pay the ex-braceros what they were owed and believed the BJM needed to work aggressively against the PAN. They also blamed President Fox for prolonging the guest workers' struggle and saw his administration's stalling as a tough blow to the movement, as many ex-braceros and their wives literally could not wait any longer for the president to address the issue. On the Fox ranch, elderly protesters once again chanted, "*No más atole con el PAN*," highlighting that they were no longer willing to work with the PAN. The misuse of power spread across the board, within several ex-bracero organizations, and many people became disillusioned with the movement. Guest-worker communities encountered problems assessing the legitimacy of organizers and weeding out the genuine activists from those who were not. Tensions within the movement grew, as organizers fought to claim ground within the larger movement and fractures surfaced within Bracero Proa.

Among those whose presence in the movement exacerbated these fractures, Carlos Marentes stood as one of the most controversial figures. Marentes had long worked for labor and immigration rights on the border, primarily through the El Paso–based organization Unión Sin Fronteras. During the early 1990s, he and his colleague Enrique Lomas began an initiative to recognize ex-bracero contributions. By the end of the decade, they had amassed a large collection of bracero contracts and identification cards. Guest workers and their families willingly gave this material to Marentes, because he had told them he was working to establish a monument, and potentially a museum, in homage to braceros, as well as establish a "Bracero Day." Furthermore, he established the Bracero Project as an initiative to promote the recognition of the historical contribution of braceros. From 1996 to 1997, Marentes and Lomas worked with over 300 ex-braceros in the states of Coahuila and Chihuahua. In 1997, Marentes created a web-based work entitled "Las Raices del Trabajador Agrícola [The Roots of the Agricultural Worker]," focused on the history of the Bracero Program. On November 22, 1997, Bracero Day was celebrated, with approximately 250 people turning up to pay homage to ex-braceros in a ceremony that included handing out diplomas and a banquet.[58] Enrique Lomas passed away in

1998, but Marentes continued working on the project. Marentes collected even more bracero documents through PRI support. Although Lomas was adamantly against the PRI, Marentes had formed a relationship with the party, from which he received support for his project.[59]

Although he declined to work with Gutiérrez, Marentes continued to collect more and more bracero documents. His collection later complicated bracero communities' perception of the Smithsonian Institution's Bracero History Project because they assumed that it coincided with Marentes's project; this led many ex-braceros to view the Smithsonian project skeptically.[60] While collecting oral histories and scanning documents for the Bracero History Project, I encountered many individuals who were wary of sharing their documents with me. To quell their apprehensions, I scanned documents directly in front of them, so that their documents were always in plain view. One ex-bracero in Monterrey recalled that when he gave Marentes his documents in the 1990s, he never imagined that braceros would actually see monetary compensation for the 10 percent that was taken from them. For this ex-bracero, his documents were just old pieces of paper that were no longer useful to him.[61] When the Mexican government finally published payment requirements, individuals from guest-worker communities pleaded with Marentes to return their documents, since one of the central requirements for compensation was the presentation of original identification, a contract, or a pay stub. For several days in March 2006, approximately 200 to 300 individuals lined up outside of Marentes's office in an effort to recover their documents and register for payouts from the Mexican Congress.[62] Marentes declined to give the documents to anyone other than the original owner, but in many cases in which the guest worker had passed away, the ex-bracero's wife or children asked Marentes to turn the documents over to them. This became particularly problematic when the Mexican government allowed widows and children of guest workers to claim the government payout owed to their husband or father; these documents became central to a family's claim.

In a protest on August 4, 2008, a group of women who wanted their family members' documents demonstrated against Marentes, hoping to warn others about his collection and his refusal to return these papers. Marentes's followers—media coverage reported that they were predominantly male—confronted this group by calling the women "*marijuanas* [stoners]" and "*borrachas* [drunks]."[63] Women staked their claims as "daughters" of braceros and demanded that more be done. In his own defense, Marentes stated, "I've never let down the people."[64] Marentes also accused the PAN of giving priority to payouts for the communities of ex-braceros who supported the PAN, such as those in Guanajuato, Jalisco, and Queretaro.[65] His early alignments with the PRI made activists in Monterrey suspicious of his role within the BJM. Politics aside, many within the bracero community were generally suspicious of government officials, as they felt that their wage theft was a direct result of a corrupt government.

Interpersonal conflicts with leadership caused several organizers to leave Bracero Proa. Baldomero Capiz left in 2001 and, along with several others, established La Unión Binacional de Ex-Braceros in Los Angeles. Interpersonal conflicts between Ventura Gutiérrez and Rosa Marta Zárate caused a large gendered split as several women followed Zárate and formed La Alianza de Ex-Braceros del Norte in 2007.[66] Under Zárate's leadership, BJM's networks extended further into Washington, Nevada, and Arizona.[67] She claimed that in Mexico many unscrupulous lawyers offered their services in exchange for exorbitant fees, which they wanted to charge to each ex-bracero, promising that they would be able to ensure the return of their back wages. After Wells Fargo proved that they in fact had sent the money to Mexico, she felt that much of the organizing should focus on public action in Mexico. By the time she started her own group, she explained that since the focus had moved to Mexico, her organization would deal mainly with bracero communities on the U.S. side of the border. Zárate stated, "We saw that in the movement a lot of attention was given to braceros in Mexico, and no one was responding to the concrete reality of the braceros residing in the United States. They needed to go and register in Mexicali or in their hometowns without transportation, the physically disabled *señores*, with no money . . . and some with no papers."[68] Bracero communities involved with La Unión Binacional de Ex-Braceros and La Alianza de Ex-Braceros del Norte continued to focus their public demonstrations in front of Mexican consul offices in cities such as Los Angeles and San Diego.

The Bracero Justice Movement and Zapatismo

Various organizations within the BJM found support in the Zapatista movement. Zapatistas understood that these movements crossed paths, as the state strove to erase the historical claims of both indigenous communities and guest-worker communities.[69] Of course, as I have recounted, the communities were not mutually exclusive, given that indigenous populations also participated in the program and joined the BJM. In September 2005, Bracero Proa held a press conference in San Cristóbal de las Casas, Chiapas, announcing its alignment with the EZLN and with La Otra Campaña (The Other Campaign).[70] La Otra Campaña aimed to create coalitions between marginalized groups committed to promoting social change outside of electoral politics. Both organizations experienced a deep disillusionment with electoral politics, feeling that the Mexican political establishment did not work to address their needs. Bracero Proa and the Zapatistas felt that their situations had come about because of an ethically bankrupt political system in which the Mexican government did not protect the interests of its own citizens but instead folded under U.S. imperial demands. Both of these groups acknowledged the Bracero Program as one example of this capitulation. Ventura Gutiérrez, as well as the leadership of other ex-bracero organizations, pursued efforts to incorporate ex-bracero activists into La Otra Campaña. Leadership in Bracero Proa traveled from various states in Mexico and the United States to assist Zapatista-led workshops in Chiapas. Organizer Alba Nidia Rubio Leyva cites these workshops as a central experience for her, indelibly shaping her sense of social justice and the strong ties between the activist struggles of indigenous communities in Mexico and those of the ex-braceros.[71]

Although Bracero Proa created ties with the EZLN, the Asamblea Nacional de Ex Braceros (ANB) was the closest ally of La Otra Campaña. Established in 2003 in Tlaxcala, the ANB was led by Luz Rivera and created chapters in six Mexican states. Felipe Muñoz Pavón, a founding member of the ANB, explained how the movement began in Tlaxcala: "It [news about the back wages] came out in a newspaper, in a Los Angeles newspaper. The article was acquired by the son of an ex-bracero, who sent it. He sent the newspaper to his father, who is from a town in Tlaxcala."[72] The ex-bracero, Maurelio, shared the news he received from his son with his *compadre* and Muñoz Pavón. Muñoz Pavón, in turn, told his neighbor and a nephew, both ex-braceros. The three of them proceeded to find others who had participated in the Bracero Program. Muñoz Pavón explained, "The three of us went to a loudspeaker to announce the news of the article that had come about braceros. If any *compañeros* present there . . . had been braceros, they should go to [Muñoz Pavón's home]. Well that's how it was . . . some came by."[73] The newly formed group sent members to government officials in the state of Tlaxcala to inquire about the back wages. Muñoz Pavón placed the onus directly on the Mexican government to identify those persons who were owed money. The government could have alerted ex-braceros about their withheld compensation through the radio or newspaper during the run of the program, Muñoz Pavón noted, but instead "the government kept silent."[74]

After many frustrated attempts, they decided to approach Luz Rivera, who agreed to assist them. As Muñoz Pavón recounted, "We are very grateful, she was interested in helping us. She, herself, made us, not all of us but some of us, tell others, every township of Tlaxcala. . . . Groups went to distinct . . . municipalities."[75] At the first meeting, about fifty men attended; by the eighth meeting, over 5,000 ex-braceros were there.[76] Chapters soon developed in Tlaxcala, Guerrero, Oaxaca, San Luis Potosí, Jalisco, Hidalgo, and el Estado de México. Organizers also focused on bringing ex-bracero communities together for meetings and protests. They protested at: Los Pinos (the president's residence), el Zócalo, la Ciudadela, la Cámara de Diputados, Gobernación, and El Banco Nacional de México. During all of these travels, "everyone paid their travel fare, their expenses and copies. . . . What helped us a lot is that the *licenciada* [Luz Rivera] didn't charge, we didn't give her anything. We still haven't given her anything. . . . That helped us a lot, that she didn't receive a dime from us."[77] Instead they pitched in money to cover the travel costs of representatives to take paperwork to the state capital and Mexico City. They even went so far as to send a team, which included Muñoz Pavón, to the Archivo General de la Nación to conduct research on the whereabouts of their savings. Muñoz Pavón explained, "All of that contributed to the government taking precautions."[78] The staff of the archives eventually denied entry to the research team, and Muñoz Pavón believes it was at the request of government officials in higher positions of power.

Soon after, the EZLN came out strongly in support of the ANB. In February 2006, Subcomandante Marcos, head of the EZLN, asked that ex-braceros unite with him on a march during El Día del Trabajo (Labor Day). To be sure, these were not mutually exclusive communities.[79] At a meeting of the ANB, Subcomandante Marcos articulated what ex-braceros had told him, "Hey, *sub*, they treat us like we are old wrapping paper in this system, as if we were an old piece of furniture that no longer works, and they have us in a corner, waiting to see if the animal eats us or the climate ruins us; like we are put aside, hindering them. And we weren't born elderly. We worked and we worked hard, generating riches and now we are not useful, they want to put us aside, they want to kill us."[80] The ex-braceros felt as if the Mexican government had pushed aside their demands, hoping and waiting for more of these men and their widows to pass away soon. Identifying with this sinister form of state silencing by slow attrition, the Zapatistas viewed the plight of the ex-bracero as similar to their own. During a large meeting of the ANB, Delegado Zero, a representative of the EZLN, illustrated how the experiences of ex-braceros resonated with those of the Zapatistas: "Like [they do with] the indigenous people, they are waiting until we disappear, for us to die like Indian people, for us to lament our color, our language, our culture. That is how they are waiting for the older generation, the braceros who were in the United States, to die and then the problem with you will cease."[81] Delegado Zero drew upon the intersections between oppressive labor and racial structures that relegate this exploited class of workers to a problem of the past that the state wants to forget. He also points to the overlapping narratives of racial marginalization, explaining that ex-braceros are made to lament their "color," suggesting that they were exploited because of race. The statement serves as a challenge to the national project of mestizaje and reveals its failure in establishing political and economic equality. His use of "they" recognizes a ruling class that has distanced itself from indigeneity. Delegado Zero makes visible that color—that is, indigenous ancestry—unites Zapatista indígenas, braceros mestizos, and finally bracero indígenas. Just as the Zapatista movement strove to expose the contemporary marginalization of indigenous communities in their efforts to gain autonomy, Delegado Zero called for a reexamination of the disposability of these guest workers in order to address their claims.

The Legal Battle in the United States

The question of the legal rights of ex-braceros in the United States remained unanswered. In 2008, the American-based Mexico Solidarity Network sought to call attention to the plight of the ex-braceros by arranging a speaking tour for ex-bracero Felipe Muñoz Pavón. During the tour, Muñoz Pavón asked American college students to put their energy toward pressuring their government to intercede on behalf of ex-braceros. But neither the Mexico Solidarity Network nor Muñoz Pavón were fully aware that the Chicago law firm of Hughes, Socol, Piers, Resnick, and Dym had already settled a class-action lawsuit with the Mexican government. In the early years of the BJM, leaders such as Ventura Gutiérrez communicated with lawyers at this law firm, but the communication became strained due to the slow pace of court proceedings. Years earlier, in 2001, the law firm had filed a class-action lawsuit on behalf of a former bracero against Wells Fargo, which was responsible for withholding the savings from laborers' paychecks and transferring the money to Mexican authorities. The law firm had garnered a national reputation for working on high-profile social justice and civil rights cases. Its lawyers first heard about the issue from paralegal Raúl

Ross during a suit against Money Gram and Western Union for inflating currency conversion and fees, which specifically affected migrant workers in the United States who were sending money to their families in Mexico and Central America.[82]

Ross initially became aware of the plight of the ex-braceros when individuals in the money-transfer suit approached him with questions about the legal avenues for ex-bracero communities. Although the lawyers were unsure of the outcome, the firm felt compelled to accept the challenge of settling one of the largest cases of withheld back wages for guest workers.[83] The case represented a complex legal puzzle that involved countless hours of investigation and transnational archival research. In the course of pursuing their investigation, the lawyers sought to find the withheld back wages and identify legal avenues to force those who had them to fulfill the terms of the original bracero contracts. In the early years of this research, Bracero Proa had more contact with the law firm, but by the time lawyer Joshua Karsh began working on the case in 1999, contact between the lawyers and activists had dwindled. For Karsh, there did seem to be a disconnect between the American class-action suit and the social movement headed by ex-bracero organizations, as there was little communication between them in the final period.[84]

One of the first major challenges to the case was the statute of limitations, which threatened to end the whole enterprise of winning the back wages, but the law firm's lawyers overcame this hurdle. They proposed and got passed a statute at the General Assembly in California stating that any claims filed by December 2005 would be deemed timely. This statute gave them the opportunity to get past the statute of limitations and present the case in the U.S. District Court in the Northern District of California in San Francisco. Although they could have chosen to file the case in various district courts across the country, they chose this district court in Northern California because of its liberal reputation.[85] They proceeded with a lawsuit against Wells Fargo because it had, at the time, been responsible for deducting and holding the original 10 percent of the braceros' wages. Despite this, the case was dismissed on August 23, 2002, after Judge Charles R. Breyer found that lawyers had failed to state a convincing claim against the bank.[86] The firm attempted to get the ruling overturned, but in June 2003 Judge Breyer let it stand.[87] Wells Fargo provided the evidence that the bank had transferred the funds to the Mexican government through the Banco Nacional de Crédito Rural.

The law firm proceeded with the lawsuit, believing it could hold accountable the Banco Nacional de Crédito Rural and the Patronato del Ahorro Nacional. The lawyers presented that case to Judge Charles R. Breyer, who needed to determine what body of law applied to this case: Would it be Mexican law, international law, or California state law? Judge Breyer explained the complexity of the case: "Defendants Banco Nacional de Credito Rural, S.A. and Patronato del Ahorro Nacional move for dismissal arguing that the exercise of personal jurisdiction over them would be unconstitutional. Plaintiffs reply that, as instrumentalities of Mexico, the defendant banks are not 'persons' within meaning of Due Process Clause."[88] On March 30, 2005, Judge Breyer dismissed the case, believing that the matter would be best handled through Mexican law. Judge Breyer stated:

> The Court agrees with defendants that Mexico has a more significant relationship to the parties and the alleged wrongs. Although the labor producing the savings funds was performed in the United States (and partially in California), plaintiffs were at the time of employment Mexican citizens who, pursuant to the braceros' individual contracts, were required to return to Mexico in order to recover the funds. Defendants are, of course, located in Mexico and the alleged refusal to return the savings funds is occurring in Mexico. Taken together both the parties and the claimed wrongs have a more significant relationship with Mexico than with California.[89]

Through Mexican law, the law firm would have little recourse because the Mexican statute of limitations could limit legal resolution in that country. Lawyer Joshua Karsh feared taking the case through the Mexican judicial system, because there seemed to be very few allies in Mexico.[90] Luckily, Judge Breyer stated that California held an interest in the outcome as it was still home to a significant population affected by the case. This statement provided the cornerstone for the firm to return to court and argue that the case needed to be heard in California under state law because the outcome bore significant consequences for California residents.

The law firm began negotiations with the Mexican federal government, and on October 10, 2008, it received preliminary approval from the federal court for the settlement. The Mexican government would admit no wrongdoing, but offered ex-braceros who had worked in the United States from 1942 to 1946 an opportunity to register for the same compensation their Mexican counterparts had received. A registration period was set from October 23, 2008, to January 5, 2009. As long as ex-braceros residing in the United States met the requirements established in Mexico, and had not already registered in Mexico, they were eligible to receive this money in the United States.[91] At the time of Muñoz Pavón's speaking tour, the law firm sent out a call to all ex-braceros residing in the United States who could be included in the settlement. It tapped into Latino television networks and newspapers, hoping more ex-braceros would join the settlement.

On February 6, 2009, a fairness hearing took place in the U.S. District Court of Northern California. The members of the class-action lawsuit were given the opportunity to voice any objections to the settlement. The legal adviser for the Mexican Ministry of Foreign Affairs, Joel Hernández, stated, "We are happy that we were able to reach a settlement agreement with the plaintiffs. We think it's very important to reach that stage in order to make it possible that any potential applicant may file an application for social support."[92] The media coverage of this settlement, as well as the official website for the bracero legal representation, claimed that those eligible for monetary compensation were ex-braceros who worked from 1942 to 1946. But, according to Verónica Cortez, legal assistant for the law firm Hughes, Socol, Piers, Resnick, and Dym, the Mexican government asked that the lawyers only publicize a call for ex-braceros who worked from 1942 to 1946, although they could include guest workers who came after that period in the settlement.[93] Mexican officials asked that this request not be made public, for fear of facing an overwhelming number of plaintiffs. Furthermore, the Mexican government continued to frame the monetary compensation as social support, since the meager $3,500 represented much less than the actual 10 percent of the wages withheld within this period.

The Battle Continues

Despite the distance, ex-braceros such as Antonio Aragón in southern Mexico worked alongside women like Rubio Leyva in the northern areas and American-based organizers like Ventura Gutiérrez. They phoned, emailed, and networked in their efforts to recuperate the back wages. Organizations, such as the ANB, La Unión Binacional de Ex-Braceros, and La Alianza de Ex-Braceros del Norte, also played key roles in the BJM. They called attention to the exploitation experienced by the ex-braceros and the injustice inherent in the denial of their back wages. Though their efforts are unfortunately incomplete, and activists are still working toward the full recovery of wages for all ex-braceros, they won more than just partial victories of monetary and social resources for ex-bracero communities.

The BJM called for further attention to the historical importance of the Bracero Program and the contributions ex-braceros had made to Mexico and the United States. The "official" acknowledgment of the Bracero Program triggered community examinations of the hardships and exploitation that ex-braceros endured. Narratives about families were used to humanize these men. These narratives were juxtaposed with images and stories of alienation, toxic DDT sprays, and unchecked labor exploitation, in order to disrupt logics that naturalize their bodies as "beasts of burden." To this end, the BJM furthered a platform and multiple avenues for guest workers' families to connect with each other and publicly acknowledge the impact of the Bracero Program on their lives. Although communities could not right the wrongs committed against ex-braceros in the past, they could work toward a more just treatment of the plight of these men in the present. Through the BJM, entire families fought alongside one another to address the injustice experienced by ex-braceros and its lingering consequences. These communities defiantly transformed the image of a generation of single, migratory laborers, cast adrift to the north and forgotten in the south, into a population of men and women attached to local and transnational communities, fiercely committed to protecting the contemporary interests of these guest laborers and their families.

Rooted in indigenous radical politics of Zapatismo, *la política de la dignidad* recognizes the racist ideologies behind the Bracero Program that placed these men in exploitative positions. Through these politics, the BJM focuses on much more than back wages. It uses tropes of family to incriminate a government that "sold" its sons and did not protect them abroad. It is a politics that constantly grapples with the past to make arguments about a corrupt and failing government in the present. Shaped by the rhetoric of Zapatista's indigenous modernities and autonomy, activists with the BJM critique the Mexican government's treatment of indigenous and campesino communities. Through *la política de la dignidad*, the BJM purposely builds historical narratives around the exploitative plight of braceros, leaving narratives about adventure and pleasure on the sidelines, in order to shed light on the Mexican conditions that led to the program and an American labor system unwilling to accept culpability for creating waves of Mexican guest workers and undocumented labor.

INTERLUDE Performing Masculinities

One of my most memorable experiences collecting oral histories was
the day I recorded my Tío Juan as part of the Bracero History Project.
This was not the first time he served as my interviewee. He recalled an
oral history assignment that I carried out as an undergrad. But this time
it was different. We sat in a conference room at the National Museum
of Mexican Art in Chicago with a fancy recording device between us.
Somewhere between the questions and the answers, I got a glimpse of
how my Tío Juan made sense of this period in his life. I had grown up
hearing some of the stories of his time as a bracero, but I have to admit
that I did not know all of the ones he told that day. He enrolled in the
program as a single eighteen year old, and I could tell that he wanted
to demonstrate that during those years he was the dutiful eldest son by
saying, "Every fifteen days I sent my mother as much as I could."[1] In the
arc of his life story, it would be these qualities that would lead him to
become a good father, brother, uncle, and patriarch.

When I asked about leisure, he brought the interview back to themes
of labor and sacrifice, asserting, "I never went out to a movie or to a
dancehall or to hang out in town. I only went to buy clothes or buy food;
that was all. But that I would say, 'Right now, today, I will go to this fiesta,
today I will go to the rodeo,' no. During that time I absolutely deprived
myself of every kind of diversion."[2] Fun and enjoyable moments could
not coexist with this particular narrative about exploitative work, medical
exams, racial segregation, and a deep sense of alienation. I have listened
to the interview countless times and talked to other family members.
From them, I have heard stories about different periods of my Tío's life.
They tell stories about my Tío wearing fashionable clothes to the *baile*,

169

the dancehall, when he was a youngster in Mexico and then again when he settled in Chicago. They describe my uncle as a youth who enjoyed a late-night party. I have tried to make sense of these two very different portrayals of who my uncle is. And I have come to believe that my uncle did not lie to me about his experience as a bracero. What he did is render memories that allowed him to perform a particular masculinity, the version of manhood rooted in family and sacrifice that the program promoted. The traumatic exploitation he experienced could not coexist with leisure and pleasure in this narrative about the program. It was as if acknowledging enjoyment had the potential to dilute the pain and alienation he wanted to express. He created a narrative arc about his life that allows him to make sense of these experiences and, in turn, tell the version of this period in his life that he wants me to remember. While some braceros remembered the program in a similar manner, luckily others did not. Some treated the interview as a confession, while other approached it as a survey. Certainly most braceros were not facing their kin armed with a recorder.

EPILOGUE

Representing Memory: Braceros in the Archive and Museum

Hubo momentos de gusto, alegría, conocimientos, pero también hubo momentos de tristeza y de ser imponente [impotente] por no poder hacer algo para remediar la situación. (There were moments of joy, happiness, and knowledge, but there were also moments of sadness, of being impotent because nothing could be done to remedy the situation.)

—FELIPE MUÑOZ PAVÓN

[Memory] has come to resemble the revenge of the underdog or injured party, the outcast, the history of those denied the right to History.

—PIERRE NORA

In the spring of 2005, the National Museum of American History (NMAH) created a consortium of institutions to preserve the history of bracero communities in Mexico and the United States. The NMAH had acquired a strong collection of images of the Bracero Program taken by the photographer Leonard Nadel in 1956, but now the museum sought to expand its physical collection while also creating a digital archive of bracero documents and oral histories. The Bracero History Consortium developed the Bracero History Project, which resulted in the Bracero History Archive and NMAH's exhibition, "Bittersweet Harvest: The Bracero Program, 1946–1964." Both of these would mediate the memories of bracero communities for the general public's understanding of the Bracero Program. This project contributed to the creation of a "public memory" of Mexican guest workers, while also contributing to a national political dialogue about guest workers in the United States, as part of a potential solution to immigration reform.

The political discussions that lie at the core of public memory about the Bracero Program reveal the inherent contradictions of a social system. As John Bodnar explains, "Public Memory is produced from a political discussion that involves not so much specific economic or moral problems but rather fundamental issues about the entire existence of a society: its organization, structure of power, and the very meaning of its past and present."[1] Public memory around the Bracero Program highlighted the tension between the guest workers' relationship to the nation and the human-rights abuses and exploitative labor practices they experienced in the United States because they were not American citizens. If, as former President Bush claimed, the temporary worker took the jobs that U.S. citizens deemed undesirable, then the real problem with exploitative work and the capitalist desire for a class or workforce without rights would not need to be addressed. Bracero public memory calls attention to already-existing questions about the role of Mexican immigrants in the United States and the limited rights guest workers have in a nation addicted to cheap labor and reluctant to provide the protection to this class of workers that it accords to its own citizens. There can be no pathway for incorporation or citizenship for these workers, as that would be both counterproductive and a potential liability for a system that is reluctant to revise its labor practices. Residency and citizenship would mean that these workers would have more legal avenues to resist exploitation and employers would not be able to use the fear of deportation to create a docile workforce. Guest workers have to stand apart from discourses of undocumented migration because their authorized entry makes them the ideal "tractable workforce."[2]

Curators in the Bracero History Project strove to preserve and display the history of the Bracero Program within the parameters of a traveling exhibit and the politics of commemoration, while keeping a keen eye on the exploitative aspects of the program. For the exhibit, deviancy would have to be intentionally curated out. For example, complicated stories that showed how individuals could oscillate between being documented and undocumented could make it more difficult to commemorate their contribution. They could not recognize larger trends of bracerismo, that is, the formal and informal ways Mexican workers entered the United States, or even the reality that the term "braceros" had been used before the program to refer to Mexican laborers.[3] Furthermore, including deviancy or subjects who could not be contained by the logics of patriarchal mestizaje could potentially challenge the logic that these heroic patriarchs came to work in order to send back remittances. Highlighting themes of adventure and pleasure might seem offensive to the very communities at the core of this history, bracero communities who were entrenched in narratives about exploitation. These decisions were carefully made as curators toed the line between creating a history that appealed to a general audience and keeping a critical eye on the gross human-rights violations braceros experienced.

What was clear to me while collecting oral histories was that the curators were committed to creating an exhibit narrative that highlighted the governmental role in creating policy that shaped immigration patterns. They wanted to challenge the idea that waves of Mexican immigrants came to the United States as undocumented workers by highlighting a period in which Mexicans were sought out as guest workers. The archive, on the other hand, could provide the flexibility and an opportunity that the exhibit—with its limited panels, words, and images—could not. The archive could also depart from the politics of commemoration that required the subjects that were included to be appropriate and respectable. It could contain the stories and images of illicit spaces and experiences, and it was not constrained by issues of morality. It could chronicle defiance through the fluidity of oral history. The potential vastness of the archive could provide complexity that the exhibit and the collective memory produced by the Bracero Justice Movement could not.

When the NMAH began the Bracero History Project, ex-braceros were already engaged in the struggle to retrieve their garnished pay. Their "savings" became both the material and the symbolic heart of the Bracero Justice Movement as activists worked toward recuperating this money. By the early 2000s, several other ex-bracero organizations had also emerged to create the Bracero Justice Movement. Public-history efforts then coalesced with activist efforts, as the Bracero History Project utilized the networks and communities created and reinvigorated by the Bracero Justice Movement to access ex-braceros and their families in order to preserve oral histories, digitize documents, and collect objects. They purposely excluded workers who had never come under temporary labor contracts—that is, men who had labored solely as undocumented workers.

NMAH curators, the Bracero Justice Movement, and policy makers thus have engaged in the solidification of a "bracero" identity that purposely divorces itself from that of the undocumented laborer. But, acknowledging that the flow of Mexican temporary workers was intricately tied to that of undocumented workers, or how easy it was to move in and out of these categories, would have made creating a cohesive narrative about bracero history difficult. The stories of men like Luis Barocio Ceja, who labored in the United States throughout the duration of the program as a bracero and occasionally as an undocumented worker, were left out of the history presented to the public. While his experience as a bracero could be told and retold to provide a cohesive narrative, the contradiction of entering as an undocumented worker could not be as easily acknowledged. His bracero subjectivity marked him in valuable ways, while his subjectivity as an undocumented worker was counterproductive to these political projects. This distinction is further problematized by the contemporary undocumented children and grandchildren of ex-braceros who followed their routes north.

The Bracero Justice Movement drew lines between undocumented laborers and braceros to strengthen legal claims to back wages, while policy makers propped up the program as a way to address the need for laborers in undesirable work areas and to address employers' interests in immigration reform. The Smithsonian Institution, for its part, received heavy criticism in the 1990s from Latinos for its failure to include them in any of the museum's collections, and the Bracero History Project, encompassing both the exhibit and the archive, quickly became one among many projects attempting to rectify this absence.[4] This process has helped shape the collective memory of braceros, where the divide between authorized and unauthorized migration became necessary. Unlike braceros' individual memories, the collective memory highlights the uniqueness of the guest workers' experiences without including stories of adventure, desire, pleasure, and bracero difference. Politically, deviance and pleasure could detract attention from the high degree of exploitation they suffered and the state's complicity in alienating these men. Thus, the nuances of regional, cultural, racial, and ethnic difference become less important in the collective memory of braceros. The collective narrative is part of a political project that is attempting to reinsert the bracero into Mexican and American national narratives; even as it may seem inclusionary, this narrative, like national narratives, has rested on exclusions.

The efforts to view documented and undocumented workers as distinctly separate groups drew on key moments of the Mexican guest-worker experience that contrasted with the perceived narrative journey of undocumented workers. Leonard Nadel, whose work provided the visual cornerstone of the exhibit, illustrated the plight of the Mexican guest worker through photography.[5] Although he documented the family lives of braceros, the contracting process, and the work conditions, the images that are most widely circulated include those that draw visual distinctions between the bracero and the undocumented worker: conditions in recruitment centers, medical exams, DDT sprayings, and closed work sites. These images provided a visual to key components of the bracero narrative that, as one guest worker argued, everyone "needed to go through to become braceros."[6] This process became a rite of passage for migrant workers who claimed a bracero identity. During the process of documenting bracero oral histories, many elderly men pulled out bracero identifications from their wallets as proof that they had, in fact, entered the United States as guest workers at some point. The flexible lines between the documented bracero and the undocumented Mexican laborer were drawn darker by the museum's efforts to focus on braceros, and by braceros distinguishing themselves as a separate class of workers. In many ways, the figure of the "legal" bracero becomes a foil to the "undocumented" worker, and thus places the guest worker in higher regard.[7] Even if the same bracero eventually became an undocumented worker, his needed labor as a guest worker discursively justified his presence in the United States, and for all of these political projects he was forever marked as a bracero.

Ultimately, all of these discussions were rooted in discourses that created a respectable bracero subject in contrast to the undocumented subject, whose entry to the United States is viewed by many as criminal and thus an indication of moral character. For public historians, deeming these men "good" subjects validates their worthiness for commemoration in American history. The worth of their very humanity is framed through their labor and its relationship to family, as if without these they would be considered less valuable. The collective public narratives that can arise from this context are limited by these parameters. As Lisa Cacho explains, for certain racially undesirable populations, their humanity is represented as something that one becomes, achieves, or earns because it cannot just be.[8] For migrant laborers, their place in American public life could be earned through "legal" entry and work. Braceros experienced the dehumanization of existing as "arms" of labor only to have their humanity restored in the contemporary period by NMAH through narratives that stressed their legal entry to the United States and their "lawful" contribution as laborers. The possibility of replicating the Bracero Program as a solution to immigration reform rests on untangling a vision of a temporary work program from narratives of illegality and its perceived immorality, with immigration reform presented as a type of "reward." A temporary work program would have to be detached from the immorality and criminality of undocumented labor in order to gain wider acceptance. The false logic that the exhibit presented is that lawful entry leads to entry into public life and public history, because the Bracero Program was ultimately a guest-worker program in which "guests" eventually returned to their homes. These tensions between the exhibit and the archive center on the aims of each and the politics of commemoration, which the exhibit cannot escape. Even as these nonconformist narratives did not make their way into the exhibit, deviance and contemporary immigration debates colored the reactions of some visitors.

From Archive to Exhibit

On September 9, 2009, the exhibition "Bittersweet Harvest: The Bracero Program, 1942–1964" opened at the National Museum of American History. Peter Liebhold, curator at NMAH, described the exhibit as "modest but powerful."[9] It consisted of fifteen freestanding banners with bilingual text and images and two audio stations. At the NMAH, curators added objects and images to the opening show that would not travel to other venues hosting the exhibit. The team of curators working on "Bittersweet Harvest" consciously decided to simplify the traveling exhibit so that more institutions could afford the shipping and other costs associated with hosting. They suggested that other institutions collect objects that would illustrate their local bracero history to add to "Bittersweet Harvest" when hosting the exhibit. The topic of the show and the affordable cost stirred so much interest in the exhibition that the NMAH created a duplicate to simultaneously travel to additional venues. Institutions in the Southwest, South, Midwest, and East Coast agreed to host the traveling exhibit through 2015.

Because the oral histories could not anchor the exhibit visually, curators drew on the Leonard Nadel collection in the NMAH archives. Nadel had been deeply moved and inspired by Ernesto Galarza's political vision of documenting exploitation in the Bracero Program, which led him to retrace some of Galarza's research footsteps.[10] A grant from the Fund for the Republic allowed him to expand this vision by traveling to Mexico and documenting the journey of braceros, from their sending communities, through contracting sites, working in fields in the United States, and enjoying limited leisure time in labor camps and towns in California. He began his six-month trip in the summer of 1956.[11] Nadel's images anchored not only the exhibit, but also the digital archive, as they provided a visual representation of bracero experiences.

Nadel was clearly fascinated with camp life, though it would not be apparent to someone who only saw the NMAH exhibit. The most-circulated images are those tied to the contracting process and labor, while those left in the margins are the images depicting braceros in the private homosocial spaces of the camp or at rest. His full collection features dozens of photographs of braceros lounging on their beds, playing cards, and smoking cigarettes

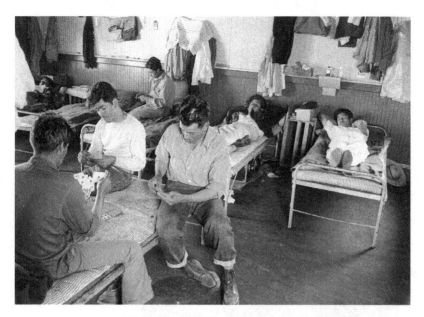

ILLUSTRATION 11 Leonard Nadel, "Braceros Playing Cards." Leonard Nadel Bracero Photographs, Archives Center, National Museum of American History, Smithsonian Institution.

(ill. 11). These images depict the bracero body not as arms of labor, but as sexualized subjects with potential desires and participating in acts of rest and pleasure. These images do not entirely support a respectable image of braceros, nor do they tell the story of "exploitation and opportunity" that ended up becoming the theme of the exhibit.

Instead, the exhibit and the public-history project's promotional materials featured images of Nadel that both critiqued the high level of exploitation these workers experienced in the Bracero Program and highlighted the opening it provided for entry into the United States. Curators chose aesthetically appealing images, such as a photograph that depicts one bracero as a contented worker casually resting a *cortito*, a short-handled hoe, over his shoulder (ill. 12). His Mexican hat complements his American work jacket as he smiles subtly for the camera. The careful composition of the photograph communicates a type of organization and structure in his labor. Both his attire and his carefully combed, coiffed hair present him in a light of respectable masculinity. He seems content to have the short handle, an object that requires the user to bend over and causes a tremendous amount of pain. Supervisors in the fields liked the short handle hoe because they could look down the row and spot anyone who stopped working and stood up.[12]

ILLUSTRATION 12

Leonard Nadel, "Short Handle Hoe." Leonard Nadel Bracero Photographs, Archives Center, National Museum of American History, Smithsonian Institution.

In Cesar Chavez's vivid words, "The short hoe is the nail they use to hang us from the cross."[13] The aesthetic appeal of the photograph seems to be the worker's face, framed by the field and the *cortito*. Bound by the parameters of the exhibition, curators juxtaposed that image with an enlarged photograph of men going through DDT sprayings and in contracting centers, providing an implicit critique of the program.

Curators were committed to also highlighting that ex-braceros who put down roots in the United States were the fathers, grandfathers, and great-grandfathers of a generation of Mexican Americans. Some stayed in the United States as undocumented workers, while others found avenues to obtain residency and even U.S. citizenship. They provided a counternarrative that aimed to challenge perceptions that all contemporary Mexican American immigrant families came to the United States "illegally" by highlighting this period of massive authorized entry into the country. In this way, the curators made the line between historically documented braceros and contemporary undocumented communities more flexible.

Some who attended the opening of the "Bittersweet Harvest" exhibit felt moved by the Leonard Nadel images and the objects collected, such as bunk beds from a labor camp that had housed braceros. Hilda Solis, the U.S. labor secretary at the time of the exhibit, sobbed during the opening of the exhibit as she stated, "My father was a bracero."[14] As the official voice on labor policy in the United States, she was emotionally shaken by the images of the exploitation that people like her father had faced. She would later overturn many of the Bush-era policies on Mexican guest workers entering the United States with H-2A visas.[15] Her own family history highlighted the strong ties many Mexican American families have to the Bracero Program. Indeed, the comment books at the exhibition are filled with statements from visitors who, like Hilda Solis, have uncles, fathers, and grandfathers who were braceros.[16] Those guests saw the NMAH exhibit as legitimating their own family histories. Graduate student Teresa Ramirez, for example, viewed "Bittersweet Harvest" shortly after it opened and was surprised to see an exhibit depicting such a controversial topic. The photographs and text moved her, as she thought of her own bracero grandfather working in the United States. As she explained to me, "I kept thinking about my grandfather stooped over in the fields."[17] She saved photographs of the exhibit on her camera for months after her visit as a reminder of her grandfather's struggles as a bracero, which she realized she had known so little about. These familial relations ignited affectual responses that critiqued the exploitation guest workers endured but also validated their sacrifice through narratives of family uplift and opportunity, embodied by someone like Hilda Solis, the daughter of a bracero who was able to rise to prominence in the U.S. government.

Although one of the goals of the "Bittersweet Harvest" exhibit was to examine the experience of bracero workers and their families in order to provide "rich insight into Mexican American history and historical background to today's debates on guest worker programs,"[18] the audience seemed less concerned with the contours of the Bracero Program and the differences between guest workers and other groups of migrant workers. According to an NMAH report that analyzes the exhibit comment books, "Quite unexpectedly, the perception of the Bracero Program itself received very little attention from the visitors in their comments."[19] Rather, many of the comments reflected current concerns with immigration, to the degree that "a surprising number of people used the term 'immigrant' to address a guest worker."[20] They preferred to see these men as "immigrants," implying that they came to the United States in order to build permanent lives in this

ILLUSTRATION 13 "Bittersweet Harvest" exhibition entry. Courtesy of the National Museum of American History, Smithsonian Institution.

country. While some men did settle in the United States, many other guest workers returned home. Despite the fact that the exhibit featured stories of men who went back to Mexico after the termination of the program, all were perceived as having settled in the United States. Visitors tied the experience of braceros to contemporary discussions on immigration reform, and guests from geographic areas where these debates are heated were more likely to leave a written response to the exhibit. By and large, the majority of those who chose to record comments about their experience visiting the exhibit in Washington, D.C., were from the southwestern United States.

A smaller number of visitors expressed outrage that the NMAH would create an exhibit about "illegal" Mexicans. Despite the carefully chosen words of curators like Stephen Velasquez, these braceros' contributions were lost when visitors did not read the text or listen to the audio stations. Braceros became conflated with any and all undocumented migrants from Mexico. To these visitors, the nuances of the guest-worker experience were lost. Although many visitors enjoyed the exhibit, there was a small group that felt insulted by the presence of the exhibit in the nation's history museum. Nineteen-year-old Samantha, from Montclair, Virginia, wrote, "I do not see the need for this when American citizens need work!! If they will come back as legal americans, then *GREAT*! Until then lets give the americans work in this economy, tax paying, law abiding americans."[21] Her logic as-

ILLUSTRATION 14 "Bittersweet Harvest" exhibition exit. Courtesy of the National Museum of American History, Smithsonian Institution.

sumes that there are only two statuses for Mexican migrants, "illegal" and "American." Here, "American" implies "legal" but excludes a myriad of possible statuses, such as "resident" and "guest worker." An anonymous visitor responded to Samantha's comment by writing directly underneath it, "Are 'Americans' willing to do back breaking work? I think not!" Another attendee wrote, "Amen Sista!"[22] This type of comment and response interaction was not unique; it was indicative of a broader public discussion concerning Mexican migration. The anonymous visitor considered the labor performed by undocumented workers to be labor that "Americans" are unwilling to perform, unintentionally agreeing with President Bush's justification for a guest-worker program that would allow migrants to take on labor roles that are perceived to be unwanted by the general population. The polemical discussion here says very little about the attendees' perceptions of the Bracero Program, communicating instead the present-day debate about the role of Mexican laborers in American society.

Rights bestowed by access to American citizenship also became central to the conversation, as visitors viewed Mexican immigrants as unwanted in a land that is not their own. Forty-eight-year-old Joe, of Paradise, California, explained, "I have always had great respect for people who are willing to work hard. I also have a duty to abide by the law. American citizens have rights. People who are not citizens do not have and should not be afforded the rights of citizens. People who break the law should be punished. People who are in this country illegally should be deported. Period."[23] According to Joe, undocumented migrants should not be granted the same protection under the law as citizens, as their very presence in the United States is implicitly "criminal." Criminalization here abrogates any human-rights protections under the law. Others went further and criminalized all Mexicans, regardless of citizenship status, demanding, "Send all Mexicans back to Mexico Now, Before It's Too Late!"

The exhibit provoked Helen from Washington, D.C., to personalize the way Mexican immigration affected her. She wrote, "I think that the US used guest workers because they were cheaper then [than] paying regular help. The practice has not helped me at all. They should stay in their own country and not hurt our wadges [wages]. It hurt my family because we lost our business."[24] A thirty-two-year-old Iraq veteran echoed Helen's concerns: "I lost my job, my home and my friends due to low cost labor. . . . I just can't figure it out anymore. Foreigners can get set up and I lose everything." Perhaps he viewed the conditions in the labor camps as tolerable or even comfortable, that the experience of braceros was not so bad, or perhaps he was responding to contemporary Mexican immigration, in which case he felt that he was the one being negatively impacted by this migration. Ultimately, he wrote, "I have nothing against anyone of any ethnic background or culture but, I blame the practices of are [our] government for allowing the labor or jobs [to] go for lower cost and cheap wages."[25]

These strong reactions point to how Latinos have become conflated with larger issues of immigration, perhaps justifying the curators' decision not to acknowledge the complicated nature of documented and undocumented migration during the Bracero Program. The importance of defining the history and role of braceros inadvertently centers on drawing lines of distinction between the "problem" of undocumented immigration and the "solution" that temporary labor programs offer, as well as the absolution that fails to call into question the systems of labor exploitation that created both. Ultimately, as David Lowenthal explains of Americans' sense of the past, "if recognizing the past's difference promoted its preservation, the act of preserving made that difference still more apparent."[26] Making migrant difference failed to recognize the fluidity of these roles and the complicated experience of the guest worker in the United States. The nature of commemorating has also caused a flattening of bracero difference with respect to race, class, gender, sexuality, and political worldviews. The goal of this book is not to pay homage to these guest workers but to humanize the experience of this community through a critical examination of the deviance and defiance of braceros. Their defiance opens up new avenues to think about state power and resistance that can dislodge mestizo and heteronormative tropes that rely on lauding particular types of masculinity and patriarchy.

Bracero Futures

The introduction of Mexican guest workers into the United States did not end in 1964, as employers found new ways to bring in Mexican laborers via temporary work contracts obtained through the H-2A visas specifically designated for agricultural work. A recent *Los Angeles Times* article profiled H-2A worker Rudolfo Benito Coy Garcia, who travels from Tamaulipas, Mexico, to work for the North Carolina Growers Association for ten months out of every year to help cultivate Christmas trees. He explains, "We come here to support our families and provide our kids with a better education."[27] Advocates of the growers' association report that most Americans quit working on these jobs within their first two days. Although Garcia faithfully completes his contracts, he has no chance of becoming a citizen in the country where he has spent most of his life.[28] Other guest workers in North Carolina defy the political parameters and join the unionizing efforts of the Farm Labor Organizing Committee, which in 2004 finally won the right to represent over 8,000 seasonal workers in the state.[29]

Not only has bracerismo masked itself through the United States' H-2A program, it has extended beyond the American border. Nearly a decade after the termination of the Bracero Program, Mexican laborers found themselves traveling even further north as the Mexican government brokered yet another deal, this time with the Canadian government, to allow brown bodies to continue picking produce. Every year, 17,000 laborers leave home to fulfill eight-month contracts, working seven days a week for ten or more hours a day in the fields and greenhouses of Canada.[30] Preference is once again given to married men with young children whose families reside in Mexico.[31] Family men—patriarchs—are again the prized workers as administrators believe affectual ties of kinship will ensure that these men return to their homeland. Once more, wages are withheld, placed in a Canadian pension fund, and available upon return to Mexico. A reporter for the *Washington Post* has described their conditions: "In Canada, the workers live like monks, sleeping in trailers or barracks, under contractual agreements that forbid them from drinking alcohol and having female visitors, or even socializing with other Mexican workers from different farms."[32] Their sexual life, social life, modes of pleasure, and movements are under strict control. It is as if the Canadian government and growers studied the Bracero Program and found a mechanism through which they could still further control men's bodies, making them more efficient arms of labor. Anthropologist Leigh Binford notes that, despite this, these workers "engage in erotic and sometimes emotional relationships with female Mexican migrants, local Mennonite women, prostitutes, and (occasionally) white Canadian females."[33] Their private spaces and social interactions mirror the homosocial spaces of the American Bracero Program, as these men resist total control by growers and the state.

Meanwhile, agricultural workers back in Mexico—specifically those labeled as the brownest, the marginal, the indigenous—continue to toil under degrading conditions in their homeland. The North American Free Trade Agreement ushered in a boom in industrialized agriculture in Mexico. The poorest of the poor need not seek agricultural exploitation by becoming contracted or undocumented laborers in the United States or Canada; they can find it in their home country. During an eighteen-month investigation of Mexican mega-farms, *Los Angeles Times* reporter Richard Marosi found that "many farm laborers are essentially trapped for months at a time in rat-infested camps, often without beds and sometimes without functioning toilets. Some camp bosses illegally withhold wages to prevent workers from leaving during peak harvest periods."[34] The worst companies are those that have been lauded by the Mexican government.[35] And, again, the Mexican government intercedes very little on behalf of these workers and has yet to address and truly integrate the indigenous in Mexico. The celebrated promises of mestizaje have once again failed the indigenous bodies that surface as those left on the fringes of the Mexican economy. The fruits of their labor arrive at our local Wal-Mart, Whole Foods, Subway, and Safeway, glistening, washed of the fingerprints of exploitation. The products that make their way into our lunch boxes and onto our dinner tables connect almost every American to indigenous Mexico. As for the guest workers in the United States and Canada, they are virtually citizens of no country as the Mexican government brokers their arms one at a time, hoping that they will send their remittances faithfully back to the families awaiting their return. Current guest workers are the metaphoric, but also literal, children and grandchildren of braceros in places like Tlaxcala, Mexico, who fight alongside their elders for back wages, reparations, recognition, and justice.

NOTES

ABBREVIATIONS USED IN NOTES

AGN   Archivo General de la Nación, Mexico City
ALM   Fondo Adolfo López Mateos
ARC   Fondo Adolfo Ruíz Cortínes
BHA   Bracero History Archive
EGP   Ernesto Galarza Papers, Special Collections and
      University Archives, Stanford University
IPS   Fondo Investigaciones Políticas y Sociales
MAC   Fondo Manuel Ávila Camacho
MAV   Fondo Miguel Alemán Valdés
SWC   Southwest Collection, Texas Tech University

Note: the majority of interviews cited here come from the Bracero History Archive and were not carried out by the author. The bibliography includes the name of the interviewer for each oral history.

INTRODUCTION

1. Herrera-Sobek, *The Bracero Experience*.

2. Stephen Pitti first coined the term Bracero Justice Movement to describe the organization's strategies to recuperate the back wages of Mexican guest workers. For more, see Stephen J. Pitti, "Legacies of Mexican Contract Labor."

3. Personal conversation and interview with Luis Barocio Ceja.

4. For more on Bracero/Mexican-American social relations, see Garcia, *A World of Its Own*; and David Gutiérrez, *Walls and Mirrors*.

5. Garcia y Griego, *Importation of Mexican Contract Laborers to the United States*.

6. Personal conversation and interview with Luis Barocio Ceja. Luis Barocio Ceja: *Los Americanos son racistas, ... nos quieren cuando les servimos, cuando trabajamos bien.*

7. *Mestizaje* refers to the historical mixing of Spaniards with Indigenous populations. For more on Mestizaje as a national project in Mexico, see chapter 2.

8. "President Bush Proposes New Temporary Worker Program."

9. For more on braceros and capitalist desires for a tractable workforce, see Schmidt Camacho, *Migrant Imaginaries*, 27.

10. Hahamovitch, *No Man's Land*, 2.

11. Fred Eldridge, "Helping Hands from Mexico," *Saturday Evening Post*, August 10, 1957, 63.

12. Ibid.

13. Ibid.

14. Ibid.

15. Ibid.

16. For another example, see Blake Brohy, "Bracero… A Story of Success," *Arizona Republic*, November 22, 1959.

17. Eileen J. Suárez Findlay explores issues of fatherhood, transnational labor, and remittances in Puerto Rico. See Suárez Findlay, *We Are Left without a Father Here*.

18. Martínez, "Impact of the Bracero Program," 59–60.

19. "Newsletter—Bishops' Committee for the Spanish Speaking," June 1958, box 21, folder 5, EGP.

20. Deborah Cohen, "Caught in the Middle," 114.

21. Deborah Cohen, *Braceros*, 24.

22. Ibid.; Ana Elizabeth Rosas, *Abrazando El Espíritu*.

23. For more on tropes of indigeneity and alcohol, see Toner, *Alcohol and Nationhood in Nineteenth-Century Mexico*.

24. Cullather, *Hungry World*, 50.

25. Ruiz, *Americans in the Treasure House*, 145.

26. Weber, "Historical Perspectives on Mexican Transnationalism."

27. Interview with Heriberto Flores Sotelo.

28. For more on intra-ethnic Mexican migrant and Mexican-American tensions, see Garcia, *A World of Its Own*; and David Gutiérrez, *Walls and Mirrors*.

29. Gamio, *Forjando Patria*, 28.

30. Cruz-Manjarrez, *Zapotecs on the Move*; Holms, *Fresh Fruit, Broken Bodies*; Gil Martínez de Escobar, *Fronteras de Pertenencia*; Rivera-Sánchez, *Belongings and Identities*; Stephen, *Transborder Lives*.

31. Letter from Benito Hernández to José Hernández Serrano, September 9, 1951, box 17, folder 11, EGP.

32. The Bracero History Project was created by the National Museum of American History, the Roy Rosenzweig Center for History and New Media at George Mason University, the Institute of Oral History at the University of Texas at El Paso, and the Center for the Study of Race and Ethnicity at Brown University.

33. Nora, *Conflicts and Divisions*, 8.

34. Ibid.

35. Taylor, *The Archive and the Repertoire*, 19.

36. Doss, *Memorial Mania*, 49.

37. Taylor, *The Archive and the Repertoire*, 20.

38. Halbwachs, *On Collective Memory*, 172–73.

39. Ibid., 53.

40. Megill, *Historical Knowledge, Historical Error*, 48.

41. Ibid.

42. Cacho, *Social Death*, 167.

43. Cathy J. Cohen, "A New Research Agenda for the Study of Black Politics," 42.

44. For more on modernity and the Bracero Program, see Deborah Cohen, *Braceros*; and Ana Elizabeth Rosas, *Abrazando El Espíritu*.

45. For more on women and the Bracero Program, see Ana Elizabeth Rosas, *Abrazando El Espíritu*.

46. For more on American historical discourses on sexuality, see Chauncey, *Gay New York*, 14.

47. Bracero Proa deploys a discourse that illustrates what scholar Gilberto Rosas terms "writing against Mexico," which reveals Mexican state powers' complicit actions toward furthering the marginalization of migrants. For more, see Gilberto Rosas, *Barrio Libre*.

INTERLUDE *Me modernicé*

1. Interview with Pedro Domínguez. Pedro Domínguez: *¿Yo, por qué me va dar pena? ¿Yo, pa' qué voy a decir que soy español, pues yo soy indígena?*

CHAPTER ONE

1. Jesús Topete, *Aventuras de un Bracero*, 52.
2. Ibid.
3. Horacio Labastida, "¿La economía indígena: Un límite de la Revolución?" *Novedades*, November 23, 1952.
4. Doremus, "Nationalism, Mestizaje, and National Identity," 381. As the national project, mestizo identity was utilized to marginalize indigenous communities and render peoples of African descent invisible.
5. Ana Elizabeth Rosas, *Abrazando El Espíritu*, 20.
6. Buffington, *Criminal and Citizen in Modern Mexico*, 144.
7. Ibid., 164.
8. Interview with Orfa Noemi Soberanis.
9. Stephen, *Transborder Lives*, 96.
10. Niblo, *Mexico in the 1940s*, 24.
11. Indigenous communities from Mexican border states experienced longer histories with border crossings. For more, see Meeks, *Border Citizens*.
12. The migration routes of these guest workers shaped contemporary immigration patterns, as several scholars have traced present-day Mixtec, Zapotec, and Mayan immigration to regions of the Pacific Northwest, Southern California, New York, and then south to the Bracero Program. In her ethnography, Rocio Gil Martínez de Escobar followed contemporary Mixtec families from Santa María Tindú, Oaxaca, to towns in Oregon and Southern California. She argued that these families stepped into the same transnational employment circuits that their parents and grandparents forged during the Bracero Program. In some cases, such as migration to New York, the children and grandchildren of braceros did not follow the same route of migration to a particular destination, but their descendants claim connections to the United States through their families' experience with the Bracero Program. Activists within the Bracero Justice Movement argue that children

of braceros are following in the footsteps of their parents and are reclaiming this experience as an explanation for their own migration and claims of belonging. For more, see Gil Martínez de Escobar, *Fronteras de Pertenencia*; and Rivera-Sánchez, *Belongings and Identities*.

13. Cruz-Manjarrez, *Zapotecs on the Move*; Holms, *Fresh Fruit, Broken Bodies*; Rivera-Sánchez, *Belongings and Identities*; Stephen, *Transborder Lives*.

14. Letter to the President from Antonio Toledo Martínez et al., March 6, 1944, microfilm box 793_6_6, MAC, AGN.

15. Summary of Letter to the President from Antonio Toledo Martínez, February 29, 1944, microfilm box 793_6_6, MAC, AGN.

16. Letter to the President from Antonio Toledo Martínez et al., March 6, 1944, microfilm box 793_6_6, MAC, AGN.

17. Summary of Letter to the President from Estela Merino et al., April 26, 1944, microfilm box 793_6_6, MAC, AGN.

18. Letter to the President from Josefina González Flores, April 4, 1948, vol. 593, exp. 546.6/15, MAV, AGN.

19. Summary of Letter to the President from Félix Aguilar, February 29, 1944, microfilm box 793_6_6, MAC, AGN.

20. Letter to the President from Abel Matamoros, August 7, 1959, vol. 715, exp. 546.6/15, ALM, AGN.

21. Interview with Julio Valentín May-May; interview with Pedro Domínguez.

22. Ruiz, *Americans in the Treasure House*, 145; Weiner, *Race, Nation, and Market*, 39.

23. Ruiz, *Americans in the Treasure House*, 145.

24. Buffington, *Criminal and Citizen in Modern Mexico*, 163.

25. For more on mestizaje, see Vasconcelos, *The Cosmic Race/La Raza Cósmica*.

26. Doremus, "Nationalism, Mestizaje, and National Identity," 380.

27. Sánchez, *Becoming Mexican American*, 119.

28. Ibid., 122.

29. Bonfil Batalla, *México Profundo*, 115.

30. Molina, *How Race Is Made in America*, 6.

31. Bonfil Batalla, *México Profundo*, 115.

32. Gamio, *Forjando Patria*, 28.

33. Doremus, "Nationalism, Mestizaje, and National Identity," 377.

34. Ibid.

35. Needler, *Mexican Politics*, 13.

36. Cullather, *Hungry World*, 50.

37. Niblo, *Mexico in the 1940s*, 313.

38. Cullather, *Hungry World*, 54.

39. Ibid.

40. Greaves, "La Política y el Proyecto de Educación Indígena del Avilacamachismo," 101.

41. Niblo, *Mexico in the 1940s*, 105.

42. For more on indigenismo, see Tarica, *The Inner Life of Mestizo Nationalism*.

43. Urías Horcasitas, *La Historia Secreta del Racismo en Mexico*.

44. Alanis Enciso, *El Primer Programa Bracero y el Gobierno de Mexico, 1917–1918*.

45. Deborah Cohen, *Braceros*, 4.

46. Sánchez, *Becoming Mexican American*, 116.

47. Garcia y Griego, *Importation of Mexican Contract Laborers to the United States*; Ana Elizabeth Rosas, *Abrazando El Espíritu*; Schmidt Camacho, *Migrant Imaginaries*.

48. Niblo, *Mexico in the 1940s*, 34.

49. Fixico, *Urban Indian Experience in America*, 10.

50. Ibid.

51. *Hoy* 747 (June 16, 1951).

52. For more on Mexican indigeneity in the United States, see Menchaca, *Recovering History, Reconstructing Race*; for more on "racial scripts," see Molina, *How Race Is Made in America*.

53. Ruiz, *Americans in the Treasure House*, 50.

54. Molina, *How Race Is Made in America*, 26.

55. Mraz, "Today, Tomorrow, and Always," 116–58.

56. Jesús Topete, *Aventuras de un Bracero*.

57. Lawrence and Sylvia Martin, "To Earn 'Miracle' Wages," *Post*, July 11, 1943, box 25, folder 6, EGP.

58. Ibid.

59. Interview with Gabriel Martínez Angel.

60. Report of Progress by Henry P. Anderson, January 1–December 31, box 17, folder 4, EGP.

61. *Huaraches* are Mexican handmade sandals.

62. Cline, *The United States and Mexico*.

63. Lewis, *Life in a Mexican Village*, 201.

64. For more on the role of Mexican social workers in bracero families, see Ana Elizabeth Rosas, *Abrazando El Espíritu*.

65. Lucile Rood, "Changes for Mexican Families as Men Return from U.S. Work," *Christian Science Monitor*, November 17, 1944, 12.

66. Ibid.

67. "A Study of Mexican Nationals in the Nine Camps of the Cucamonga, Upland, Ontario, and Chino Districts of San Bernardino County, California," summer 1944, box 17, folder 8, EGP.

68. Garcia, *A World of Its Own*, 131.

69. "A Study of Mexican Nationals in the Nine Camps of the Cucamonga, Upland, Ontario, and Chino Districts of San Bernardino County, California," summer 1944, box 17, folder 8, EGP.

70. Garcia, *A World of Its Own*, 136.

71. "A Study of Mexican Nationals in the Nine Camps of the Cucamonga, Upland, Ontario, and Chino Districts of San Bernardino County, California," summer 1944, box 17, folder 8, EGP.

72. This was not the first Mexican feature film set in Janitzio, as there was also a 1934 film titled *Janitzio*.

73. Interview with Pedro Domínguez. Pedro Domínguez: *Ese patrón no creía que yo era de allí. 'No, tú no eres de allí, pues allí ha de vivir pura gente rica porque se ve pues muy bonito en la película. . . . Yo soy de allí. . . . Yo me sentía muy orgulloso.*

74. Ibid. Pedro Domínguez: *Nadie sabía que yo era indígena.*

75. Ibid. Pedro Domínguez: *Tenían mucho interés ellos de que se enseñaran eso, Tarasco.*

76. Ibid. Pedro Domínguez: *¿Yo, por qué me va dar pena? ¿Yo, pa' qué voy a decir que soy español, pues yo soy indígena?*

77. Roediger and Esch, *Production of Racial Difference*, 15.

78. Interview with Elvon De Vaney by Jeff Townsend on March 9, 1974, SWC.

79. Ibid.

80. Interview with Rosendo Alarcón Carrera. Rosendo Alarcón Carrera: *Sabía mucho inglés y él nos platicaba.*

81. Leonard Nadel, "An Official Examines a Bracero's Hands for Calluses during Processing at the Monterrey Processing Center, Mexico," Item #1592, http://bracero archive.org/items/show/1592 (January 8, 2015), BHA.

82. Roediger and Esch, *Production of Racial Difference*, 8.

83. "They Helped Feed America," *Today's Health*, October 1957.

84. Interview with Nemecio Meza. Nemecio Meza: *Los contrataban porque no eran gente muy alta, eran chaparritos. Aguantaban mucho la temperatura, como su tierra de ellos era bastante caliente.*

85. "Problems of the Mexican Nationals in the Nine Camps of Cucamonga, Upland, Ontario, and Chino Districts of San Bernardino County, California," summer 1944, box 17, folder 8, EGP.

86. Ibid.

87. Report on Antonio Feliciano Ramirez, undated, box 17, folder 9, EGP. For more on the Railroad component of the Bracero Program, see Driscoll de Alvarado, *The Tracks North.*

88. Report on Antonio Feliciano Ramirez, undated, box 17, folder 9, EGP.

89. Ibid.

90. "A Study of Mexican Nationals in the Nine Camps of the Cucamonga, Upland, Ontario, and Chino Districts of San Bernardino County, California," summer 1944, box 17, folder 8, EGP.

91. Sarricolea Torres, "Cuerpos Masculinos en Tránsito," 247.

92. Interview with Nemecio Meza. Nemecio Meza: *Pero en diez personas buscaban a un oaxaqueño que hablara su idioma, el zapoteco, y español para que podría interpretar a sus gente. Y ya el mayordomo le preguntaba al intérprete del grupo de diez personas, oaxaqueños, les decía lo que tenía que hacer o cómo se trabajaba. Bueno todo lo que quería el mayordomo de aquel le decía al interprete de ellos. Así se entendían en ese tiempo.*

93. For more on special contracts, see Ana Elizabeth Rosas, *Abrazando El Espíritu*, 66.

94. Interview with Alonso Ayala. Alonso Ayala: *A mi papá no le gustaba que hablemos maya, y mi mamá hablaba maya. El nos hablaba así, en castellano y ella en maya.*

95. Ibid. Other indigenous bracero families shared similar experiences with the hacienda system. See Interview with Orfa Noemi Soberanis.

96. Interview with Alonso Ayala. Alonso Ayala: *Pos porque aquí estaba dura la cosa. Está duro el trabajo de aquí y se ganaba poco.*

97. Ibid. Alonso Ayala: *A muchos . . . les da pena hablar maya.*

98. Interview with Patricia Sahera.

99. Interview with Isaias Sánchez. Isaias Sánchez: *No sabes leer, no sabes escribir.*

100. Ibid. Isaias Sánchez: *Mira chaparrito, tú tienes chanza de aprender aunque sea a firmar. Yo te voy a enseñar.*

101. Ibid. Isaias Sánchez: *Ese hombre me enseñó. Fue a la tienda me trajo un pizarrón, de esos de la Coca-Cola. Y ahí empezó a poner las letras y todo eso.*

102. Ibid. Isaias Sánchez: *Vamos a renovar contrato y no vas a poner el dedo.*

103. Interview with Pedro Domínguez. Pedro Domínguez: *Estaban los de Oaxaca también pero ellos nos platicaban, pero no les entendíamos porque ellos hablan de otra forma y uno no puede entenderles, pues a ellos también. Yo creo ni ellos también nos entendían a nosotros.*

104. Ibid. Pedro Domínguez: *Sí, nos buscábamos, como que no estábamos contentos . . .*

105. Interview with Felix Flores. Felix Flores: *Él le decía en la barraca... 'Mira muchachos, paisanos, aquí están otros los paisanos, se van a tratar como gente, se van a tratar como hermanos, se van a tratar como sobrinos. No se van a pelear y ellos hablan otro idioma y ustedes otro idioma y otros otro idioma.*

106. Ibid. Felix Flores: *Que nosotros éramos Bolcheviques.*

107. Ibid. Felix Flores: *Cálmense, no hagan caso, que si hacemos caso nos avientan hasta allá.*

108. Ibid. Felix Flores: *Ellos son altos y nosotros chaparros.*

109. Interview with Isaias Sánchez. Isaias Sánchez: *Los primeros que vinieron en 1945, los primeros hombres que vinieron aquí, fueron unos que llegaron allá y dijeron que Estados Unidos '[es]ta bien suave, [hay] mucho trabajo y gana mucho dinero.'*

110. Mize and Swords, *Consuming Mexican Labor*, 8.

111. Interview with Isaias Sánchez. Isaias Sánchez: *Los humillaban, les decían cosas.*

112. Ibid. Isaias Sánchez: *Yo les decía, 'No les digan nada. Lo que están hablando ellos, ellos lo que hablan porque ellos así se entienden.' 'Y tú, ¿[por] qué te metes?' 'Tú no tienes ningún derecho de ofenderlos.' 'Y tú, ¿quién eres?' 'Porque yo soy parte de ellos.' Nos agarramos a fregazos.*

113. Ibid. Isaias Sánchez: *Pues los insultaban, les decían malas palabras, y eso no se vale, no se vale.*

114. Ibid. Isaias Sánchez: *'Si los insultas,' le digo 'ni te entienden. Porque ellos saben hablar poco castellano, pero poco.*

115. Interview with Julio Valentín May-May. Julio Valentín May-May: *Ya le caí mal.*

116. Ibid. Julio Valentín May-May: *Porque no oigan los otros.*

117. Ramirez Cuevas, "Cuando los Braceros se Fueron a Huelga en California."

118. Ibid.

119. Interview with Isaias Sánchez. Isaias Sánchez: *Paisano, no nos dejes, si tú te vas a ir, nos vamos contigo. Tú nos vas a decir cuando vamos a cambiar el dinero, cuando nos vamos a ir a Oaxaca. Tú nos ayudas.*

120. Ibid. Isaias Sánchez: *Seguro que sí.*

INTERLUDE *¡Yo le digo!*

1. Personal conversations with Gustavo Eloy Reyes Rodríguez.

CHAPTER TWO

1. Ted Le Berthon, "At the Prevailing Wage," *Commonwealth*, November 1, 1957.

2. Martínez, "Impact of the Bracero Program."

3. Garcia, *A World of Its Own*, 178.

4. Gamboa, *Mexican Labor and World War II*, 116.

5. Harry Klissner, "Mexican Aid Vital to Local Farmers," *Los Angeles Times*, September 23, 1956, F4; Lucile Rood, "Changes for Mexican Families as Men Return from U.S. Work," *Christian Science Monitor*, November 17, 1944, 12.

6. Deborah Cohen, "From Peasant to Worker."

7. D'Emilio, "Capitalism and Gay Identity," 108.

8. Cantú, *The Sexuality of Migration*, 21.

9. Rodríguez, *Next of Kin*, 12.

10. These were not all mutually exclusive categories, as guest workers could become undocumented and migrants could see themselves as zoot suiters.

11. Alvarez, *The Power of the Zoot*, 111.

12. Vaughan, "Modernizing Patriarchy," 201.

13. "Pamphlet: The Legend of Pancho Sanchez," undated, box 18, folder 1, EGP.

14. Kunzel, *Criminal Intimacy*, 9.

15. Gutmann, "Seed of the Nation," 195.

16. Suárez Findlay, *We Are Left without a Father Here*, 116.

17. Braceros who married women in the United States could achieve respectable domesticity. Marrying American women could also lead to gaining residency more rapidly, providing an exit from bracero camp life.

18. Shah, *Contagious Divides*, 13.

19. Ana Elizabeth Rosas, *Abrazando El Espíritu.*

20. José Natividad Rosales, "De Bracero, Sobre La Ruta de La Tragedia Mexicana," *Siempre! Presencia de México* 3, no. 26 (December 19, 1953): 32–34.

21. Ibid.

22. Letter to President from Isidora Botello, January 26, 1959, vol. 715, exp. 546.5/37, ALM, AGN.

23. Examples of these can be found in the papers of Miguel Alemán Valdés (MAV), Adolfo López Mateos (ALM), and Manuel Ávila Camacho (MAC), all in AGN.

24. Letter to the President from María Consuelo Miranda Luna, January 5, 1962, vol. 715, exp. 546.5/37, ALM, AGN.

25. For more on underage entry into the Bracero Program, see Interview with José Alvarez Munguía.

26. Report written by Eduardo Ampudia V, May 24, 1944, vol. 91, exp. 5, IPS, AGN.

27. MAV, ALM, and MAC, all in AGN.

28. Letter to the President from Maria Concepción Rosales, undated, vol. 587, exp. 545.3/98, MAV, AGN.

29. Ibid.

30. Ibid.

31. Ibid.

32. Letter from Vicente Peralta to José Hernández Serrano, June 8, 1945, box 19, folder 6, EGP.

33. Interview with Asterio López León. Asterio López León: *Dio la orden [el Presidente de México] de que echaran todos los braceros para fuera. Porque había muchos que ya no mandaban dinero a sus familias, nada, que todo lo gastaban aquí. [Quería] que los echaran todos afuera para mandar braceros nuevos.*

34. "Mal les Fue a los Braceros: Muchos que regresan de Estados Unidos hallaron sus hogares destruidos," *El Universal*, box 24, folder 17, EGP.

35. Personal conversations and interview with Hilario Martínez Cortez. Hilario Martínez Cortez: *Es que cuando me salía, la dejaba cubierta . . . así no me la ganaban, pos ya la trampa estaba ocupada.*

36. Ibid.

37. Personal conversations and interview with Roberto Guardado Montelongo.

38. Interview with José Torres Gracian. José Torres Gracian: *Tú te vas a ir y ya no vas a regresar.*

39. Ibid. José Torres Gracian: *Mira si quieres voy a dejar mi ropa . . . para que veas que voy a regresar.*

40. Ibid. José Torres Gracian: *No llévate tu ropa que yo sé que no vas a regresar.*

41. Ibid. José Torres Gracian: *Hasta me dieron ganas de bajarme [de la troca] pero no ya tiene la mente que me iba venir a Michoacán.*

42. Ibid. José Torres Gracian: *Por allí iba a las cantinas, a los parties.*

43. Ibid. José Torres Gracian: *Mujeres me querían enlazar para arreglarme papeles.*

44. Ibid. José Torres Gracian: *De hecho, una allá en Los Ángeles quería que, este, que me casara, este, con ella . . . le dije, 'mira yo no puedo casarme contigo' digo 'porque, porque yo soy casado en México y tú sabes que yo soy casado en México. 'No no importa' dice, 'mira, este, nos casamos, o sea que a tu señora, a tu familia no le va ser falta nada,' dice, 'nosotros le vamos a estar mandando [dinero],' dice, 'cada quince días, cada mes, como tú quieras, como tú decidas. No le va a hacer falta nada.'*

45. Ibid.

46. Lytle Hernández, *Migra*, 179.

47. The San Luís Group and the Renters Union of the State of Baja California.

48. Letter from Grupo de San Luís and La Unión de Inquilinos to Adolfo Ruíz Cortínes, November 6, 1956, vol. 893, exp. 548.1/124, ARC, AGN.

49. Ibid.

50. Fussel, "Tijuana's Place in the Mexican Migration Stream," 148.

51. Bender, *Run for the Border*, 71.

52. Ibid.

53. Martínez, "Impact of the Bracero Program."

54. Interview with Juan Topete. Juan Topete: *Sí, me la robe.*

55. Ibid. Juan Topete: *Bueno, porque ya teníamos mucho tiempo noviando y pues yo le había dicho que tenía que venirme y me dijo: 'No te vayas,' Y empezó ella, usted sabe, a decirme. Entonces le digo: 'No,' le digo, 'Pos nos podemos casar si tú quieres y si no,' le digo, 'pos a ver qué pasa.' Y me dijo: 'Está bueno.'*

56. Ibid. Juan Topete: *¿Pues y, esta muchacha?*

57. Ibid. Juan Topete: *'Pues ella viene conmigo' le digo. '¿Cómo que viene con[tigo]?' 'Sí,' le dijo. Dice 'Pues yo te quería mandar pa' los Estados Unidos,' dice, 'pero esta mujer la vas a llevar a 'onde te la trajiste. Tienes que llevarla con su papá o su mamá," dice. Y 'No,' le digo. Entonces ya en la noche platiqué con ella. 'No, si quieres yo me voy,' dice, 'nomás llegando allá,' dice, 'pos me escribes.' 'Sí' le dije, 'está bien.' Pues me fui de vuelta pa' mi tierra a llevarla con la mamá, ellos me querían mucho a mi, la mamá de ella y pues, la señora no tenía esposo.*

58. Ibid. Juan Topete: *Pues él me dijo que . . . solo que no quería que la dejara por ahí en algún lugar sin conocer ella a nadie.*

59. Ibid. Juan Topete: *Verá, verá que cuando yo salí en 1949, salí pa' Mexicali y la miré a ella. La miré en un lugar que le decían, El Patio, 'onde iba, allí caían todos los braceros y todo eso. Ahí caían a bailar y voy oyendo que dicen: 'Esta canción va dedicada para Margarita . . .' Dije: 'Pos ¿qué anda haciendo aquí?' Sí, ella era, ella era . . . Sí, pues agarró la vida, la vida alegre y no, pos ya. Estaba yo sentado tomando una cerveza cuando llegó y me miró, soltó el ruedo y se sentó conmigo y me abrazó y pues no, pero de todos modos ya no, ya no seguimos ella y yo, porque, porque no, pues no. Ya no.*

60. Garcia, *A World of Its Own*, 178.

61. Ibid.

62. Ibid.

63. Interview with Juan Topete. Juan Topete: *Y muchos terminaban su contrato y lo terminaban y así como entraron, así salían; sin nada, ey.*

64. Ibid. Juan Topete: *'Taba, 'taba mal, porque pos no guardaban nada. Eso sí, se divertían, pues bien, pero no guardaban nada . . . Pues muchos, muchos en ese tiempo dejaron sus familias por . . . porque ellos aquí se les hacía fácil todo, no mandaban nada.*

65. Bohulano Mabalon, *Little Manila Is in the Heart*, 84.

66. "'City of Sin' Label Tacked on Tijuana," *Pasadena Independent*, November 17, 1959.

67. Herzog, *Where North Meets South*, 99.

68. "Prostitution Isn't Profitable in SC County, Drobac Claims," *Santa Cruz Sentinel*, November 5, 1959.

69. Ibid.

70. Guadalupe Cano Quiroz, bracero paycheck stub, item #810, BHA, http://braceroarchive.org/items/show/810 (July 8, 2015).

71. "Prostitution Isn't Profitable in SC County, Drobac Claims," *Santa Cruz Sentinel*, November 5, 1959.

72. Anderson, "The Bracero Program in California," 173.

73. Interview with José Baltazar Sánchez. José Baltazar Sánchez: *Ah sabe por qué iban, ya me recuerdo porque razón. Había un reporte de que había hombres que llevaban mujeres a los campos, eso es, por esa razón iban . . . Porque hombres que llevan mujeres a los campos o al baile . . . la inmigración y la policía llegó a ir . . . pero que yo me di cuenta no se llevaron a nadie.*

74. Ibid. José Baltazar Sánchez: *El patrón tenía una cantina . . . uno de los mayordomos no el patrón, que se llamaba el Café Sonora, y allí era cantina y allí íbamos a tomar cerveza. No nos cobraban [para cambiar el cheque], pero allí gastábamos el cheque.*

75. Health Attitudes and Practices of Braceros, January 1–December 31, 1957, box 17, folder 4, EGP.

76. For more on narratives of morality during the Bracero Program, see Deborah Cohen, *Braceros.*

77. Gina Marie Pitti, "A Ghastly International Racket," 16.

78. "Newsletter—Bishops' Committee for the Spanish Speaking," June 1958, box 21, folder 5, EGP.

79. Ibid.

80. Ibid.

81. Interview with Susan González.

82. Alamillo, *Making Lemonade Out of Lemons*, 60.

83. Ibid.

84. Ibid.

85. Interview with Julius Lowenberg.

86. Interview with Sebastian Martínez.

87. Report by Joseph R. Hellmer, undated, box 17, folder 10, EGP.

88. Ibid.

89. Ibid.

90. For more on Afro-Mexican history, see Menchaca, *Recovering History, Constructing Race*; and Velásquez, *La Huella Negra en Guanajuato.*

91. Report by Joseph R. Hellmer, undated, box 17, folder 10, EGP.

92. Ibid.

93. "City Launches Drive on Vice," *Lubbock Evening Journal*, January 20, 1954, 1.

94. Interview with Rosendo Alarcón Carrera. Rosendo Alarcón Carrera: *Los fines de semana cuando sabían que les pagaban, ya llegaban como a las doce o una de la mañana, porque nunca llegaban temprano.*

95. Ibid. Rosendo Alarcón Carrera: *Sabrá Dios cuantas enfermedades tengan.*

96. Interview with Dr. Pedro A. Ortega.

97. Ibid.

98. For more on public health and the U.S.-Mexico border, see Mckiernan-González, *Fevered Measures.*

99. Nate Haseltine, "Meeting the Health Threat of Mexican Migrants," *Washington Post*, February 25, 1959.

100. Ibid.

101. Ibid.

102. Interview with Juan Virgen Díaz. Juan Virgen Díaz: *La tenía acostada en un colchón allí y pos, este, de repente yo sentí como que sí quería yo con ella.*

103. Ibid. Juan Virgen Díaz: *¿Vas a ir con la mujer esa? Ni te metas.*

104. Gutmann, "Seed of the Nation."

105. Cantú, "De Ambiente," 140.

106. Interview and personal conversations with Gustavo Eloy Reyes Rodríguez. Gustavo Eloy Reyes Rodríguez: *Mire, en el [19]60 cuando yo estuve en Blythe, en ese tiempo este, pos se oían hablar muy poco de, de esa gente, ¿no? Pero antes, pues se veían muy poco de, de esa gente, ¿no? Pero antes pues se veía muy pocos, o muy pocos había. Pero en el campo, en la barraca donde yo estaba, donde yo dormía, allí estaba un, un chavo que también estaba viviendo en la misma barraca, en la entrada de la barraca que allí un día se fue la luz, pero no sabíamos por que razón hasta que después hubo una discusión, una alegata ahí entre ellos, que estaban a la puerta y a otro día se aclaró por qué fue. Ese muchacho se llamaba Porfirio, era del estado de Oaxaca y este, y se aclaró que él era el, como le llaman ahora, los gays, o sea homosexual o así. Entonces ese muchacho se aclaró que así era, y se aclaró que apagó la luz porque estaba con una pareja de hombre con hombre. Y después le llamamos la atención en el fil, que en el trabajo, como dice uno, ¿no? Que entonces le llamaba uno los files, los campos onde trabajábamos. Entonces él dijo que sí, que él era de, de esa . . . era gay.*

107. Ibid.

108. Ibid. Gustavo Eloy Reyes Rodríguez: *Él hacía los ademanes como que se declaraba públicamente que, que él sí, porque es muy declarado . . . hasta el modo de caminar ¿no? Y sí, él no dijo que no, él no dijo que no, él dijo que sí. Y él sí, pero le dijimos que no, le dijo uno de Michoacán que, por favor que ya se fuera yéndose allí. Con palabras pesadas porque le dijo: 'Te vas a largar mucho de aquí,' dice. Entonces allí le dijo que, que sí. Pero era trabajador, ¿cómo se iba ir? Así es que él no se fue, siguió. Nomás que ya no cometió el error de cortar la luz. Pero sí, entonces fue que se aclaró como, que era el muchacho. Pero no se negó, dijo que sí.*

109. Ibid.

110. Ibid.

111. Sarricolea Torres, *Cuerpos Masculinos en Tránsito*, 234.

112. Maciel, *El Bandolero, El Pocho, y La Raza*, 100.

113. Fox, *Fence and the River*, 101.

114. Ibid.

115. Patiño Gómez, *Pito Pérez Se Va De Bracero.*

116. Ibid.

117. Ibid.

118. Galarza, *Strangers in Our Fields*, 2.

INTERLUDE Documenting

1. Interview with Luis Estrada.

2. Interview with José Santos Guevara Rodríguez. José Santos Guevara Rodríguez: *No le pagaba mucho y . . . después que estábamos en una alianza.*

CHAPTER THREE

1. Cuestionario, undated, box 18, folder 7, EGP.

2. "Two Mexican Generals Fight It Out for the Presidency amid Talk of Revolution," *Life*, July 1, 1940.

3. Stephen J. Pitti, *The Devil in Silicon Valley*, 144.

4. Valdés, *Organizing Agriculture and the Labor Movement before the UFW*, 224.

5. Ibid., 223.

6. Letter from Benito Hernández to José Hernández Serrano, September 9, 1951, box 17, folder 11, EGP.

7. Personal conversation and interview with Luis Barocio Ceja.

8. For more on the Good Neighbor Policy, see Pike, *FDR's Good Neighbor Policy*.

9. Personal conversation and interview with Luis Barocio Ceja.

10. Ngai, *Impossible Subjects*, 162; Stephen J. Pitti, *The Devil in Silicon Valley*.

11. Letter from José Hernández Serrano to Manuel Ávila Camacho, October 18, 1943, vol. 598, exp. 546.6/418, MAV, AGN.

12. Ibid.

13. Ibid.

14. Ibid.

15. Ibid.

16. "Circular a Los Braceros Mexicanos: Para que cooperen de manera más efectiva en los Estados Unidos," *La Prensa*, March 2, 1944.

17. Deborah Cohen, *Braceros*, 120.

18. Letter from José Hernández Serrano to Manuel Ávila Camacho, October 18, 1943, vol. 598, exp. 546.6/418, MAV, AGN.

19. Jesús Topete, *Aventuras de un Bracero*.

20. Niblo, *Mexico in the 1940s*, 114.

21. Ibid., 99.

22. Letter from José Hernández Serrano to Ernesto Galarza, undated (summer 1953), box 19, folder 6, EGP.

23. Memorandum to C. Lamberto Ortego Peregina from M. Rios Thivol, May 10, 1949, vol. 84, exp. 2, IPS, AGN.

24. Ibid.

25. Flyer: Volante de Orientacion, undated, vol. 84, exp. 2, IPS, AGN.

26. Letter to José Hernández Serrano from Ricardo Castro Sainz, August 10, 1944, box 19, folder 6, EGP.

27. Letter from Consul Vincent Peralta to José Hernández Serrano, June 8, 1945, box 19, folder 6, EGP.

28. "No se ha Dispuesto la Disolución de un Grupo," *La Prensa*, May 18, 1946.

29. "Una Alianza que solo Explota a Braceros," *La Prensa*, May 19, 1946.

30. Letter from Alianza Executive Committee to Miguel Alemán Valdés, November 11, 1948, vol. 587, exp. 545.3/98, MAV, AGN.

31. Ibid.

32. Memorandum to C. Lamberto Ortego Peregina from M. Rios Thivol, May 10, 1949, vol. 84, exp. 2, IPS, AGN.

33. Niblo, *Mexico in the 1940s*, 200.

34. Flyer: Volante de Orientacion, undated, vol. 84, exp. 2, IPS, AGN.

35. Memorandum to C. Lamberto Ortego Peregina from M. Rios Thivol, May 11, 1949, vol. 84, exp. 2, IPS, AGN.

36. Ibid.

37. Letter from Alianza Executive Board to Miguel Alemán Valdés, November 11, 1948, vol. 587, exp. 545.3/98, MAV, AGN.

38. Ibid.

39. Niblo, *Mexico in the 1940s*.

40. Letter from José Hernández Serrano to H. L. Mitchell, December 19, 1949, box 19, folder 6, EGP. For more on the National Agricultural Workers Union and the National Farm Labor Union and their work with braceros, see Galarza, *Farm Workers and Agri-Business in California, 1947–1960*; Mitchell, *They Saved the Crops*; and Valdés, *Organizing Agriculture and the Labor Movement before the UFW*.

41. Letter from José Hernández Serrano to H. L. Mitchell.

42. A *coyote* is a person who brings people into the United States for a large fee.

43. Letter from José Hernández Serrano to Manuel García, December 15, 1949, box 19, folder 6, EGP.

44. *Enganchadores* are illegal work contractors in the United States.

45. Letter from José Hernández Serrano to Manuel García, December 15, 1949, box 19, folder 6, EGP.

46. González, *Mexican Consuls and Labor Organizing*, 210.

47. Letter from José Hernández Serrano to Manuel García, December 15, 1949, box 19, folder 6, EGP.

48. García y Griego, *Importation of Mexican Contract Laborers to the United States*; Ngai, *Impossible Subjects*.

49. Letter from José Hernández Serrano to Miguel Alemán Valdés, January 25, 1950, box 19, folder 6, EGP.

50. Ibid.

51. Ibid.

52. Ibid.

53. Letter from José Hernández Serrano to H. L. Mitchell, October 7, 1950, box 19, folder 6, EGP.

54. Letter from Ernesto Galarza to José Hernández Serrano, October 12, 1950, box 19, folder 6, EGP.

55. Letter from José Hernández Serrano to Ernesto Galarza, April 14, 1950, box 19, folder 6, EGP.

56. Ibid.

57. Letter from Ernesto Galarza to José Hernández Serrano, October 21, 1950, box 19, folder 6, EGP.

58. Ibid.

59. Letter from José Hernández Serrano to Ernesto Galarza, May 9, 1950, box 19, folder 6, EGP.

60. Letter from José Hernández Serrano to Ernesto Galarza, November 28, 1950, box 19, folder 6, EGP.

61. Niblo, *Mexico in the 1940s*, 203.

62. Letter from José Hernández Serrano to Ernesto Galarza, November 28, 1950, box 19, folder 6, EGP.

63. Ibid.

64. Letter from Ernesto Galarza to H. L. Mitchell, January 8, 1949, box 23, folder 5, EGP.

65. Niblo, *Mexico in the 1940s*, 240.

66. Letter from Ernesto Galarza to H. L. Mitchell, February 4, 1951, box 24, folder 6, EGP.

67. Press Release, October 18, 1948, box 23, folder 4, EGP.

68. Letter from Ernesto Galarza to Mae and Eli, January 29, 1951, box 24, folder 6, EGP.

69. Letter from Ernesto Galarza to H. L. Mitchell, undated, box 24, folder 6, EGP.

70. Ibid.

71. Letter from Ernesto Galarza to Mae and Eli, January 29, 1951, box 24, folder 6, EGP.

72. Niblo, *Mexico in the 1940s*, 4.

73. Ibid., 253.

74. Letter from Ernesto Galarza to H. L. Mitchell, January 30, 1951, box 24, folder 6, EGP.

75. Letter from Ernesto Galarza to H. L. Mitchell, undated, box 24, folder 6, EGP.

76. Ibid.

77. Manifiesto, undated, box 22, folder 6, EGP.

78. Letter from Ernesto Galarza to H. L. Mitchell, January 30, 1951, box 24, folder 6, EGP.

79. Ibid.

80. Letter from José Hernández Serrano to Benjamín Tobón, February 1, 1951, box 24, folder 6, EGP.

81. Galarza, *Farm Workers and Agri-Business in California, 1947–1960*, 156.

82. Letter from Ernesto Galarza to H. L. Mitchell, January 30, 1951, box 24, folder 6, EGP.

83. Galarza, *Farm Workers and Agri-Business in California, 1947–1960*, 156.

84. Stephen J. Pitti, *The Devil in Silicon Valley*, 144.

85. Letter from Ernesto Galarza to H. L. Mitchell, undated, box 24, folder 6, EGP.

86. Letter from Ernesto Galarza to H. L. Mitchell, February 4, 1951, box 24, folder 6, EGP.

87. Letter from Ernesto Galarza to H. L. Mitchell, January 30, 1951, box 24, folder 6, EGP.

88. Letter from Ernesto Galarza to H. L. Mitchell, February 1, 1951, box 24, folder 6, EGP.

89. Letter from Ernesto Galarza to H. L. Mitchell, January 30, 1951, box 24, folder 6, EGP.

90. Ibid.

91. Galarza, *Farm Workers and Agri-Business in California, 1947–1960*, 156.

92. Letter from Ernesto Galarza to H. L. Mitchell, February 4, 1951, box 24, folder 6, EGP.

93. Ibid.

94. Letter from Ernesto Galarza addressed to "Estimados Compañeros," February 6, 1951, box 24, folder 6, EGP.

95. Telegram from José Hernández Serrano to Ernesto Galarza, February 25, 1951, box 19, folder 6, EGP.

96. Deborah Cohen documents growers' communist accusations of union supporters within the 1947 DiGiorgio strike. Deborah Cohen, *Braceros*, 149.

97. Letter from José Hernández Serrano to Robert T. Creasy, April 19, 1951, box 19, folder 6, EGP.

98. Press Release, March 14, 1951, box 19, folder 6, EGP.

99. Ibid.

100. Ibid.

101. Letter from Ernesto Galarza to John F. Shelley, March 9, 1951, box 19, folder 6, EGP.

102. Letter from Pedro Cerón González to Ernesto Galarza, May 10, 1951, box 17, folder 11, EGP.

103. Letter from A. J. Clark to Galarza, May 26, 1951, box 19, folder 6, EGP.

104. Galarza, *Farm Workers and Agri-Business in California, 1947–1960*, 158.

105. Galarza explains further how growers used braceros as strikebreakers despite the international agreement prohibiting this.

106. Calavita, *Inside the State*, 63.

107. Ibid., 64.

108. Galarza, *Farm Workers and Agri-Business in California, 1947–1960*, xi.

109. Ibid., 164.

110. Letter from José Hernández Serrano to Galarza, June 13, 1951, box 22, folder 7, EGP.

111. Valdés, *Organizing Agriculture and the Labor Movement before the UFW*, 221.

112. Ibid., 223.

113. Manifiesto a los Braceros Contratados Mexicanos, May 25, 1951, box 8, folder 5, EGP.

114. Instructivo Confidencial y Reservado Número 1, May 11, 1951, box 17, folder 11, EGP.

115. Registro de Filiación, August 31, 1951, box 17, folder 11, EGP.

116. Letter from José Hernández Serrano to Ernesto Galarza, June 13, 1951, box 22, folder 7, EGP.

117. Letter from José Hernández Serrano to Ernesto Galarza, June 8, 1951, box 19, folder 6, EGP.

118. Letter from Pedro Cerón González to Ernesto Galarza, June 30, 1951, box 19, folder 6, EGP.

119. Ibid.

120. Letter from Ernesto Galarza to Benjamín Tobón, March 8, 1951, box 19, folder 6, EGP.

121. Galarza, *Farm Workers and Agri-Business in California, 1947–1960*, 166.

122. "La Union Es Nuestra Fuerza," undated, box 8, folder 5, EGP.

123. Ibid.

124. Program on Nationals, undated, box 19, folder 6, EGP.

125. Ibid.

126. Letter to Eugenio Pezqueira from José Hernández Serrano, July 29, 1951, box 19, folder 6, EGP.

127. "Congreso de Campesinos en Salinas," *La Opinión*, August 12, 1951, box 9, folder 2, EGP.

128. Letter from Jesus Hernández Uresti to Ernesto Galarza, September 27, 1951, box 17, folder 11, EGP.

129. Circular de Orientación, September 9, 1951, box 22, folder 7, EGP.

130. Ibid.

131. As shown by Sarah Wald's work, Galarza's discourse would later change, and *Strangers in Our Fields* signals a rhetorical shift. See Wald, "The Nature of Citizenship."

132. Letter from Benito Hernández to José Hernández Serrano, September 9, 1951, box 17, folder 11, EGP.

133. Ibid.

134. Letter from Ernesto Galarza to José Hernández Serrano in Salinas, California, October 12, 1951, box 17, folder 11, EGP.

135. "Los Encomenderos de 1951," undated, box 8, folder 5, EGP.

136. Ibid.

137. Letter from Ernesto Galarza to José Hernández Serrano in Salinas, California, October 12, 1951, box 17, folder 11, EGP.

138. Letter from José Frias Briones to José Hernández Serrano, September 29, 1951, box 17, folder 11, EGP.

139. Letter from Joaquin Gutierres to José Hernández Serrano, October 2, 1951, box 17, folder 11, EGP.

140. "Impugnan los Socialistas la Contratación," *Novedades*, February 5, 1951, box 22, folder 6, EGP.

141. Letter from Benito Hernández to José Hernández Serrano, September 9, 1951, box 17, folder 11, EGP.

142. Emergency Mass Meeting, November 23, 1951, box 23, folder 7, EGP.

143. Ibid.

144. Ibid.

145. Galarza, *Farm Workers and Agri-Business in California, 1947–1960*, 166.

146. Ibid., xi.

147. David Gutiérrez, *Walls and Mirrors*, 197.

148. Letter from José Hernández Serrano to Ernesto Galarza, undated (summer 1953), box 19, folder 6, EGP.

149. González, *Mexican Consuls and Labor Organizing*, 205.

150. Carr, *Marxism and Communism in Twentieth-Century Mexico*, 116.

151. Letter from José T. Rocha to Ernesto Galarza, April 13, 1935, box 19, folder 6, EGP.

152. Letter from José Hernández Serrano to Ernesto Galarza, undated (summer 1953), box 19, folder 6, EGP.

153. Ibid.

154. Ibid.

155. Ibid.

156. Ibid.

157. Ibid.

158. Letter from José Hernández Serrano to Antonio Rivas Ramirez, September 28, 1954, box 19, folder 6, EGP.

159. Ibid.

160. Ibid.

161. Ibid.

162. Letter from Ernesto Galarza to José Hernández Serrano, May 3, 1955, box 19, folder 6, EGP.

163. Letter from Ernesto Galarza to José Hernández Serrano, October 12, 1955, box 19, folder 6, EGP.

164. Ibid.

165. Garcia, *From the Jaws of Victory*, 23.

166. Established by the Ford Foundation in 1952, the Fund for the Republic funded, according to Mitchell, "research and action in favor of expanding speech and other civil rights in the midst of McCarthyism." See Mitchell, *They Saved the Crops*, 248.

167. Stevens Street, *Photographing Farmworkers in California*, 173.

168. Letter from José Hernández Serrano to Richard H. Frank, March 16, 1957, box 19, folder 6, EGP.

169. Box 19, folder 6, EGP.

170. There is no correspondence between Alianza and Galarza in the 1960s in EGP.

171. Memorandum to Miguel Alemán Valdéz from José Hernández Serrano et al., August 2, 1948, vol. 587, exp. 545.3/98, MAV, AGN; Letter to Adolfo López Mateos from Chilacachapa, Guerrero, chapter of Alianza, December 21, 1958, vol. 715, exp. 546.6/8, ALM, AGN.

172. Memorandum to Miguel Alemán Valdéz from José Hernández Serrano et al., August 2, 1948.

173. Letter to Adolfo López Mateos from Chilacachapa, Guerrero, chapter of Alianza, December 21, 1958, vol. 715, exp. 546.6/8, ALM, AGN.

174. Ibid.

175. "Braceros Look to Canada for Work," *Modesto Bee*, March 14, 1966, 2.

INTERLUDE Ten Percent

1. Interview with Felipe Hernández Cruz. Felipe Hernández Cruz: *Esta gestión . . . ya tiene años . . . Pues basta, porque somos gente del campo, somos campesinos.*

2. Ibid. Felipe Hernández Cruz: *Yo le voy a traducir. Ahorita voy a decir [en español] lo que yo dije. Ya tiene tiempo que hemos venido con esta gestión, y hasta la fecha no hemos logrado. Ojala que el presidente de la república, o gobernador, que nos tome en cuenta pues porque nosotros somos gente necesitado.*

CHAPTER FOUR

1. Driscoll de Alvarado, "10% Solution."

2. Pam Belluck, "Settlement Will Allow Thousands of Mexican Laborers in the U.S. to Collect Back Pay," *New York Times*, October 15, 2008.

3. Ibid.

4. Letter from José Martínez Valtierra to Manuel Ávila Camacho, January 19, 1950, vol. 593, exp. 546.6/1–13, MAV, AGN.

5. Letter from Antonio Vasquez de Casas to Adolfo Ruíz Cortines, December 8, 1958, vol. 715, exp. 546.6/3, ALM, AGN.

6. Personal conversations with braceros in Salinas, California, on July 28, 2005.

7. Summary of Letter to the President from Juan Vega Olvera, May 31, 1944, microfilm box 793_2_6, MAC, AGN. According to historian Barbara Driscoll de Alvarado, the well-kept records on railroad braceros made it far more likely that "more railroad braceros than agricultural workers received their savings accounts." For more, see Driscoll de Alvarado, "10% Solution."

8. Letter to the President from Altagracia Estrada Flores, May 23, 1944, microfilm box 793_2_6, MAC, AGN.

9. Interview with Ventura Gutiérrez, June 30, 2008, Acapulco, Guerrero.

10. Driscoll de Alvarado, "10% Solution."

11. Stephen J. Pitti, "Legacies of Mexican Contract Labor."

12. Interview with Rosendo Alarcón Carrera. Rosendo Alarcón Carrera: *Pos sí, nosotros sabíamos perfectamente que nos estaba rentando como animales . . . Pues fondo de ahorro, . . . ¿pa' quién? Pues pa' el gobierno mexicano yo creo.*

13. Ibid.

14. O'Neil, *Two Nations Indivisible*, 26.

15. Stephen, *Zapata Lives*, xxvi.

16. Bellinghausen Enviado, "Invita *Marcos* a Ex Braceros."

17. Interview with Antonio Aragón.

18. Astorga Morales, "Breve historia del movimiento social de ex braceros en México."

19. Mize, "Power (In)-Action."

20. Randal C. Archibold, "Owed Back Pay, Guest Workers Comb Past," *New York Times*, November 23, 2008.

21. Ibid.

22. Activists in other bracero organizations, such as Carmen Martínez of La Alianza de Ex-Braceros del Norte, recognize Gutiérrez as the founder of the movement. Personal conversation with Carmen Martínez on April 28, 2009, Santa Paula, California.

23. Ibid.

24. Interview with Ventura Gutiérrez, June 30, 2008, Acapulco, Guerrero.

25. From 1974 to 1980, Cárdenas served as senator of Michoacán, then as governor from 1980 to 1986, and then unsuccessfully ran for president in 1988. With several leftist Mexican parties, he founded the Partido de la Revolución Democrática (PRD).

26. Interview with Ventura Gutiérrez, June 30, 2008, Acapulco, Guerrero.

27. Ibid.

28. For more on this bailout, see Edmonds-Poli and Shirk, *Contemporary Mexican Politics*, 220.

29. Personal conversation with Ventura Gutiérrez, December 21, 2007, Merida, Yucatán.

30. Ibid. Ventura Gutiérrez: *El Primer Robaproa, No fue el Fobaproa, Sino el Braceroproa*.

31. Mitchell, *They Saved the Crops*, chap. 11.

32. Interview with Alba Nidia Rubio Leyva.

33. Personal conversations with braceros in Salinas, California, July 28, 2005.

34. Bobby Cuza, "Bracero Rights Activist Says He Was Kidnapped in Mexico," *Los Angeles Times*, April 26, 2000.

35. Julián Sánchez, "Niegan Existencia De Ahorros De Bracero," *El Universal*, April 7, 2000.

36. Bobby Cuza, "Bracero Rights Activist Says He Was Kidnapped in Mexico," *Los Angeles Times*, April 26, 2000.

37. Henck, *Subcommander Marcos*, 342.

38. Araceli Martínez, "Anuncian Caravana De Ex Braceros a México: Planean Demandar a Fox Que Exija El Pago De Sus Ahorros Detenidos Entre 1943 y 1964," *El Universal*, March 30, 2002.

39. Personal conversation with Ventura Gutiérrez, June 30, 2008, Acapulco, Guerrero.

40. Ibid.

41. "Allanan Rancho De Fox," *El Siglo de Torreón*, February 8, 2004; Stephen J. Pitti, "Legacies of Mexican Contract Labor."

42. Interview with Ventura Gutiérrez, June 30, 2008, Acapulco, Guerrero.

43. "Cabildean Partida Especial Para Ex Braceros," *El Universal*, June 22, 2004.

44. Interview with Alba Nidia Rubio Leyva.

45. Personal conversation with Antonio Aragón, July 2, 2008, Oaxaca, Oaxaca.

46. Interview with Alba Nidia Rubio Leyva. Alba Nidia Rubio Leyva: *Casi las que estábamos en frente somos todas mujeres*.

47. "Insensible, El Gobierno Busca Pagar en Abonos el Bracero Proa," *La Jornada*, August 26, 2009.

48. Personal conversation with Ventura Gutiérrez, June 30, 2008, Acapulco, Guerrero.

49. The Palacio Legislativo is the House of Representatives.

50. Jorge Escalante, "Vence Cero e ex-Braceros," *Reforma*, November 21, 2004.

51. Martin Diego and Claudio Banuelos, "Pago De 100 Mil Pesos a Cada Ex Bracero, Compromiso Asumido Por Gobernación," *La Jornada*, May 28, 2005.

52. Jesus Aranda, "Ordena la Corte Incluir en Padrón a todos los Ex Braceros o sus Familiares: Plantea Como Requisito que hayan Trabajado Legalmente en EEUU entre 1942 y 1964," *La Jornada*, May 10, 2007.

53. Personal communication with Juan Loza, January 22 and 25, 2009.

54. Email correspondence from Ventura Gutiérrez, February 12, 2009.

55. Personal communication with Juan Loza, January 22 and 25, 2009.

56. Ibid.

57. Ibid.

58. "On the Day of the Bracero."

59. Kent Paterson, "New Movement Demands Justice for Farmworkers," *Border-lines* 10 (December 1998).

60. While documenting oral histories within bracero communities, I often encountered individuals who interrogated me in order to discover the relationship of my work to Marentes's collection.

61. Conversation with a bracero, June 21, 2008, Monterrey, Nuevo Leon.

62. Louie Gilot, "Lines Grow but Bracero Sign Ups Are Over," *El Paso Times*, March 24, 2006.

63. Angélica Bustamante, "Reciben con gritos a Carlos Marentes," *El Mexicano*, August 4, 2008.

64. Ibid.

65. Two of these states also happen to be the states that sent the largest numbers of men to the Bracero Program.

66. Interview with Ventura Gutiérrez, June 30, 2008, Acapulco, Guerrero.

67. For more on Rosa Martha Zárate's activism, see Medina, *Las Hermanas*, 110–17.

68. Personal conversation and interview with Rosa Martha Zárate. Rosa Martha Zárate: *Veíamos que en el movimiento mucho se enfocaba en los braceros que estaban en México, y no se estaba dando respuesta a la realidad concreta de los braceros radicando en Estados Unidos. Que tenían que irse a registrar hasta Mexicali o hasta sus lugares de origen sin transporte, los señores incapacitados físicamente, sin dinero ... mucho sin documentos.*

69. Bellinghausen Enviado, "Invita *Marcos* a Ex Braceros."

70. Reynoso, "Alianza Braceroproa Joins La Sexta Declaración De La Selva Lacandona."

71. Personal communication with Alba Nidia Rubio Leyva on December 21, 2007, in Merida, Yucatán.

72. Interview with Felipe Muñoz Pavón. Felipe Muñoz Pavón: *Salió en un periódico de Los Ángeles, California, una nota del ahorro del 10 por ciento de los braceros. Esa nota la adquirió un hijo de un bracero, y la mandó. Mandó el periódico a su papá, que es de un pueblo de Tlaxcala.*

73. Ibid. Felipe Muñoz Pavón: *Ya los tres fuimos a un aparato de sonido a anunciar de ese periódico que había salido de los braceros. Que si algunos compañeros que estaban allí presente ... que habían sido braceros, que se acercaran a la dirección de la casa de usted* [meaning his house]. *Pues así fue ... se acercaron algunos.*

74. Ibid. Felipe Muñoz Pavón: *El gobierno guardó siempre el silencio.*

75. Ibid. Felipe Muñoz Pavón: *Le agradecemos mucho, tomó interés en ayudarnos. Ella misma hizo que fuéramos, aunque no fuéramos todos pero fuéramos algunos, a hacer conocimiento a los, a todos los municipios de Tlaxcala ... fueron grupos a distintos ... municipios.*

76. Ibid.

77. Ibid. Felipe Muñoz Pavón: *Cada quien pagaba su pasaje, sus gastos no, las copias también ... lo que nos ayudó mucho, que a la licenciada no, no cobró, no le*

dimos, no. Hasta la presente no le damos nada . . . eso fue lo que nos ayudado mucho, que ella no recibe ni un centavo de nosotros.

78. Ibid. Felipe Muñoz Pavón: *Todo eso contribuyó a que el gobierno tomara precauciones.*

79. Ex-braceros like Felipe Muñoz Pavón saw themselves as supporters of the Zapatista Movement and the Bracero Justice Movement. Personal conversation with Felipe Muñoz Pavón on November 8, 2008, in Chicago, Illinois.

80. Bellinghausen Enviado, "Invita *Marcos* a Ex Braceros."

81. Enlace Zapatista, http://enlacezapatista.ezln.org.mx/la-otra-campana/207/.

82. Personal conversation with Joshua Karsh on November 3, 2009, in Chicago, Illinois.

83. Ibid.

84. Ibid.

85. Ibid.

86. Barbara Whitaker, "Judge Dismisses Mexican Laborers' Suit for Savings Taken from Pay in 40's," *New York Times*, August 30, 2002.

87. Driscoll de Alvarado, "The 10% Solution."

88. Memorandum and Order Granting Mexican Defendants' Motion to Dismiss, March 30, 2005, Legal Documents for *Case No. 01–892-CRB in United States District Court Northern District of California.*

89. Ibid.

90. Personal conversation with Joshua Karsh on November 3, 2009, Chicago, Illinois.

91. Personal communication with Verónica Cortez, January 8, 2009, Chicago, Illinois.

92. Belluck, "Settlement Will Allow."

93. Personal communication with Verónica Cortez, January 8, 2009, Chicago, Illinois.

INTERLUDE Performing Masculinities

1. Interview with Juan Loza. Juan Loza: *Cada quince días yo le mandaba a mi mamá todo lo que yo podía.*

2. Ibid. Juan Loza: *Nunca salí a un cine o a un centro de baile o a dar la vuelta al pueblo, solamente iba para comprar ropa o comprar comida, era todo. Pero de que yo dijera: 'Ahora, hoy yo voy a esta fiesta, hoy yo voy a este rodeo, no. Durante todo ese tiempo yo me privé en lo absoluto de cosas de diversión.*

EPILOGUE

1. Bodnar, *Remaking America*, 14.

2. Schmidt Camacho, *Migrant Imaginaries*, 27; Hahamovitch, *No Man's Land*, 50.

3. For more on bracerismo, see Bonfil Batalla, *México Profundo*, 154.

4. Smithsonian Institution Task Force on Latino Issues, *Willful Neglect.*

5. Stevens Street, *Everyone Had Cameras*, 373.

6. Informal conversation with Raúl Canela, San Jose, California, July 27, 2005: "*Todos necesitábamos pasar eso para ser braceros.*"

7. Ngai, *Impossible Subjects.*

8. Cacho, *Social Death*, 6.

9. Informal conversation with Peter Liebhold, September 30, 2009, Washington, D.C.

10. Street, *Everyone Had Cameras*, 373.

11. Ibid.

12. Pawel, *The Crusades of Cesar Chavez*, 17.

13. Bruns, *Cesar Chavez*, 92.

14. Wayne G. Clough, "From the Castle: Our Plan," *Smithsonian Magazine*, December 2009.

15. "Forced Labor," *New York Times*, September 7, 2010, A26.

16. "Bittersweet Harvest Comment Book," National Museum of American History, Washington, D.C. (September 9, 2009–January 3, 2010).

17. Personal conversation with Teresa Ramirez, October 16, 2009, Irvine, California.

18. "Bittersweet Harvest: The Bracero Program, 1942–1964."

19. Ferry, "Bittersweet Harvest Comment Book Analysis," 7.

20. Ibid., 11.

21. "Bittersweet Harvest Comment Book," National Museum of American History.

22. Ibid.

23. Ibid.

24. Ibid.

25. Ibid.

26. Lowenthal, *The Past Is a Foreign Country*, xvii.

27. Semuels, "For U.S. Farmers and Mexican Workers, It's Tough Being Legal."

28. Ibid.

29. Reyes, "8000 'Guest Workers' Join Farm Labor Union in North Carolina."

30. Sook Lee, *El Contrato.*

31. Miroff, "Canada's Guest Worker Program Could Become Model."

32. Ibid.

33. Binford, *Tomorrow We're All Going to the Harvest*, 113.

34. Marosi, "Hardship on Mexico's Farms, a Bounty for U.S. Tables."

35. Ibid.

BIBLIOGRAPHY

PRIMARY SOURCES

Manuscript Collections

College Park, Maryland
  National Archives
Detroit, Michigan
  Special Collections, Wayne State University
    Collections of the United Farm Workers of America
Digital Archive
  Bracero History Archive
Guanajuato, Mexico
  Archivo Histórico del Estado de Guanajuato
Lubbock, Texas
  Southwest Collection, Texas Tech University
Mexico City, Mexico
  Archivo General de la Nación
    Fondo Adolfo López Mateos
    Fondo Adolfo Ruíz Cortínes
    Fondo Investigaciones Políticas y Sociales
    Fondo Manuel Ávila Camacho
    Fondo Miguel Alemán Valdés
San Bruno, California
  National Archives
Stanford, California
  Special Collections and University Archives, Stanford University
    Ernesto Galarza Papers

Newspapers and Magazines

Agricultural Life	*El Universal*
Arizona Republic	*Hoy*
Christian Science Monitor	*Indy Media*
Commonwealth	*La Jornada*
El Mexicano	*La Opinión*
El Paso Times	*La Prensa*
El Siglo de Torreón	*Life*

Los Angeles Times
Lubbock Evening Journal
Modesto Bee
New York Times
Novedades
Pasadena Independent
Reforma

Santa Cruz Sentinel
Saturday Evening Post
Siempre! Presencia de México
Smithsonian Magazine
Today's Health
Washington Post

Oral Histories

Alarcón Carrera, Rosendo. Interview for Bracero History Archive by Laureano Martínez on May 28, 2003, in Durango, Durango.

Aragón, Antonio. Interview for Bracero History Archive by Mireya Loza on July 2, 2008, in Oaxaca, Oaxaca.

Ayala, Alonso. Interview for Bracero History Archive by Mireya Loza on July 9, 2008, in Cansahcab, Yucatán.

Barocio Ceja, Luis. Interview for Bracero History Archive by Mireya Loza on June 28, 2008, in Jiquilpan, Michoacán.

Bentura Cortez, Audelia. Interview for Bracero History Archive by Mireya Loza on June 26, 2008, in Janitzio, Michoacán.

Delgado Garfia Tiburcio. Interview for Bracero History Archive by Mireya Loza on June 27, 2008, in Patzcuaro, Michoacán.

De Vaney, Elvon. Interview for Southwest Collection at Texas Tech University by Jeff Townsend on March 9, 1974, in Lubbock, Texas.

Domínguez, Pedro. Interview for Bracero History Archive by Mireya Loza on June 27, 2008, in Patzcuaro, Michoacán.

Estrada, Luis. Interview for Bracero History Archive by Susana Salgado on May 25, 2006, in Perris, California.

Flores, Felix. Interview for Bracero History Archive by Mireya Loza on June 26, 2008, in Janitzio, Michoacán.

Flores Sotelo, Heriberto. Interview for Bracero History Archive by Violeta Mena on July 22, 2002, in Mexico City, Mexico.

Gómez, Mauro. Interview for Bracero History Archive by Myrna Parra-Mantilla on June 12, 2003, in Meoqui, Chihuahua.

González, Susan. Interview for Bracero History Archive by Kristine Navarro on May 22, 2006, in Blythe, California.

Guardado Montelongo, Roberto. Interview for Bracero History Archive by Mireya Loza on June 21, 2008, in Monterrey, Nuevo León.

Guevara Rodríguez José Santos. Interview for Bracero History Archive by Violeta Domínguez, May 12, 2002, in Mexico City, Mexico.

Gutiérrez, Ventura. Interview for Bracero History Archive by Mireya Loza on December 21, 2007, in Merida, Yucatán.

Gutiérrez, Ventura. Interview for Bracero History Archive by Mireya Loza on June 30, 2008, in Acapulco, Guerrero.

Hernández Cruz, Felipe. Interview for Bracero History Archive by Alma Carrillo on December 14, 2007, in Tamulté de las Sabanas, Tabasco.

López León, Asterio. Interview for Bracero History Archive by Violeta Mena on May 22, 2006, in Blythe, California.

Lowenberg, Julius. Interview for Bracero History Archive by Richard Baquera on March 19, 2003, in El Paso, Texas.

Loza, Cayetano. Interview for Bracero History Archive by Mireya Loza on July 30, 2007, in El Sitio de Maravillas, Guanajuato.

Loza, Juan. Interview for Bracero History Archive by Mireya Loza on August 31, 2005, in Chicago, Illinois.

Loza González, Maria Concepción. Interview for Bracero History Archive by Mireya Loza on July 30, 2007, in El Sitio de Maravillas, Guanajuato.

Martínez, Sebastian. Interview for Bracero History Archive by Karim Ley Alarcón on November 12, 2005, in El Paso, Texas.

Martínez Ángel, Gabriel. Interview for Bracero History Archive by Edwin R. Ubeda on September 1, 2005, in Chicago, Illinois.

Martínez Cortez, Hilario. Interview for Bracero History Archive by Mireya Loza on June 22, 2008, in Monterrey, Nuevo León.

May-May, Julio Valentín. Interview for Bracero History Archive by Mireya Loza on July 9, 2008, in Cansahcab, Yucatán.

Meza, Nemicio. Interview for Bracero History Archive by Mireya Loza on May 12, 2006, in Los Angeles, California.

Munguía, José Alvarez. Interview for Bracero History Archive by Veronica Cortez on May 25, 2006, in Perris, California.

Muñoz Pavón, Felipe. Interview for Bracero History Archive by Alma Carrillo on November 8, 2008, in Chicago, Illinois.

Ortega, Dr. Pedro A. Interview for Bracero History Archive by Richard Baquera on March 21, 2003, in El Paso, Texas.

Reyes Rodríguez, Gustavo Eloy. Interview for Bracero History Archive by Mireya Loza on July 3, 2008, in San Pedro Ixtlahuaca, Oaxaca.

Rubio Leyva, Alba Nidia. Interview for Bracero History Archive by Alma Carrillo on December 21, 2007, in Merida, Yucatán.

Sahera, Patricia. Interview for Bracero History Archive by Mireya Loza on July 29, 2008, in Salem, Oregon.

Sánchez, Isaias. Interview for Bracero History Archive by Alma Carrillo on May 20, 2006, in Coachella, California.

Sánchez, José Baltazar. Interview for Bracero History Archive by Veronica Cortez on May 22, 2006, in Blythe, California.

Soberanis, Orfa Noemi. Interview for Bracero History Archive by Mireya Loza on July 9, 2008, in Cansahcab, Yucatán.

Topete, Juan. Interview for Bracero History Archive by Grisel Murillo on May 24, 2006, in Heber, California.

Torres Gracian, José. Interview for Bracero History Archive by Alma Carrillo on December 20, 2007, in Caruso Madrazo, Quintana Roo.

Villareal, Severiano. Interview for Bracero History Archive by Verónica Cortez on May 22, 2006, in Blythe, California.

Virgen Díaz, Juan. Interview for Bracero History Archive by Anaís Acosta on May 24, 2006, in Heber, California.
Zárate, Rosa Martha. Interview for Bracero History Archive by Mireya Loza on August 8, 2011, in Colton, California.

Legal Documents

Case No. 01–892-CRB in United States District Court Northern District of California.
Memorandum and Order Granting Mexican Defendants' Motion to Dismiss. March 30, 2005.
Transcripts of Proceeding. October 21, 2008.
Plaintiff's Notice of Motion, Motion and Memorandum in Support of Final Approval of Class Settlement. February 6, 2009.
Transcripts of Proceedings. February 6, 2009.

Web and Multimedia Sources

Bellinghausen Enviado, Hermann. "Invita *Marcos* a Ex Braceros a Reuniones con Mexicanos que Trabajan en EU." *La Jornada*, February 21, 2006, http://www.jornada.unam.mx/2006/02/21/index.php?section=politica&article=020n1pol (November 23, 2015).
"Bittersweet Harvest: The Bracero Program, 1942–1964." Smithsonian Institute Traveling Exhibit Service, http://www.sites.si.edu/exhibitions/exhibits/bracero_project/main.htm (November 25, 2015).
Enlace Zapatista, http://enlacezapatista.ezln.org.mx/la-otra-campana/207/ (August 5, 2013).
Labor Notes, September 30, 2004, http://www.labornotes.org/2004/09/8000-%E2%80%98guest-workers%E2%80%99-join-farm-union-north-carolina (November 23, 2015).
Marosi, Richard. "Hardship on Mexico's Farms, a Bounty for U.S. Tables." *Los Angeles Times*, December 7, 2014, http://graphics.latimes.com/product-of-mexico-camps/ (November 25, 2015).
Miroff, Nick. "Canada's Guest Worker Program Could Become Model for U.S. Immigration Changes." *Washington Post*, January 5, 2013, http://www.washingtonpost.com/world/canadas-guest-worker-program-could-become-model-for-us-immigration-changes/2013/01/05/2b82a468-551b-11e2-89de-76c1c54b1418_story.html (November 25, 2015).
"On the Day of the Bracero." *The Farmworkers Website*, November 22, 1997, http://www.farmworkers.org/thebday.html (November 23, 2015).
Patiño Gómez, Alfonso. *Pito Pérez Se Va De Bracero*. Mexico, 1948. Film.
"President Bush Proposes New Temporary Worker Program." January 7, 2004, http://georgewbush-whitehouse.archives.gov/news/releases/2004/01/20040107-3.html (April 2, 2014).
Ramirez Cuevas, Jesus. "Cuando los Braceros se Fueron a Huelga en California." *La Jornada* (October 19, 2003), http://www.jornada.unam.mx/2003/10/19/mas-jesus.html (November 23, 2015).

Reyes, Téofilo. "8000 'Guest Workers' Join Farm Labor Union in North Carolina."
Reynoso, Maricela. "Alianza Braceroproa Joins La Sexta Declaración De La
    Selva Lacandona." *Indy Media*, September 14, 2005, http://www.indybay.org/
    newsitems/2005/09/14/17672041.php (November 23, 2015).
Semuels, Alana. "For U.S. Farmers and Mexican Workers, It's Tough Being Legal."
    Los Angeles Times, March 30, 2013, http://www.latimes.com/nation/la-na
    -guest-worker-20130331-dto-htmlstory.html (November 23, 2015).
Sook Lee, Min. *El Contrato* (Canada, 2003), DVD.

SECONDARY SOURCES

Alamillo, José M. *Making Lemonade Out of Lemons: Mexican American Labor
    and Leisure in a California Town, 1880–1960*. Urbana: University of Illinois
    Press, 2006.
Alanis Enciso, Fernando Saul. *El Primer Programa Bracero y el Gobierno de
    Mexico, 1917–1918*. San Luis Potosi: Colegio de San Luis, 1999.
Alvarez, Luis. *The Power of the Zoot: Youth Culture and Resistance during World
    War II*. Berkeley: University of California Press, 2008.
Anderson, Henry P. "The Bracero Program in California, with Particular
    Reference to Health Status, Attitudes, and Practices." Berkeley, Calif.: Berkeley
    School of Public Health, 1961.
Aster, Richard Frederick. "The Termination of the Bracero Program—Its Impact
    on Welfare and Education in Santa Barbara County." M.A. Thesis, University of
    California, Santa Barbara, 1965.
Astorga Morales, Abel. "Breve historia del movimiento social de ex braceros en
    México." Revista Historia Autónoma 5 (2014): 133–47.
Bender, Steve W. *Run for the Border: Virtue in U.S.-Mexico Border Crossing*. New
    York: New York University Press, 2012.
Binford, Leigh. *Tomorrow We're All Going to the Harvest: Temporary Foreign
    Worker Programs and Neoliberal Political Economy*. Austin: University of Texas
    Press, 2013.
"Bittersweet Harvest Comment Book." National Museum of American History,
    Washington, D.C. (September 9, 2009–January 3, 2010).
Bodnar, John. *Remaking America: Public Memory, Commemoration, and
    Patriotism in the Twentieth Century*. Princeton: Princeton University Press,
    1992.
Bohulano Mabalon, Dawn. *Little Manila Is in the Heart: The Making of the
    Filipina/o Community in Stockton, California*. Durham: Duke University Press,
    2013.
Bonfil Batalla, Guillermo. *México Profundo: Reclaiming a Civilization*. Austin:
    University of Texas Press, 1996.
Boyer, Christopher R. *Becoming Campesinos: Politics Identity and Agrarian
    Struggle in Postrevolutionary Michoacan, 1920–1935*. Palo Alto: Stanford
    University Press, 2003.
Bruns, Roger. *Cesar Chavez: A Biography*. Westport: Greenwood Press, 2005.

Buffington, Robert M. *Criminal and Citizen in Modern Mexico*. Lincoln: University of Nebraska Press, 2000.

Cacho, Lisa M. *Social Death: Racialized Rightlessness and the Criminalization of the Unprotected*. New York: New York University Press, 2012.

Calavita, Kitty. *Inside the State: The Bracero Program, Immigration, and the I.N.S.* New York: Routledge, 1992.

Cantú, Lionel. "De Ambiente: Queer Tourism and the Shifting Boundaries of Mexican Male Sexualities." *GLQ: A Journal of Lesbian and Gay Studies* 8, nos. 1–2 (2002): 140.

———. *The Sexuality of Migration: Border Crossing and Mexican Immigrant Men*. New York: New York University Press, 2009.

Carr, Barry. *Marxism and Communism in Twentieth-Century Mexico*. Lincoln: University of Nebraska Press, 1992.

Chauncey, George. *Gay New York: Gender, Urban Culture, and the Making of the Gay Male World, 1890–1940*. New York: Basic Books, 1994.

Cline, Howard F. *The United States and Mexico*. Boston: Harvard University Press, 1953.

Cohen, Cathy J. "A New Research Agenda for the Study of Black Politics." *Du Bois Review: Social Science Research on Race* 1, no. 1 (2004): 42.

Cohen, Deborah. *Braceros: Migrant Citizens and Transnational Subjects in the Postwar United States and Mexico*. Chapel Hill: University of North Carolina Press, 2011.

———. "Caught in the Middle: The Mexican State's Relationship with the United States and Its Own Citizen-Workers, 1942–1954." *Journal of American Ethnic History* 20 (2001): 110–32.

———. "From Peasant to Worker: Migration, Masculinity, and the Making of Mexican Workers in the U.S." *International Labor and Working-Class History* 69 (Spring 2006): 81–103.

Cruz-Manjarrez, Adriana. *Zapotecs on the Move: Cultural, Social, and Political Processes in a Transnational Perspective*. New Brunswick: Rutgers University Press, 2013.

Cullather, Nick. *The Hungry World: Americans' Cold War Battle against Poverty in Asia*. Boston: Harvard University Press, 2010.

D'Emilio, John. "Capitalism and Gay Identity." In *Powers of Desire: The Politics of Sexuality*, edited by Ann Snitow, Christine Stansell, and Sharan Thompson, 100–113. New York: Monthly Review Press, 1983.

Doremus, Anne. "Nationalism, Mestizaje, and National Identity in Mexico during the 1940s and the 1950s." *Mexican Studies/Estudios Mexicanos* 17, no. 2 (Summer 2001).

Doss, Erika. *Memorial Mania: Public Feeling in America*. Chicago: University of Chicago Press, 2010.

Driscoll de Alvarado, Barbara. "10% Solution: Bracero Program Savings Controversy." *ReVista: Harvard Review of Latin America* (Autumn 2003).

———. *The Tracks North: The Railroad Bracero Program of World War II*. Austin: CMAS Books, Center for Mexican American Studies, University of Texas at Austin, 1999.

Edmonds-Poli, Emily, and David A. Shirk. *Contemporary Mexican Politics.* Lanham: Rowman and Littlefield, 2012.

Ferry, Daniel. "Bittersweet Harvest Comment Book Analysis." National Museum of American History, Washington, D.C., Summer 2010, 7.

Fixico, Donald L. *The Urban Indian Experience in America.* Albuquerque: University of New Mexico Press, 2000.

Fox, Claire F. *The Fence and the River: Cultural Politics at the U.S.-Mexico Border.* Minneapolis: University of Minnesota Press, 1999.

Frye, David L. *Indians into Mexicans: History and Identity in a Mexican Town.* Austin: University of Texas Press, 1996.

Fussel, Elizabeth. "Tijuana's Place in the Mexican Migration Stream: Destination for Internal Migrants or Stepping Stone to the United States?" In *Crossing the Border: Research from the Mexican Migration Project,* edited by Jorge Durand and Douglas S. Massey. New York: Russell Sage Foundation, 2006.

Galarza, Ernesto. *Farm Workers and Agri-Business in California, 1947–1960.* Notre Dame: University of Notre Dame Press, 1977.

———. *Merchants of Labor: The Mexican Bracero Story: An Account of the Managed Migration of Mexican Farm Workers in California, 1942–1960.* San Jose: Rosicrucian Press, 1964.

———. *Spiders in the House and Workers in the Field.* Notre Dame: University of Notre Dame Press, 1970.

———. *Strangers in Our Fields.* Washington, D.C.: Joint United States–Mexico Union Committee, 1956.

———. *Tragedy at Chualar: El Crucero de las Treinta y Dos Cruces.* Santa Barbara: McNally and Loftin, 1977.

Gamboa, Erasmo. *Mexican Labor and World War II: Braceros in the Pacific Northwest, 1942–1947.* Columbia Northwest Classics. Seattle: University of Washington Press, 2000.

Gamio, Manuel. *Forjando Patria: Pro Nationalismo.* Boulder: University of Colorado Press, 2010.

———. *The Mexican Immigrant: His Life Story.* Chicago: University of Chicago Press, 1931.

———. *Mexican Immigration to the United States: A Study of Human Migration and Adjustment.* Chicago: University of Chicago Press, 1930.

Garcia, Matt. "Cain contra Abel: Courtship, Masculinities, and Citizenship in Southern California, 1942–1964." In *Race, Nation, and Empire in American History,* edited by James Campbell, Matthew Guterl, and Robert Lee. Chapel Hill: University of North Carolina Press, 2007.

———. *From the Jaws of Victory: The Triumph and the Tragedy of Cesar Chavez and the Farm Workers Movement.* Berkeley: University of California Press, 2012.

———. *A World of Its Own: Race, Labor, and Citrus in the Making of Greater Los Angeles, 1900–1970.* Studies in Rural Culture. Chapel Hill: University of North Carolina Press, 2001.

García y Griego, Manuel. *The Importation of Mexican Contract Laborers to the United States, 1942–1964.* In *Between Two Worlds: Mexican Immigrants in the*

United States, edited by David G. Gutíerrez. Wilmington: Scholarly Resources Inc., 1996.

Gil Martínez de Escobar, R. *Fronteras de Pertenencia: Hacia la Construcción del Bienestar y el Desarollo Comunitario Transnacional de Santa María Tindú, Oaxaca*. Mexico City: Universidad Autonoma Metropolitana, 2006.

González, Gilbert G. *Guest Workers or Colonized Labor? Mexican Labor Migration to the United States*. Boulder: Paradigm Publishers, 2007.

———. *Mexican Consuls and Labor Organizing: Imperial Politics in the American Southwest*. Austin: University of Texas, 1999.

González, Gilbert G., and Raul A. Fernandez. *A Century of Chicano History: Empire, Nations, and Migration*. New York: Routledge, 2003.

Greaves, Cecilia. "La Política y el Proyecto de Educación Indígena del Avilacamachismo." In *Historias, Saberes Indígenas y Nuevas Etnicidades en la la Escuela*, edited by María Bertley Busquets, 95–119. Mexico City: CIESAS, 2006.

Gutiérrez, David. *Walls and Mirrors: Mexican Americans, Mexican Immigrants, and the Politics of Ethnicity*. Berkeley: University of California Press, 1995.

Gutiérrez, Natividad. *Nationalist Myths and Ethnic Identities*. Lincoln: University of Nebraska Press, 1999.

Gutmann, Matthew C. *The Meanings of Macho: Being a Man in Mexico City*. Berkeley: University of California Press, 1996.

———. "Seed of the Nation: Men's Sex and Potency in Mexico." In *The Gender Sexuality Reader: Culture History Political Economy*, edited by Roger N. Lancaster and Micaela di Leonardo, 194–206. Chicago: Routledge, 1997.

Hahamovitch, Cindy. *No Man's Land: Jamaican Guestworkers in America and the Global History of Deportable Labor*. Princeton: Princeton University Press, 2011.

Halbwachs, Maurice. *On Collective Memory*. Chicago: University of Chicago Press, 1992.

Henck, Nick. *Subcommander Marcos: The Man and the Mask*. Durham: Duke University Press, 2007.

Henderson, Amy, and Adrienne Lois Kaeppler. *Exhibiting Dilemmas: Issues of Representation at the Smithsonian*. Washington, D.C.: Smithsonian Institution Press, 1997.

Herrera-Sobek, Maria. *The Bracero Experience: Elitelore versus Folklore*. Los Angeles: UCLA Latin American Center Publications, University of California, 1979.

Herzog, Lawrence A. *Where North Meets South: Cities, Space, and Politics on the U.S.-Mexico Border*. Austin: University of Texas Press, 1990.

Holms, Seth M. *Fresh Fruit, Broken Bodies: Migrant Farmworkers in the United States*. Berkeley: University of California Press, 2013.

Kunzel, Regina. *Criminal Intimacy: Prison and the Uneven History of Modern American Sexuality*. Chicago: University of Chicago, 2008.

Lewis, Oscar. *Life in a Mexican Village: Tepoztlan Restudied*. Urbana: University of Illinois Press, 1951.

Lowenthal, David. *The Past Is a Foreign Country*. New York: Cambridge University Press, 1999.

Lytle Hernández, Kelley. *Migra: A History of the U.S. Border Patrol*. Berkeley: University of California Press, 2010.

Maciel, David R. *El Bandolero, El Pocho, y La Raza*. México: Siglo Ventiuno Editores, 2000.

Martínez, Daniel. "The Impact of the Bracero Program on a Southern California Mexican-American Community," M.A. Thesis, Claremont Graduate School, 1958.

Mckiernan-González, John. *Fevered Measures: Public Health and Race at the Texas-Mexico Border, 1848–1942*. Durham: Duke University Press, 2012.

Medina, Lara. *Las Hermanas: Chicana/Latina Religious-Political Activism in the U.S. Catholic Church*. Philadelphia: Temple University Press, 2004.

Meeks, Eric V. *Border Citizens: The Making of Indians, Mexicans, and Anglos in Arizona*. Austin: University of Texas Press, 2007.

Megill, Allan. *Historical Knowledge, Historical Error: Contemporary Guide to Practice*. Chicago: University of Chicago Press, 2007.

Menchaca, Martha. *The Mexican Outsiders: A Community History of Marginalization and Discrimination in California*. Austin: University of Texas Press, 1995.

———. *Recovering History, Constructing Race: The Indian, Black, and White Roots of Mexican Americans*. Austin: University of Texas Press, 2001.

Mitchell, Don. *They Saved the Crops: Labor, Landscape, and the Struggle over Industrial Farming in Bracero-Era California*. Athens: University of Georgia Press, 2012.

Mize, Ronald L. "Power (In)-Action: State and Agribusiness in the Making of the Bracero Total Institution." *Berkeley Journal of Sociology* 50 (2006): 76–119.

Mize, Ronald L., and Alicia C. S. Swords. *Consuming Mexican Labor: From the Bracero Program to NAFTA*. Toronto: University of Toronto Press, 2011.

Molina, Natalia. *How Race Is Made in America: Immigration, Citizenship, and the Historical Power of Racial Scripts*. Berkeley: University of California Press, 2014.

Mraz, John. "Today, Tomorrow, and Always: The Golden Age of Illustrated Magazines." In *Fragments of a Golden Age: The Politics of Culture in Mexico since 1940*, edited by Gilbert M. Joseph, Anne Rubenstein, and Eric Zolov, 116–58. Durham: Duke University Press, 2001.

Mraz, John, and Jaime Velez Storey. *Uprooted: Braceros in the Hermanos Mayo's Lens*. Houston: Arte Publico, 1996.

Needler, Martin C. *Mexican Politics: The Containment of Conflict*. Westport: Praeger Publishers, 1995.

Ngai, Mae M. *Impossible Subjects: Illegal Aliens and the Making of Modern America*. Politics and Society in Twentieth-Century America. Princeton: Princeton University Press, 2004.

Niblo, Stephen. *Mexico in the 1940s: Modernity, Politics, and Corruption*. Wilmington: SR Books, 2000.

Nora, Pierre. *Conflicts and Divisions*. Vol. I of *Realms of Memory: The Construction of the French Past*. New York: Columbia University, 1996.

———. "Reasons for the Current Upsurge in Memory." In *The Collective Memory Reader*, edited by Jeffrey K. Olick, Vered Vinitzky-Seroussi, and Daniel Levy. New York: Oxford University Press, 2011.

O'Neil, Shannon K. *Two Nations Indivisible: Mexico, the United States, and the Road Ahead*. New York: Oxford University Press, 2013.

Pawel, Miriam. *The Crusades of Cesar Chavez: A Biography*. New York: Bloomsbury Press, 2014.

Pike, Fredrick B. *FDR's Good Neighbor Policy: 60 Years of Generally Gentle Chaos*. Austin: University of Texas Press, 1995.

Pitti, Gina Marie. "'A Ghastly International Racket': The Catholic Church and the Bracero Program in California, 1942–1964." Working Paper Series: Cushwa Center for the Study of American Catholicism, Series 33, no. 1 (Fall 2001).

Pitti, Stephen J. *The Devil in Silicon Valley: Northern California, Race, and Mexican Americans*. Princeton: Princeton University Press, 2003.

———. "Legacies of Mexican Contract Labor." Lecture given at Repairing the Past: Confronting the Legacies of Slavery, Genocide, and Caste. New Haven, Connecticut, 2005.

Rivera-Sánchez, Liliana. "Belongings and Identities: Migrants between the Mixteca and New York." Ph.D. diss., New School University, 2001.

Rodríguez, Richard T. *Next of Kin: The Family in Chicano/a Cultural Politics*. Durham: Duke University Press, 2009.

Roediger, David, and Elizabeth D. Esch. *The Production of Difference: Race and the Management of Labor in U.S. History*. New York: Oxford, 2012.

Rosas, Ana Elizabeth. *Abrazando El Espíritu: Bracero Families Confront the US-Mexico Border*. Berkeley: University of California Press, 2014.

Rosas, Gilberto. *Barrio Libre: Criminalizing States and Delinquent Refusals of the New Frontier*. Durham: Duke University Press, 2012.

Ruiz, Jason. *Americans in the Treasure House: Travel to Porfirian Mexico and the Cultural Politics of Empire*. Austin: University of Texas Press, 2014.

Saldivar, José David. *Border Matters: Remapping American Cultural Studies*. Berkeley: University of California Press, 1997.

Sánchez, George J. *Becoming Mexican American: Ethnicity, Culture, and Identity in Chicano Los Angeles, 1900–1945*. New York: Oxford University Press, 1993.

Sarricolea Torres, Juan Miguel. "Cuerpos Masculinos en Tránsito: Una Etnografía con Hombres, Mujeres, y Familias Migrantes de Jerez, Zacatecas, 1940–1964." Ph.D. diss., El Colegio de Michoacán, 2014.

Schmidt Camacho, Alicia. *Migrant Imaginaries: Latino Cultural Politics in the U.S.-Mexico Borderlands*. New York: New York University Press, 2008.

Shah, Nayan. *Contagious Divides: Epidemics and Race in San Francisco's Chinatown*. Berkeley: University of California Press, 2001.

———. *Stranger Intimacy: Contesting Race, Sexuality, and Law in the North American West*. Berkeley: University of California Press, 2012.

Smith, Robert C. *Mexican New York: Transnational Lives of New Immigrants*. Berkeley: University of California Press, 2006.

Smithsonian Institution Task Force on Latino Issues. *Willful Neglect: The Smithsonian Institution and U.S. Latinos*. Washington, D.C.: Smithsonian Institutions, May 1994.

Stephen, Lynn. *Transborder Lives: Indigenous Oaxacans in Mexico, California, and Oregon*. Durham: Duke University Press, 2007.

———. *Zapata Lives! Histories and Cultural Politics in Southern Mexico*. Berkeley: University of California Press, 2002.

Stevens Street, Richard. *Everyone Had Cameras: Photography and Farmworkers in California, 1850–2000*. Minneapolis: University of Minnesota Press, 2008.

———. *Photographing Farmworkers in California*. Palo Alto: Stanford University Press, 2004.

Suárez Findlay, Eileen J. *We Are Left without a Father Here: Masculinity, Domesticity, and Migration in Postwar Puerto Rico*. Durham: Duke University Press, 2014.

Tarica, Estelle. *The Inner Life of Mestizo Nationalism*. Minneapolis: University of Minnesota Press, 2008.

Taylor, Diana. *The Archive and the Repertoire: Performing Cultural Memory in the Americas*. Durham: Duke University Press, 2003.

Toner, Deborah. *Alcohol and Nationhood in Nineteenth-Century Mexico*. Lincoln: University of Nebraska Press, 2015.

Topete, Jesús. *Aventuras de un Bracero*. Monterrey, Mexico: Gráfica Moderna, 1961.

Urías Horcasitas, Beatriz. *La Historia Secreta del Racismo en Mexico (1920–1950)*. Mexico City: Tusquets, 2007.

Valdés, Dionicio Nodín. *Organizing Agriculture and the Labor Movement before the UFW: Puerto Rico, Hawai'i, California*. Austin: University of Texas Press, 2007.

Vargas, Zaragosa. *Proletarians of the North: A History of Mexican Industrial Workers in Detroit and the Midwest, 1917–1933*. Berkeley: University of California Press, 1993.

Vasconcelos, José. *The Cosmic Race/La Raza Cósmica*. Baltimore: Johns Hopkins University Press, 1997.

Vaughan, Mary Kay. "Modernizing Patriarchy: State Policies, Rural Households, and Women in Mexico, 1930–1940." In *Hidden Histories of Gender and the State in Latin America*, edited by Elizabeth Dore and Maxine Molyneaux, 194–214. Durham: Duke University Press, 2000.

Vázquez Castillo, María Teresa. *Land Privatization in Mexico: Urbanization, Formation of Regions, and Globalization in Ejidos*. New York: Routledge, 2004.

Velásquez, María Elisa. *La Huella Negra en Guanajuato*. Guanajuato: Ediciones La Rana, 2007.

Wald, Sarah. "The Nature of Citizenship: Race, Citizenship, and Nature in Representations of Californian Agricultural Labor." Ph.D. diss., Brown University, 2009.

Weber, Devra. "Historical Perspectives on Mexican Transnationalism: With Notes from Angumacutiro." Special issue, *Social Justice* 2, no. 3 (77) (Fall 1999): 39–58.

Weiner, Richard. *Race, Nation, and Market: Economic Culture in the Porfirian Mexico*. Tucson: University of Arizona Press, 2004.

INDEX

Page numbers in italics indicate illustrations.

138–39; Bracero Program impact on, 64, 65; breakup of, 8, 68, 72–73, 83; at collective memory periphery, 148; disregarding economic needs, 93; documents sought by, 159; focus on nuclear families, 155–56; involvement in Bracero Justice Movement, 147; narratives about, 167; relocation in border towns, 68, 69, 93; role in Bracero Proa, 151–52

Bracero History Archive, 12, 18, 175–76

Bracero History Project: Bracero Project confused with, 159; creation of, 12, 186n32; development of, 171; goal of, 174; indigenous participation in, 21, 27; interviews for, 2, 169; selective presentation of history, 172–74

Bracero Justice Movement: achievements, 166–67; attempt to recover bracero wages, 2, 17–18, 137, 140, 148–57, 173, 174; bi-national trajectory of, 142; Bracero Proa and, 143–48; collective memory emerging from, 18, 140–41, 173; competing organizations, 148; conflicts within, 157–60; critiques by, 139; embracing by defiance, 142; ex-bracero action through, 143; gains for, 151; goals of, 4–5, 167; historical narratives ignored by, 5; indigenous community ties to, 27; international attention sought by, 155; leadership, 148; meetings arranged by, 61, 135; Mexico, activities in, 21; rise of, 139, 173; term, 2, 139, 185n2; voices silenced by, 11; Zapatista movement and, 140, 160–63, 167

Bracero Proa: alignment with Zapatista movement, 160–61; banks targeted by, 148–49; broadening sought by bracero document recognition scope, 157; compared to other organizations, 154; conflicts within, 157–58; contact with law firm, 164;

establishment of, 149; membership identification cards issued by, 153, 154; overview of, 143–48; protests and media coverage, 149–51, 155; wage theft investigated by, 18

Bracero Program: aftermath of, 4; bracero rights limited under, 103–4; collective amnesia about, 139; communism presence alleged in, 117; contemporary work programs compared to, 183–84; creating collective memory about, 140–41, 142, 148; critiques of, 8, 63–64, 82–83, 93–94, 107, 161, 178; documented and undocumented migration during, 182; early arguments for, 6–7; exhibits, 12, 18, 171, 172, 175–83, 180, 181; exploitation in, 176; extension of, 111–12, 119; historical importance of, 167, 172; images of, 171; intergenerational transmission through U.S. connections, 27, 187–88n12; investigation of problems, 129–30; labor interests excluded from discussions of, 113, 115; Mexican American family ties to, 179; Mexican opinions concerning, 7; modernization through, 9, 15, 31, 32, 40, 150; national and racial identity in, 35–36; negotiations, growers' association participation in, 115; patriotic propaganda, 101; perceptions of, 179; publications on, 93–94, 100, 123, 130, 131, 145, 201n131; public memory of, 171–72; public narratives concerning, 147; racist ideologies of, 167; replication of, 175; rules and regulations, failure to enforce, 129; SANTA place within, 111; termination attempts, 17, 100, 131, 133; termination of, 127, 129, 131, 132, 183; Texas growers barred from, 108; worker lives controlled through, 5; worker perspective on, 19

Bracero Project, 158, 159

17; pressure regarding, 82; surplus income spent on, 80

dealings with, 150; family ranch, protests at, 142, 150–51, 155
Fund for the Republic, 130, 176

Galarza, Ernesto: Alianza, involvement with, 17, 97, 98–99, 100, 107, 109, 110–11, 117–18, 129; as American labor advocate, 111–12; background and education, 99; bracero organizing attempts by, 124; change in discourse, 123, 201n131; correspondence, 97, 98; ex-braceros and *aspirantes*, contact with, 113; Hernández Serrano, J., dealings with, 122, 123, 127–28; indigenous populations studied by, 49; information gathering by, 129–30; labor organization arrangement negotiated by, 121; local union leadership, dealings with, 126; manager perceptions recorded by, 46; obstacles to worker organizing, 126; position on contract renewals, 125; press coverage concerns, 116, 117; SANTA, involvement with, 106; surveillance of, 114–15; transnational labor organizing after, 144; works by, 93–94, 100, 116, 123, 130, 131, 201n131
Gambling: bracero families impacted by, 82; bracero participation in, 17, 93; in labor camps, 62; opportunities for, 65; surplus income spent on, 80
Gamio, Manuel, 10, 30, 32
Gender: challenging expectations, 15; deviance, 15; power relationships, 73; reconfiguration of norms, 63; redefined notions of, 65, 68; roles, 88
Good Neighbor Policy, 101, 102
Granjas Agricolas para ex-Braceros (Agricultural Farms for Ex-Braceros), 131–32
Growers, American. *See* American growers
Growers' associations, 115

Growers Farm Labor Association, 121
Grupo de San Luís and Unión de Inquilinos del Estado de Baja California, 77, 78
Guardado Montelongo, Roberto, 74, 76
Guest-worker program, potential, 6, 175, 179, 181
Guest-worker program, World War I era, 31
Guest workers: Alianza members as, 117; children and grandchildren of, 138–39; claims, addressing, 163; "clean" narratives concerning, 64; contracts, obtaining, 58, 118, 119, 120, 121; current conditions, 184; decision to stay in U.S. vs. return to Mexico, 28, 53, 66–67, 179–80; determining ethnicity, 43; experiences and memories of, 14; exploitation of, 100; fight for better working conditions, 5; H-2A visas for, 179; health hazards to, 86–87; historic claims of, 160; image of respectable, 98; indigenous, 49; injustices against, 103; jobs taken by, 172; Mexican American community fracturing, accusations of, 78; Mexican government attitude toward, 25; Mexican government failure to protect, 11, 98; Mexicans sought out as, 173; migration routes of, 27, 187n12; organizing attempts, 123, 126, 131; plight of, 93–94, 99; programs for, 133; proof of status as, 148; public image vs. reality, 11; race and sex work issues, 84–85; return of, 66–67; rights of, 130, 172; shifting of legal status, 66, 192n10; unionizing efforts on behalf of, 112; wages for, 119
Guevara Rodríguez, José Santos, 95–96
Gutiérrez, Ventura: activism, 144–46; background and education, 144; as Bracero Proa founder, 143, 149; communication with law firm, 163; concern over grandfather's back

wages, 138–39, 145; conflicts with Rosa Marta Zárate, 160; fight for ex-bracero back wages, 149, 150; long-distance contacts, 166; at protest rally, *143*

istic, 21–22; performing, 44; poverty interwoven with, 37; racial meanings grounded in, 25; transitioning away from, challenges to, 42–43; unionizing efforts and, 16; U.S. and Mexican national-building projects, role in, 16

Indigenismo, 29–30, 31

Indigenous braceros: addressing social needs, 40; ancestry uniting, 163; difficulty determining numbers of, 25; dilemma of, 33, 33–34; discrimination against, 49, 54–57, 59; gaining literacy, 53–54; invisibility of, 25; labor activist attitudes toward, 100; language barriers, 16, 21, 47–49, 54; meetings with, 135–36; mestizo bracero attitudes toward, 51–52, 54–55; public events and entertainment for, 40–42; racialized systems for managing, 46, 49–50; reinforcing power relations over, 47; role in shaping Mexican modernization narratives, 25–26; self-representations of, 59; social isolation, 26–27, 40, 54; social networks, 16, 50, 55; Spanish language learning impact on, 52–53, 58, 59

Indigenous campesinos, 136, 140, 141

Indigenous communities: assimilation of, 30–31; bracero generation role in shaping migration, 10; Bracero Justice Movement, ties to, 27; Bracero Program impact on, 25, 36, 59; consumption impact on, 32, 59; dress styles, change in, 37; experiences of, 10; film depictions of, 42; grower perceptions of, 46; historic claims of, 160; labor activist attitudes toward, 124; language barriers, 26; language issues in managing, 42; marginalizing, 25, 29, 59, 187n4; from Mexican border states, 27, 187n11; Mexican government treatment of, 167; Mexican racial hierarchy in, 24; modernization conflict perceived with, 24; modernizing, 9, 10, 29, 31, 59–60; oppression of, 25; oral histories and digitized materials, 12; post–Mexican Revolution depictions of, 40; racial identity vis-à-vis, 9; racism faced by, 29; transformation into mestizos, 25, 37; vulnerability of, 16

Indigenous families: Bracero Program impact on, 59; language barriers, 58; in Mexico City, 27–28, 37, 40; participation in Bracero History Project, 21; perception of, 64

Indigenous identity: attitudes concerning, 28, 42–43; claiming, 27; culture and, 27, 30, 31; reasserting, 60

Indigenous languages, 42, 52, 56–58

Indigenous Mexicans: braceros depicted as, 34; challenging racial inferiority views, 30; depicted as children, 33, 33–34; in popular imagery, 33, 33–37, 35, 40–46; Spanish language learning impact on, 50–51, 52–53

Indigenous migrants, 18–19

Indigenous movements, 140, 160–63, 167; philosophies rooted in, 139

Indigenous peasants, 25–26, 27–28

Indigenous populations: attitudes toward, 29, 40–46; in Bracero Justice Movement, 160; in hacienda system, 51; hierarchy and tensions within, 46; integration of, 16, 32–33; modernization and integration of, 16; participation in sexual economies, 87; racist views concerning, 40–46; taking on mestizo cultural identity, 31; in Zapatista movement, 140

Indigenous subjects, 8–9, 25

Indigenous women: abandonment of, 68, 69; attitudes toward, 23–24; Bracero Program impact on, 37, 40; husband modernization noted by, 26; portrayal of, 41; preparation for modernity, 40

Indigenous workers: decision to stay in U.S. vs. return to Mexico, 28, 53; exploitation of, 29; jobs and tasks deemed suitable for, 26, 45–46; mestizo worker attitudes concerning, 9–10, 54–57; in Mexico, 184; physical characteristics of, 43; pros and cons of selecting, 45; seen as distinct from braceros and non-indigenous workers, 133

Infidelity, 73, 74

Instituto Mexicano de Seguro Social (IMSS), 151, 154

Instituto Nacional para la Atención de Adultos Mayores (INAPAM), 154

Intimacy, alternative/nonnormative, 74, 92

Intra-ethnic tensions, 9–11, 100, 124–25

Janitzio, Michoacán, 41–42

Jimenez, Lara, 101

Kinship models, normative, attachments outside boundaries of, 65, 68

Labor, 1, 18, 92, 93–94

Labor Commission, 111

Labor management: ethnic and race considerations, 43; language impact on systems of, 16, 49–50; mediation attempts in mestizo-indigenous bracero tension, 54–55; racialized system under, 26, 40, 46

Labor organizing, 10–11, 99, 118–19

Landless laborers, 109, 131, 132

Land redistribution policies, 2, 30–31, 131–32

Land reform, 30–31, 32, 66

Language: impact on indigenous bracero families, 59; indigenous identity based on, 27; modernity and, 26, 36, 47–54; as race symbol, 50–51

Language instruction, 50–51, 52–53, 59

Lara Jimenez, José, 97, 101

Law as wage recovery tool, 148, 149, 150, 163–66

"Lazy Indian" stereotype, 9

Le Berthon, Ted, 63, 64

Linguistic networks of support, 48–49, 54, 57–58

Literacy: courses and learning opportunities, 46, 52, 53–54, 59; as leadership qualification, 147; manager views of worker, 46; role in racial and ethnic identity shaping, 26; Spanish-language, 51, 58

Local union leadership, 126

Long-distance fathering, 7

López Leon, Asterio, 72

López Mateos, Adolfo, 69, 138

Lowenberg, Julius, 83–84

Loza, Juan (M. Loza's uncle), 156–57, 169–70

Luna, María Consuelo Miranda, 70

Mabalon, Dawn Bohulano, 80

Maclovia (Mexican movie), 41–42

Male sexuality, 67

"*Mal gobierno*" (term), 140

Management, communication with, 49

Managers. *See* Labor management

Manhood, redefining, 8

"March for Indigenous Dignity," 149

Marcos, Subcomandante, 162

Marentes, Carlos, 145, 158–60

Marginalization, 17, 19, 100, 108

Marginalized groups, 25, 29, 59, 161, 187n4

Marriage: benefits of, 67, 192n17; of convenience, 80; drinking threat to, 83; heterosexual relations outside of, 88; long-distance, 67

Martínez, Daniel, 8, 63–64, 78

Martínez, Sebastian, 84, 85–86

Martinez Cortez, Hilario, 73

Masculinity: alternative forms of, 66; challenging constructions of, 16, 65, 183; complex vision of, 92;

normalizing type of, 15; normative narratives tied to, 98; performing, 169–70; redefining notions of, 16, 65; respectable, demonstrating, 93; romanticized notions of, 5; ties to nuclear family, 66

Mayan community, 16

Mayan language, 51, 52, 56–57

Mayans, 27, 52

May-May, Julio Valentín, 21–22, 28, 52, 56–57

Medical border, 87

Medical examinations, 129, 141, 152–53, *153*, 174

Memory, 13–14, 19

Mestizaje: defined, 5, 185n7; failings of, 184; indigenous community transformation into, 9; Mexican push for, 10; as nation-building requirement, 10, 29–30, 42–43, 59, 163; as racial ideology, 60; racial project of, 32; rejection of, 43; romanticized notions of, 5; Spanish language as step toward, 50; spectrums of, 27, 31; as whitening project, 22

Mestizo braceros: illiterate, 58; indigenous ancestry uniting, 163; indigenous populations, attitudes toward, 51–52; labor management racialized discourses understood by, 46; racist practices of, 16; social networks, 26

Mestizo campesinos, 136, 140

Mestizo identity, 25, 31, 51, 187n4

Mestizo normativity, 98

Mestizo outlook, 100

Mestizo project, failures of, 141

Mestizos: appearance of, 23; cartoon depictions of, *33*, *34*, *35*; centrality of, 59, 60; exploitation of, 141; film depictions of, 42; heteronormative nuclear family life, 66; as ideal citizens, 25; Indian potential to become, 24; miscegenation role in creating, 29; modernity implications for men, 9; physical characteristics of, 43–44;

reinforcing racial identity of, 25; support networks, 54; transforming into indigenous communities, 25, 37, 60

Mestizo tropes, 183

Mestizo workers, 9–10, 54–57

Mexicali, families in, 69

Mexican agricultural workers, 18, 183–84

Mexican American communities, 63–64, 78

Mexican American Political Association (MAPA), 144

Mexican Americans: attitudes concerning Bracero Program, 63–64; attitudes toward braceros, 80; braceros as fathers, grandfathers, and great-grandfathers of, 178; as performers, 41; public events for, 41; work with braceros, 84

Mexican American women, 24, 41, 80

Mexican consul, 68–69, 71, 72

Mexican consulates, protests at, 151, 160

Mexican economy, 8, 32, 184

Mexican family, 60, 65

Mexican family breakups, 8

Mexican government: anti-communist campaign, 105, 111; attempts to regulate Mexican immigration, 108–9; Bracero Program amnesia on part of, 153; Bracero Program promoted by, 8; corruption of, 140; criticism of, 140; dealings with Canadian government, 183; failure to protect immigrant workers, 11, 98, 103, 161; law firm negotiations with, 165; mega-farm companies lauded by, 184; obligation toward braceros, 4–5, 139, 157, 161; organized labor climate under, 103–4; racist attitudes in, 25; repressive treatment of Alianza, 17, 99–100, 105, 114–15, 116–17, 121, 126, 127–28, 131, 133; respectable domesticity illusion created by, 66; response to bracero back wage recovery efforts, 148, 156, 162, 166; role in wage theft, 11, 18, 160; social hierarchies created by, 125; treatment of indigenous and campesino communities, 167; wage recovery system not implemented by, 18

Mexican immigrants, 9–11, 172

Mexican immigration: Alianza calls for regulation of, 108–9; incorporation into national historical narrative, 4; legal reality vs. illegal perception, 1, 4, 5, 178; perceived job loss due to, 182

Mexican labor, 1, 11, 19, 113, 132

Mexican laborers, indigenous peasant transformation into, 25–26

Mexican labor movement, 103, 127, 133

Mexican labor unions, 112, 127, 128

Mexican men, portrayal of, 41

Mexican migrant-Mexican American tensions, 59

Mexican Ministry of Foreign Affairs, 166

Mexican modernization. See Modernization, Mexican

Mexican nation-building, 10, 29–30, 42–43, 59, 163

Mexican peso, devaluation of, 139

Mexican Revolution, 29–30, 140

Mexicans: blacks as, 84–85; film depictions of, 41–42; perceived indigenous ancestry of, 34; racial discrimination against, 108; relations with African Americans, 84–85

Mexican state: bracero documentation burden of proof owed by, 157; critiques of, 19; exposing corruption, 11; narrative, defying, 92; repressive strategies of, 142–43

Mexican women, 68, 78–80

Mexican workers, 6, 46, 112, 133

Mexico: agricultural workers in, 184; Bracero Program supported by, 15;

economic conditions, 139; historical narratives ignored by, 5; oral history collecting in, 21; relations with United States, 103; shift to right by, 105; writing against, 18, 187n47

Mexico City, 27–28, 37, 40

Mexico Solidarity Network, 163

Meza, Nemecio, 21, 52–53

Middle-class white Americans, 64–65

Middle-management, 49–50, 54

Migrant descendants, 27, 187–88n12

Migrant workers: as adventure seekers, 3, 5; divisions between Mexican, 100; Mexican state obligation to, 139; U.S. exploitation of, 140

Migration, modernizing power of, 26, 31

Migration impact on indigenous bracero families, 59

Migratory Labor Committee, 129

Migratory processes, sexuality influence on, 65

Mitchell, H. L., 107, 109

Mixtec community, 16

Mixtec families, transnational employment for, 27, 187n12

Mixtecs, 27, 46

Mobility, medical border political authority control over, 87

Modernity, language of, 47–54

Modernity, mestizo, 37

Modernization: Bracero Program role in, 9, 15, 31, 32, 37, 40; bypassing of social programs addressing, 16; footwear relationship to, 36, 37; migration role in, 31; personal accounts of, 22;

Modernization, Mexican: alternative views of, 43; American ideologies meshing with, 64; attire, 26, 32, 37, 59; consumer symbols of, 37; framework of, 26; indigenous and rural peasantry as objects of, 9; indigenous communities outside, 24; indigenous role in shaping narratives of, 25–26; masculinity type tied to, 15; opportunities, 59; patriarchal nuclear family as vehicle for, 8; racial frameworks rooted in, 24–25; racialized terms of, 28, 32, 43; revolution toned down in push for, 98; as whitening project, 22

Modern Mexican, characteristics of, 32

Money-transfer companies, 149, 163–64

Movimiento Estudiantil Chicano de Aztlan (MEChA), 144

Multiculturalism, 51–52

Muñoz Barrera, Francisco, 104–5

Muñoz Pavón, Felipe, 161, 162, 163, 166

Mushroom workers' strike, 1990s, 145–46

Nadel, Leonard photo collection: bracero plight, documenting, 130, 174; brown bodies, 36; camp life, 176–77, *177*; at National Museum of American History, 171; work tools, *178*

Nahuas, 23, 27

Nahuatl language, 57

Narratives, official image, deviations in, 14

Narrator/listener, formulation of, 14

Nation, normative narratives tied to, 98

National Farm Labor Union (NFLU): Alianza dealings with, 107; attempts at guest worker elimination by, 123; bracero unionizing efforts through, 99, 116; involvement with Galarza, 99; local leadership, 126; materials produced by, 124; membership in, 115, 120; strike called off by, 122; strikes organized by, 118, 119

National Museum of American History: bracero as figure of honor at, 14; bracero exhibit opened at, 176; bracero history preservation measures, 171; Bracero History Project launched by, 173; contracting process and labor focus of, 18;

documentation and artifacts, 12; documenting bracero experience by, 2, 175; historical narratives ignored by, 5; integrating Latino migration story into national historical narrative, 4, 5

Nation-building projects, Mexican, 16, 25, 59, 98

Nation-building projects, U.S., 16

Native Americans, 30, 32–33

Nonconformist identities, 5

Nonconformist narratives, 176

Non-Spanish speakers, 26

Normative narrative, 5, 6–11, 59

Normativity, contested conceptions of, 19

Norms, worker deviation from, 15

North American Free Trade Act (NAFTA), 139, 140, 184

Nuclear family: alternatives to, 64–65; American ideologies of, 64; attempt to reconfigure extended family into, 66; bracero compensation based on visions of, 155–56; causes and consequences of breakup of, 82–83; constructions of, 77; economic survival outside, 65; heteronormative constructions of, 15, 63, 66, 82–83; masculinity tied to, 66; Mexican agricultural family differing from schema of, 65; redefining, 8

Official history, alternatives to, 5

Oral history(ies): collecting and documenting, 12–13, 18, 61; embodied practices/knowledge converted to enduring record in, 13; interviewer influence on recorded product of, 14; limitations of, 176; present influence on political and social context, 18

Ortega, Pedro A., 86–87

Otra Campaña, 161

Padua Players, 41

Pan American Union, 99

labor activist attitudes toward, 100; labor performed by, 181; narrative of, 142; rights and recourses lacking for, 104; rise of, 103, 107; standing in Bracero Justice Movement, 147–48; U.S. trade unionist attitudes toward, 126–27; wives of, 71

Unionizing efforts, 17

Unión Binacional de Ex-Braceros, 154–55, 160, 166

Unión de Trabajadores Agrícolas de Méxicali, 118, 120, 121

Unionization, 126

Union leadership, local, 126

Unions, quelling of, 98

Unión Sin Fronteras, 144, 145, 158

United Farm Workers of America (UFW), 127, 144

United Mexican American Student Organization (UMAS), 144

United States: ex-braceros residing in, 143; migrant descendant claims of connections to, 27, 187–88n12; relations with Mexico, 103; transition into life in, 28

Unjust and unequal system, 6

Upward mobility, 5

U.S. government, 4–5, 126

U.S. stay vs. return to Mexico, decision on, 28, 53, 66–67, 179–80

Vasconcelos, José, 29, 30

Vice, 64, 65

Vice, economies of, 8, 17, 93

Virgen Díaz, Juan, 88

Visitor reactions to bracero exhibit, 176, 179–82

Wages, low, 6

Wage theft: attention brought to, 137; examination of, 149; investigation

of, 18; Mexican government role in, 11, 18, 160; movement in response to, 139

Wartime cooperation period, 3

Wells Fargo Bank, 18, 148–49, 160, 163, 164

"Wetbacks," 100

Whiteness, 24, 43

Whitening projects, 29

Women: abandonment of, 70–71; Bracero Proa, role in, 151–52; Bracero Program impact on, 70–73; divorces, 72–73; as heads of household, 16, 65; migration to U.S., 69–70; participation in bracero economies, 5, 16, 68, 69, 73, 76; sexual economy changes for, 91; sexuality, 76; work opportunities for, 7, 69–70

Work, teaching value of, 29, 30–31, 32

Worker citizens abroad, Mexican nation-state obligation to, 5

Worker literacy, screener attitude concerning, 3

Worker selection, criteria for, 43–46

Workforce without rights, 172

Work habits, modern, 31

Working poor, 117

Work-related injuries, compensation denied for, 47–49

World War I, 31

World War II, 1, 77, 103

Zapata, Emiliano, 140

Zapatista indigenous movement, 139, 140, 160–63, 167

Zapotec community, 16

Zapotecs, 26, 27, 46

Zero, Delegado, 162–63

Zoot suiters, 66

CPSIA information can be obtained
at www.ICGtesting.com
Printed in the USA
LVHW101938090922
728003LV00005B/474